CONFUCIUS

THE ESSENTIAL
ANALECTS

SELECTED PASSAGES WITH
TRADITIONAL COMMENTARY

CONFUCIUS

THE ESSENTIAL
ANALECTS

SELECTED PASSAGES WITH
TRADITIONAL COMMENTARY

Translated By
EDWARD SLINGERLAND

Hackett Publishing Company, Inc.
Indianapolis/Cambridge

11 10 09 08   2 3 4 5 6 7

For further information, please address
  Hackett Publishing Company, Inc.
  P.O. Box 44937
  Indianapolis, IN 46244-0937

  www.hackettpublishing.com

Cover art: From a facsimile edition of the Songben Lunyu Zhushu
(Song Dynasty edition of the *Analects* with commentary and
subcommentary).

Cover design by Abigail Coyle
Text design by Jennifer Plumley
Composition by SNP Best-set Typesetter Ltd., Hong Kong
Printed at RR Donnelley

Library of Congress Cataloging-in-Publication Data

Confucius.
    [Lun yu. English. Selections]
    Confucius : the essential analects : selected passages with
traditional commentary /
    translated by Edward Slingerland.
       p.   cm.
    Includes bibliographical references.
    ISBN 0-87220-773-0—ISBN 0-87220-772-2 (pbk.)
    I. Slingerland, Edward G. (Edward Gilman)   II. Title.
  PL2478.L4 2006
  181'.112—dc22   2005025432

ISBN-13: 978-0-87220-773-8 (cloth)
ISBN-13: 978-0-87220-772-1 (pbk.)

CONTENTS

PREFACE

The *Analects* is not a "book" in the sense that most modern Westerners usually understand a book—that is, a coherent argument or story presented by a single author, to be digested alone in the quiet of one's study. It is instead a record—somewhat haphazardly collected and edited together at an unknown point in history—of a dynamic process of teaching, and most likely was only committed to writing many years after the primary touchstone of the process, the Master Confucius, had passed away. It probably represents an attempt by later students and followers to keep alive the memory of his teaching, which had been conveyed both verbally and by personal example. Many, if not most, of the passages are quite cryptic, and this is possibly at least partially intentional. In 7.8, the Master is reported as saying, "I will not open the door for a mind that is not already striving to understand, nor will I provide words to a tongue that is not already struggling to speak. If I hold up one corner of a problem, and the student cannot come back to me with the other three, I will not attempt to instruct him again." As we see throughout the text, Confucius' comments are often intended to elicit responses from his disciples, which are then corrected or commented upon by the Master. Therefore, these "ordered sayings" of Confucius were originally embedded in a conversational context within which their meaning could be gradually extracted.

By the late fourth century B.C.E., with the Master gone, direct conversation was no longer possible, but this merely forced the dialogue to take a different form. It is at this point that we get the beginning of what came to be an over-two-thousand-year-old tradition of commentary on the words of Confucius, which begins with such Warring States texts as the *Mencius*, *Xunzi*, and the *Record of Ritual*, and continues up to the present day—carried on for most of this time in classical Chinese, branching out into the various vernaculars of East Asian nations in the Chinese cultural sphere, and finally expanding in the eighteenth century into a wide variety of Indo-European languages. This commentarial tradition for the most part represents an attempt by later followers or admirers of the Master to find "the other three corners," now no longer in dialogue with the Master himself, but rather by embracing extant clues about the Master's possible intention, the views of previous students of the text, and the opinions of contemporaries. For later students of the *Analects*, this written commentarial tradition serves as a proxy for the original conversational environment, providing context, making connections, and teasing out implications.

Since at least the Han Dynasty (202 B.C.E.–220), no Chinese student of the text has attempted to approach the *Analects* outside of the context of this written commentarial tradition. Most modern Chinese people, of course, read the text—originally written in classical Chinese, a purely literary language—with a translation into modern Chinese as well as extensive commentaries, but even traditionally educated Chinese conversant with the classical language find it necessary to base their understanding of the text upon the foundation of earlier commentaries. Indeed, the text of the *Analects* itself is arguably so concise as to be incomprehensible without some sort of interpretative apparatus imposed upon it. As John Makeham has noted, "Unless a reader is provided with a commentarial 'context' in which flesh is added to the very spare bones of the text, [the *Analects*] frequently reads as a cryptic mixture of parochial injunctions and snatches of dry conversation. It is the commentaries which bring the text to life and lend it definition" (1997: 261). I have therefore always found it astounding that Western readers of the *Analects* have, for the most part, been left to their own devices in understanding this exceedingly difficult text, being presented with simply the bare, original passages with usually no more than a translator's introduction and occasional textual notes to rely on. Small wonder that so many have come away from the *Analects* with their impression of cryptic, mysterious Eastern "fortune cookie" wisdom reinforced. This, however, is not how the text is read in China, and is not at all how the text itself was originally meant. The passages that make up our received *Analects* were probably originally intended to be recited aloud, with teachers and students together discussing their meaning and subtleties. The commentarial tradition that has accreted around the text merely represents a written substitute for this original verbal interaction.

In the full version of this translation, published by Hackett in 2003 (*Confucius: Analects*), I attempted to give the English-language reader a hint of the richness of this context, a glimpse of the living text in its natural habitat, by presenting it with extensive running commentary. The present, shorter version that you are holding is a response to requests from some educators for a more compact edition suitable for a large world religion, philosophy, or history course, where the *Analects* represents merely one of many assigned readings. Rather than responding to this need by simply eliminating the commentary—ripping the text out of its native habitat once again—I have decided to provide selections from the *Analects* rather than the text as a whole. It is far preferable, in my mind, for students new to the thought of Confucius to acquire a full understanding of a representative selection of passages than to superficially skim over the text in its entirety. Because of the composite nature of the *Analects*—cobbled together by perhaps several generations of editors over an indeterminate span of time—there is a fair amount of repetition in the text, which makes it possible to significantly abridge it without omitting any major themes. Another variation in this edition is the separation of primary text and commentary into discrete sections, in order to provide a cleaner, less intimidating copy. This layout also allows students a chance to mull over the primary text on their own before turning to the explanatory comments, giving them their own chance to provide the "other three corners" to complete the square being hinted at by Confucius.

This solution to the problem of providing a more concise edition of the *Analects* without watering down its content was initially suggested to me by Lee Yearley over a very nice meal and bottle of Chianti, one of the many helpful nudges and excellent dinners he has bestowed on me over the years. This slim version of my translation of course owes all of the same debts as the full version; I'd just like here to mention again the particular contributions of Deborah Wilkes and Joel Sahleen. Deborah, my editor at Hackett, has been a source of constant encouragement and lucid advice, managing to skillfully balance our desire for academic integrity with the demands of common sense. Sensitive to the sometimes rather finicky needs of the author and yet thoroughly professional and efficient, Deborah has been a sheer pleasure to work with, and one could not hope for a better editor. My longtime friend and colleague Joel Sahleen generously agreed—despite the demands of new fatherhood and dissertation writing—to watch my sinological back, commenting extensively on the first draft of the full translation and saving me from innumerable embarrassing gaffs and stylistic crimes. As a result of Joel's consistent firm guidance—urging me toward clarity of expression, grammatical responsibility, and historical accuracy—his voice permeates this entire translation. In keeping with Confucius' dictum on friendship, Joel would remonstrate with me gently, desisting when I was too stubborn to listen (12.23), and so was unable to save me from all of the sinological and stylistic errors no doubt still to be found in this translation. For these, of course, I take full responsibility.

CONVENTIONS

The *pinyin* system of romanization is used throughout. In order to avoid confusion, Chinese words appearing in quotations from Western scholars have also been converted into *pinyin*, with the exception of titles of articles or books.

References to *Analects* passages are in the form x.x, where the first number refers to the "book" and the second to the passage number within the book.

Traditional Chinese commentators often make direct or oblique references to classical texts, and these I note with brackets.

To avoid cluttering the text and commentary with Chinese characters, the characters for proper names are omitted unless immediately relevant.

The disciples of Confucius are often referred to by a variety of names. Their more formal style-name (*zi* 字) is usually used in third-person narrative, whereas in first-person speech or when they are addressed by Confucius their personal name (*ming* 名) is generally used. The benefits of reflecting these differences in level of formality in the translation seem to me to be outweighed by the confusion they will create for the English reader, so throughout the translation I have kept to one form of reference—usually the style-name, but sometimes the full name when the style-name is not used or is only rarely used in the text. I have followed the same practice with other potentially confusing proper names, such as the Shang Dynasty, which is also referred to as the Yin.

In order to avoid confusion, I have adopted nonstandard romanizations of certain proper names:

Zhow 紂, for the evil last king of Shang, to distinguish him from the Zhou 周 Dynasty;

Qii 杞, for a minor state mentioned in the text, to distinguish it from the much more prominent state of Qi 齊;

Jii 姬, for the Zhou clan name, to distinguish it from the Ji 季 of the Ji Family that ruled the state of Lu in Confucius' time.

I have exclusively used the male third-person pronoun when referring to the Confucian practitioner because, as far as one can tell, the *Analects* was composed by and for men, and the idea that women might have any place in the Confucian worldview—other than as temptations to immorality, or (from the Han Dynasty on) subsidiary helpmates toward morality—has no place in an account of traditional Confucianism (refer to the commentary to 17.25). I am not at all unsympathetic toward certain modern Western attempts to make Confucianism more gender neutral, but I feel it is a scholarly disservice to obscure the gender attitudes of Warring States Confucians.

INTRODUCTION

The Text

The *Analects*, or *Lunyu* 論語 (lit. "ordered sayings"), purports to be a record of the teachings of Kongzi 孔子 and his disciples. Kongzi is more commonly known in the West by the latinization "Confucius," bestowed on him by Jesuit missionaries in the eighteenth century, and his traditional dates are 551–479 B.C.E. Traditionally, the *Analects* has been viewed as a coherent and accurate record of the teachings of the Master, recorded during his lifetime or perhaps shortly after his death, but this view of the text began to be called into question by the philologists of the Qing Dynasty (1644–1912), and modern textual critics have argued convincingly that the text actually consists of different chronological strata, assembled by an editor or series of editors, probably considerably after the death of Confucius.

The translation found in this book is based on the standard "received" text, assembled by He Yan (190–249), although occasional reference will be made to textual variants found in other versions of the text.[1] There is no doubt among contemporary scholars that this received text is a somewhat heterogeneous collection of material from different time periods, although scholars differ in their identification of the different strata, as well as in the significance they attribute to these differences. In my mind the most plausible view of the *Analects* is that, although it no doubt represents different time periods and somewhat different concerns, its various strata display enough consistency in terminological use, conceptual repertoire, and general religious viewpoint to allow us to treat the text as a whole that presents a unified vision. The probable late date of the last books in the *Analects* (especially Books Fifteen through Twenty) should always be kept in mind, but it is probably safe to view the text as a genuine representation of the state of the "School of Confucius" before the innovations of Mencius and Xunzi.

The primary distinguishing characteristic of this translation of the *Analects* is the inclusion of traditional Chinese commentary on the text, selected from the commentaries already culled by the eminent

---

[1] One of these is the so-called Dingzhou 定州 *Analects*, written on bamboo strips and found in 1973 (but not published until 1997) in a Han Dynasty tomb that was sealed in 55 B.C.E.

twentieth-century scholar Cheng Shude in his exhaustive, four-volume critical edition of the *Analects* that serves as the standard in the field. Cheng reviewed more than 140 commentaries, as well as references to the *Analects* in other early texts, and his selection seems ideal to me because he also made a conscious effort to include many sides of various debates (although he usually ends up weighing in on one side or the other), as well as unusual or unorthodox readings. The commentators cited are all listed in Appendix 2, which includes their dates and a brief biographical sketch. This is intended to give the reader some impression (however vague) of the interpretative standpoints that might inform their views of the text.

The overarching interpretative standpoint adopted in the translation as a whole—the standpoint that has determined which commentators will be cited, and when—is that of a modern, historically and philologically responsible student of the text (whether a Qing Dynasty Chinese philologist or a contemporary Asian or Western scholar), fluent in reading classical Chinese and interested in the thought of Confucius. This standpoint assumes that the text of the *Analects* is a relatively coherent whole, edited together at one time by an editor or group of editors (the "early Confucian school") in accordance with a vision they had of what their Master, Confucius, was trying to teach. In attempting to understand this vision, modern readers of the text should try to be as historically and philologically responsible as possible—that is, they should avoid imputing to the editor(s) of the text views that would have been unrecognizable to them, and whenever possible should refrain from introducing anachronistic terms or ideas. In practice, this means that our knowledge of late Spring and Autumn and Warring States language usage, society, history, and thought should delimit the parameters of possible interpretations of the text. While this set of assumptions is by no means the only angle from which one might approach the text of the *Analects*, ultimately it seems the most rewarding and historically responsible standpoint for someone interested in understanding the text in something resembling its original religious and cultural milieu.

Pre-Confucian Background

Traditional Chinese historiography presents the Xia Dynasty as the first of the legendary dynasties of the Golden Age, supposedly founded by the legendary sage-king Yu. Yu is also credited with taming the floods of the Yellow River, thereby making what we now think of as north-central China habitable for the Chinese people. The earliest Chinese civilization for which we have archaeological and written evidence, however, is the Shang Dynasty (sometimes alternately referred to as the Yin Dynasty), the traditional dates of which are 1751–1122 B.C.E. It is from the Shang that we have the first written records from China, in the form of so-called "oracle bones." These oracle bones are pieces of ox scapula or tortoise shells used in divination: questions concerning the proper course of action or requests for things such a rain, directed to the spirits of the Shang ancestors, were written upon them, and heat was then applied. The answer from the ancestors—yes, this military campaign will be successful; no, rain will not be forthcoming—were revealed in the resulting pattern of cracks decoded by the diviner, who was often the Shang king himself.

Often the ancestors were asked to intercede with the being who wielded the greatest power of all over the Shang people, the ur-ancestor known as the "Lord on High" (*shangdi* 上帝). The Lord on High seems originally to have been a nonhuman God who gradually came to be viewed as the first human ancestor of the Shang people, and therefore—by virtue of seniority—the most powerful of the ancestor spirits. The Lord on High and the other ancestor spirits of the Shang were viewed as dwelling in a kind of netherworld somewhere above the human realm (hence the Lord "on High"), from which vantage point they continued to monitor the behavior of their descendents, receive sacrificial offerings from them, hear questions and requests, and control all of the phenomena seen as lying beyond human control: weather, health and sickness, success or failure in battle, etc. Establishing and maintaining a good relationship with these spirits—especially the most powerful of them, the Lord on High—was therefore one of the primary concerns of the Shang ruler.

In the oracle bones we find a special term referring to the power accrued by a ruler who, through timely and appropriate ritual sacrifices (*li* 禮), had successfully established and preserved such a relationship with the ancestors: *de* 德. We translate this term as "Virtue,"[2] with the caveat that the reader should keep in mind the original sense of the Latin *virtus*—the particular "power" residing in a person or thing, preserved in modern English in such expressions as, "By virtue of his great intelligence, he was able to solve the problem." Virtue in the early Shang context refers to a kind of attractive, charismatic power residing

---

[2] *De* as a particular power derived from Heaven will be translated as "Virtue" in order to distinguish it from "virtue" in a more general sense, although in the *Analects* and later writings it sometimes does possess the latter sense.

in a ruler who has won the endorsement of the ancestral spirits. This power could be perceived by others, serving as a visible mark of the spirits' favor, and its attractive qualities allowed the ruler to both win and retain supporters.

Sometime near the end of the second millennium B.C.E. a people known as the Zhou invaded the Shang realm and deposed the last of the Shang kings. The traditional date of the conquest is 1122 B.C.E., but this has been the subject of great dispute, and the conquest may in fact have occurred over a period of time rather than in one fell swoop. The traditional account of the Zhou conquest credits King Wu ("The Martial King") with defeating the last of the Shang kings, the infamous Zhow 紂, and posthumously declaring his father to be the first of the Zhou kings, King Wen ("The Cultured King"). When King Wu died, his designated heir, the future King Cheng ("The Perfected King"), was not yet old enough to assume the throne. For the duration of his minority, China was ruled by King Wu's brother, the famous Duke of Zhou, a wise and strong regent who promptly ceded his position once King Cheng came of age. This triumvirate who established the early Zhou— King Wen, King Wu, and the Duke of Zhou—became bywords for virtue and wisdom.

We have much more in the way of written material from the Zhou Dynasty that helps us to understand their religious worldview. The most reliable source is the set of inscriptions that have been found on bronze ritual vessels discovered in tombs, intended as commemorations of the occasion of the making of the vessel, that reveal much about early Zhou history and thought. Less reliable—because subject to scribal changes, both intentional and unintentional—but far richer in content are the received texts that purport to date from the Zhou Dynasty. The most helpful of these are the *Book of Documents* (*shangshu* 尚書 or *shujing* 書經) and the *Book of Odes* (*shijing* 詩經), the former a collection of historical documents and governmental proclamations supposedly dating back to the earliest years of Chinese history, and the latter a collection of folk songs and official state hymns.[3] These two texts form the core of the "classics" that came to play such a central role in Confucius' system of self-cultivation.

The religious worldview of the Zhou borrowed heavily from the dynasty that they replaced. One reflection of the Zhou eagerness to

---

[3] The current belief in scholarly circles is that at least half of the *Book of Documents* is a fourth-century C.E. forgery, whereas much of the *Book of Odes* represents genuinely pre-Confucian material, probably dating to between 1000 and 600 B.C.E.

identify with the Shang was their adoption of the Shang high god, the Lord on High, who was conflated with and eventually replaced by their own tribal god, *tian* 天. Early graphic forms of *tian* seem to picture a massive, striding, anthropomorphic figure, who is from the earliest times associated with the sky. Hence "Heaven" is a fairly good rendering of *tian*, as long as the reader keeps in mind that "Heaven" refers to an anthropomorphic figure—someone who can be communicated with, angered, or pleased—rather than a physical place. Heaven possessed all of the powers of the Lord on High, and in addition had the ability to charge a human representative on earth with the "Mandate" (*ming* 命) to rule. *Ming* refers literally to a command issued by a political superior to an inferior or a decree issued by a ruler; in a metaphorical and religious sense, it refers to Heaven's command to its proxy on earth, the king, to rule the human world. Just as the Lord on High sent blessings down to those of his descendents who performed the sacrifices correctly, Heaven was believed to grant the Mandate to the ruler who maintained ritual correctness. The *Book of Odes* and *Book of Documents* claim that the Shang lost the Mandate because of gross ritual improprieties and general immorality, which motivated the Lord on High/Heaven to withdraw the Mandate from them and give it to the Zhou. In this way, the Zhou rulers presented their motivation for conquering the Shang to be merely the desire to enact Heaven's will, rather than any selfish desire for power on their part.[4] Similarly, since the holder of the Mandate was believed to also receive Virtue from Heaven as a sign of its favor, early texts present the conquest as relatively effortless: King Wu simply arrived on the battlefield with his troops, and the awesome power of his Virtue caused most of the opposing armies to immediately submit to him.[5] This is the origin of two themes in Chinese religious thought that were inherited by Confucius: that only someone who is selfless and sincere will receive Virtue from Heaven, and that political order is properly brought about only through the charismatic, noncoercive power of Virtue—the need to exert force being viewed as evidence that a ruler does not truly enjoy Heaven's favor.

---

[4] See, for instance, the *Book of Documents*–like fragment reproduced in 20.1, where Tang, mythical founder of the Shang Dynasty, humbly declares to Heaven that his vanquishing of Jie, the evil last king of the Xia, is intended merely as punishment for Jie's transgressions against Heaven's order.

[5] See, for instance, the account of the conquest given in Chapter 31 ("The Successful Completion of the War") of the *Book of Documents* (Legge 1991b: 306–316).

As in Shang times, the manner in which to assure the favor of the supreme being was through the proper observance of a set of practices referred to as "ritual" (*li* 禮), but in the Zhou conception both the scope and nature of ritual practice was understood differently. Shang ritual consisted primarily of sacrificial offerings to the spirits of the ancestors, and the main concern was that the sacrifices were performed properly—that the food and drink offered were of sufficient quality, that the proper words were intoned, etc. By Zhou times, the scope of ritual had grown significantly, encompassing not only sacrificial offerings to the spirits, but also aspects of the Zhou kings' daily lives that we might be tempted to label as "etiquette": the manner in which one dressed, took one's meal, approached one's ministers, etc. In addition, proper performance of ritual duties became more than a matter of simply observing external forms, because in order for ritual practice to be acceptable to Heaven, it was necessary that the king perform it with *sincerity*. We thus see in the Zhou the beginnings of a concern with internal state of mind—a demand that one's emotions and thoughts match one's external behavior.

Because of this concern with sincerity, in early Zhou texts we see a sort of unself-conscious skill being associated with ideal exemplars, both the military lord or gentleman (*junzi* 君子)—who throughout the *Book of Odes* is described as embodying the martial and social virtues that become his station with an effortless ease—and the more explicitly moral sage-ruler of old, such as Shun or Yao. Having attained a state of completely sincere, spontaneous, unself-conscious harmony with Heaven, they are rewarded with Virtue: a power that not only brings them personal benefit, but that also allows them to more effectively realize Heaven's will in the world. We will see this theme continued in the *Analects*, where Confucius' ideal gentleman combines both the physical mastery of the martial aristocrat in the *Odes*—although his mastery shows itself in ritual performance rather than in war—and the unself-conscious ease and selflessness of the virtuous kings of the Zhou, also sharing with them a special relationship to Heaven. This ideal spiritual state comes to be referred to in the later Chinese tradition as "wu-wei" (*wuwei* 無為). Meaning literally "no-doing" or "nondoing," wu-wei might be best translated as "effortless action," because it refers not to what is or is not being done, but to the *manner* in which something is done. An action is wu-wei if it is spontaneous, unself-conscious, and perfectly efficacious, representing a perfect harmony between one's inner dispositions and external movements, and thus being perceived by the subject to be "effortless" and free of strain. We will see that one of Confucius' primary concerns in the *Analects* is how to encourage the morally and culturally corrupt people of his age to embrace the Way of the ancients in a genuinely wu-wei fashion.

The Age of Confucius

The Zhou system resembled that of feudal Europe, where the king enjoyed the fealty of the local feudal lords—usually relatives of the royal family or favored retainers—to whom he had granted hereditary fiefdoms. Although these fiefdoms were governed independently, all of the feudal lords were bound to obey the Zhou king in times of war and to submit periodic tribute to the Zhou royal court. The beginning of the decline of the Zhou can be traced to the sack of the Zhou capital in 770 B.C.E. by barbarian tribes allied with rebellious Chinese principalities. The Zhou court was forced to flee, and a new capital was established farther east. The movement of the capital marks the beginning of the so-called "Eastern Zhou" period (770–221 B.C.E.), the latter part of which is in turn often subdivided into the "Spring and Autumn" (722–481 B.C.E.) and "Warring States" (403–221 B.C.E.) periods. The Eastern Zhou period was characterized by a gradual decline in the power of the Zhou kings, with local feudal lords and ministers gradually usurping the traditional Zhou kingly prerogatives, and more and more openly running their fiefdoms as independent states. By the time of Confucius' birth in 551 B.C.E., the Zhou kings had been reduced to mere figureheads, and even many of the feudal lords had seen their power usurped by upstart ministers. That was the case in Confucius' native state of Lu 魯, where the authority of the Dukes—who could trace their ancestry back to the Duke of Zhou himself—had been usurped by a group of powerful clans, collectively known as the "Three Families": the Ji Family, Meng Family, and Shu Family.

Not very much is known for sure about the life of Confucius. Most of the traditional details of his life are derived from a biography in the *Record of the Historian*, compiled around 100 B.C.E. by the Grand Historian Sima Qian, and much of this clearly consists of legend and literary invention. Some modern scholars have attempted to construct coherent chronologies of Confucius' life from a variety of early sources and to separate potential facts from clear fiction, but so little can be known for sure that it seems best to stick to whatever facts we might glean from the *Analects* itself. Confucius was clearly a native of Lu (18.2), of humble economic background (9.6), and seems to have been a member of the scholar-official (*shi* 士) class, the lowest of the three classes of public office holders. Originally referring to an aristocratic warrior, by the time of Confucius, *shi* had come to refer to a class of people who filled the middle and lower ranks of state governments in primarily civil posts.

Like Confucius, it seems that a subset of these scholar-officials were also *ru* 儒. This term, which later came to mean "Confucian," appears only once in the *Analects* (6.13), and referred in Confucius' time to a class of specialists concerned with transmitting and preserving the traditional rituals and texts of the Zhou Dynasty. The fact that mastery of the Zhou classics and traditional ritual etiquette was a valued skill in public officials led many aspiring scholar-officials to seek out *ru*-like training for the sake of acquiring public office and—most importantly— the salary and public prestige that went along with it. This was only one of many contemporary phenomena that troubled Confucius, who felt that training in traditional Zhou cultural forms should be pursued as an end in itself.

As portrayed in the *Analects*, Confucius saw himself as an emissary of Heaven, on a mission to restore the sort of natural, spontaneous, unself-conscious harmony that had once prevailed during the reigns of the ancient sage-kings Yao and Shun, as well as during the Golden Age of the "Three Dynasties"—the Xia, the Shang, and the Zhou. The "categorized conversations" of Confucius that constitute the *Analects* are thus a wake-up call sent from Heaven to a politically, culturally, and morally corrupted world. In Confucius' view, his contemporaries had lost sight of "the Way" (*dao* 道), an important term in the *Analects* that Confucius seems to have been the first person in early China to use in its full metaphysical sense. Referring literally to a physical path or road, *dao* also refers to a "way" of doing things, and in the *Analects* refers to *the* Way: that is, the unique moral path that should be walked by any true human being, endorsed by Heaven and revealed to the early sage-kings. More concretely, this "Way" is manifested in the ritual practices, music, and literature passed down from the Golden Age of the Zhou, which were still preserved in the state of Lu by a few high-minded, uncompromising *ru* (6.13, 19.22). The fact that "the Way of Kings Wen and Wu has not yet fallen to the ground" (19.22) serves for Confucius as a small glimmer of hope in an otherwise bleak landscape. He saw his mission to be serving Heaven by helping to reinvigorate this "Way" in his otherwise fallen and corrupt age.

A person thoroughly transformed in both behavior and thought by training in the Way of the Zhou was referred to by Confucius as the "gentleman" (*junzi* 君子). In Zhou times this title ("son of a lord") referred to a member of the military aristocracy, but it was thoroughly moralized by Confucius to refer to any culturally and morally perfected person, no matter what his social background.[6] A term closely associated with the gentleman is the overarching virtue of "Goodness" (*ren* 仁), which only the gentleman can be said to possess. The word *ren* 仁 is closely related etymologically to the general word for "human being" (*ren* 人), and is therefore sometimes translated as "humanity" or "humaneness." It is probably most accurately translated as "true humaneness" or "the state of being a perfected human"; "Goodness" has been chosen as the least infelicitous rendering. However one glosses *ren* 仁 in English, it refers to the overarching virtue of being a perfected human being—that is, having mastered and effortlessly internalized the Way of Heaven. One who possesses the quality of Goodness has thus achieved a special relationship with Heaven, and as in Zhou and Shang times was expected by Confucius to receive as a reward the power of Virtue (*de* 德). With this power, the gentleman would be able to win the admiration and support of his peers, secure the loyalty of wise ministers, and bring about the moral obedience of the common people. The ascension of such a gentleman to political power would thus bring about a restoration of the lost Golden Age—a "second Zhou in the East,"[7] as Confucius puts it in 17.5.[8]

Despite his numerous disclaimers, Confucius himself is portrayed in the *Analects* as a gentleman possessing the virtue of Goodness, and therefore presumably also "Virtue" in the sense of moral-religious power. It is a bit unclear, therefore, why he himself did not effect the transformation of Chinese society that he had in mind. Many commentators suggest that Confucius, with his respect for traditional authority, felt that only a member of the hereditary Zhou aristocracy had the moral and political right to put the Way of Heaven into practice, and that this is why he spent so much of his time and effort trying to persuade various debauched rulers to return to the true Way of their ancestors. His failure in this regard raises another question: If Confucius had

---

[6] This transformation is also seen in the English word "gentleman," which originally referred solely to a particular social class, but later came to mean anyone capable of acting with "class."

[7] The state of Lu being located to the east of the original Zhou capital.

[8] "Gongshan Furao used the stronghold of Bi to stage a revolt against the Ji Family. He summoned Confucius, and the Master was inclined to go.

Zilu was displeased, and said, 'We have nowhere else to go, that is true. But why must we go to the house of Gongshan?'

The Master replied, 'I have been summoned—how could it be for naught? If I found someone to employ me, could I not establish a new Zhou in the East?' "

truly achieved a state of wu-wei harmony with Heaven and therefore possessed the power of Virtue, how could he have been so consistently ignored by these authorities? These sorts of questions have served as constant thorns in the sides of traditional hagiographers of Confucius, some of whom claim that Confucius failed only because he had something else in mind: not actually transforming the society of his day, but rather withdrawing into private life with his disciples in order to elaborate and lay down for posterity an eternal blueprint of how to effect such a transformation—a much loftier and more lasting goal.

In any case, it is clear to historians that Confucius himself never held anything more than minor posts in his lifetime, and failed to secure the conversion of any significant contemporary figure of power. His real success was his influence on later generations. He did succeed in gathering around himself a fairly sizable group of disciples, some of whom managed to obtain high governmental posts after the Master's death. His vision was also picked up by two prominent Warring States followers, Mencius and Xunzi, the latter of whom was an extremely influential intellectual and teacher of Hanfeizi and Li Si, the two Legalist thinkers who helped the first Emperor of Qin unify China in 221 B.C.E. The Qin finally put an end to the Zhou Dynasty once and for all, and laid the groundwork for two thousand years of Chinese imperial rule by, for the first time, unifying China under a single, centrally administered government.

It was not until well into the Han Dynasty, however, that Confucius was finally officially recognized as a great sage by the rulers of China, at which time the book that purports to be the record of his teachings, the *Analects*, became required reading for any educated Chinese person. Although Confucianism was eclipsed during the Sui and Tang Dynasties by Buddhism, it continued even during this period to exert a powerful influence on the Chinese mind, and it was officially revived in the Song Dynasty by the so-called "neo-Confucian" school. During the Ming Dynasty the so-called "Four Books" assembled by Zhu Xi (1130–1200) as the core of Confucian teachings—the *Analects* and the *Mencius*, along with two chapters from the *Record of Ritual* called the "Great Learning" and the "Doctrine of the Mean," all accompanied by Zhu Xi's commentary—became the basis of China's civil service examination, and were therefore memorized by every single educated Chinese person from 1313 until the last nationwide exam in 1905. Similar national exams in Korea, Japan, and Vietnam assured the hold of the *Analects* on the minds of the educated classes in those nations as well. Therefore, although the Master had little influence during his own lifetime, the cultural legacy he left to East Asia is difficult to overestimate. As Simon Leys has observed, "no book in the entire history of the world has exerted, over a longer period of time, a greater influence on a larger number of people than this slim little volume" (1997: xvi).

Hopefully the background information provided above and the commentary provided in the translation that follows will give the reader some sense of *why* the *Analects* has been so influential, and allow him or her to see the text as more than merely a historical curiosity or collection of quaint homilies. The *Analects* gives expression to a powerful religious and moral vision—one still capable of both speaking to and instructing us today. The passages selected for this edition of the *Analects* are intended to introduce the reader to the various elements of Confucius' religious vision: his diagnosis of the causes of the fallenness of his age, the path of self-cultivation that he proposes to remedy this state of fallenness, and the characteristics of the ideal state which lies at the end of this path.

TRADITIONAL CHRONOLOGY

Below is a list of the traditional dates of major figures (some of the earliest of whom are no doubt legendary) and a rough chronology of early Chinese history.

Sage-king Yao 堯 r. 2357–2257 B.C.E.

Sage-king Shun 舜 r. 2255–2205 B.C.E.

Hou Ji 后稷 ("Lord Millet"). Supposedly Minister of Agriculture under Shun, progenitor of what became the Zhou royal line.

Xia 夏 Dynasty 2205–1766 B.C.E.
There is, as yet, no archaeological evidence for the existence of this dynasty.

Sage-king Yu 禹 2205–2197 B.C.E. Supposed founder of the Xia, also credited with taming the floods of the Yellow River, thereby making what we now think of as north-central China habitable for the Chinese people.

King Jie 桀 1818–1766 B.C.E. Evil tyrant, last of the Xia rulers.

Shang 商 Dynasty 1751–1122 B.C.E.
Alternately referred to as the Yin 殷 Dynasty, source of the first written records from China, in the form of so-called "oracle bones," and also amply attested to in the archaeological record.

King Tang 湯 1766–1753 B.C.E. Defeated the evil Jie to found the Shang Dynasty.

King Zhow 紂 1154–1122 B.C.E. Evil last king of the Shang, infamous tyrant.

(Western) Zhou 周 Dynasty 1122–770 B.C.E.
The Golden Age of China, in the view of Confucius.

King Wen 文 ("The Cultured King"). Remained loyal to the evil King Zhow, last ruler of the Shang Dynasty, hoping to reform him through virtuous example.

King Wu 武 ("The Martial King") r. 1122–1115 B.C.E. Son of King Wen, militarily defeated the evil Zhow, who showed himself incapable of reform, to found the Zhou Dynasty.

Duke of Zhou 周公. Brother of King Wu, who, after King Wu's death, served as regent for Wu's son, the future King Cheng, until he was old enough to take office.

(Eastern) Zhou Dynasty 770–221 B.C.E.
A period of decline following the sacking of the Zhou capital. Usually subdivided into two periods:

Spring and Autumn Period 722–481 B.C.E.
The period covered by the court history of the state of Lu, the *Annals* (*chunqiu* 春秋; lit. "Spring and Autumn").

Confucius 551–479 B.C.E.

Warring States Period 403–221 B.C.E.
This period begins when the Zhou kings officially recognize the partitioning of the state of Jin 晉, which inspires the rulers of former vassal states of the Zhou to assert increasing levels of autonomy, eventually usurping the title of "king" for themselves. Time of intense interstate warfare, social chaos, and intellectual innovation.

Laozi (legendary figure, but text bearing name composed in latter part of fifth c. B.C.E.)

Mozi c. 480–390 B.C.E.

Mencius fourth c. B.C.E.

Zhuangzi fourth c. B.C.E.

Xunzi c. 310–219 B.C.E.

Hanfeizi c. 280–233 B.C.E.

Qin 秦 Dynasty 221–206 B.C.E.

Founded by the self-declared First Emperor of Qin (*qinshi huangdi* 秦始皇帝) along Legalist lines, this marks the real beginning of China's imperial period, the first time it was unified under a central government. Great Wall constructed, monetary system, weights and measures, and writing system standardized. Origin of the word "China" ("Qin" is pronounced with an initial "ch" sound) in Western languages.

Former Han 漢 Dynasty 206 B.C.E.–9

After a brief power struggle, the Han Dynasty is founded in 206 B.C.E. By the first century B.C.E., a syncretic form of Confucianism becomes the state religion, and Confucian classics are made the basis of a nationwide civil service examination.

Later Han Dynasty 25–220

Buddhism introduced to China, Han imperial power begins to degenerate.

Three Kingdoms Period 220–280

China divided in three kingdoms, each struggling for dominance.

Jin 晉 Dynasty 266–316

China briefly united under weak central government.

Northern and Southern Dynasties Period 316–589

China divided along north–south lines (demarcated by the Yangzi River) and ruled by a series of short-lived dynasties. Buddhism grows in importance in Chinese religious and political life.

Sui 隋 Dynasty 581–618

China once again unified; various forms of Buddhism, Daoism, and Confucianism all enjoy official patronage.

Tang 唐 Dynasty 618–907

Although Buddhism is dominant religion in China, near end of the dynasty Confucianism begins to grow in importance as a revived civil service examination system grows in importance.

Song 宋 Dynasty 906–1279

The so-called "neo-Confucian" movement successfully puts Confucianism back at the center of elite Chinese cultural and religious life. Although it sees itself as merely a reestablishment of the thought of

Confucius and Mencius, neo-Confucianism in fact incorporates a great deal of Buddhist metaphysics and other nonclassical Confucian influences.

Yuan 元 Dynasty 1279–1368
China is ruled by a series of Mongol rulers, who gradually become sinified.

Ming 明 Dynasty 1368–1644
Reestablishment of "native" Chinese rule.

Qing 清 Dynasty 1644–1912
China again conquered by northern "barbarians," the Manchus, who also quickly adopt Chinese culture and Confucianism. Civil service examination system finally abolished in 1905.

BOOK ONE

One of the central themes of this book is that learning (xue 學) *has more to do with actual behavior than academic theory, and that virtuous public behavior as an adult is rooted in such basic familial virtues as filial piety* (xiao 孝) *and respect for elders* (ti 弟) (*lit. "being a good younger brother").*[1]

1.1 The Master said, "To learn and then have occasion to practice what you have learned—is this not satisfying? To have friends arrive from afar—is this not a joy? To be patient even when others do not understand—is this not the mark of the gentleman?"

1.2 Master You said, "A young person who is filial and respectful of his elders rarely becomes the kind of person who is inclined to defy his superiors, and there has never been a case of one who is disinclined to defy his superiors stirring up rebellion.

"The gentleman applies himself to the roots. 'Once the roots are firmly established, the Way will grow.' Might we not say that filial piety and respect for elders constitute the root of Goodness?"

1.3 The Master said, "A clever tongue and fine appearance are rarely signs of Goodness."

1.4 Master Zeng said, "Every day I examine myself on three counts: in my dealings with others, have I in any way failed to be dutiful? In my interactions with friends and associates, have I in any way failed to be trustworthy? Finally, have I in any way failed to repeatedly put into practice what I teach?"

---

[1]Although the literal meaning of the term is something like "being a good younger brother," *ti* often refers more generally to showing respect and being obedient to one's elders, and the more general rendering will be used throughout to maintain consistency.

1.6 The Master said, "A young person should be filial when at home and respectful of his elders when in public. Conscientious and trustworthy, he should display a general care for the masses but feel a particular affection for those who are Good. If he has any strength left over after manifesting these virtues in practice, let him devote it to learning the cultural arts [*wen* 文]."

1.9 Master Zeng said, "Take great care in seeing off the deceased and sedulously maintain the sacrifices to your distant ancestors, and the common people will sincerely return to Virtue."

1.10 Ziqin asked Zigong, "When our Master arrives in a state, he invariably finds out about its government. Does he actively seek out this information? Surely it is not simply offered to him!"

Zigong answered, "Our Master obtains it through being courteous, refined, respectful, restrained, and deferential. The Master's way of seeking it is entirely different from other people's way of seeking it, is it not?"

1.11 The Master said, "When someone's father is still alive, observe his intentions; after his father has passed away, observe his conduct. If for three years he does not alter the ways of his father, he may be called a filial son."

1.12 Master You said, "When it comes to the practice of ritual, it is harmonious ease [*he* 和] that is to be valued. It is precisely such harmony that makes the Way of the Former Kings so beautiful. If you merely stick rigidly to ritual in all matters, great and small, there will remain that which you cannot accomplish. Yet if you know enough to value harmonious ease but try to attain it without being regulated by the rites, this will not work either."

1.15 Zigong said, "Poor without being obsequious, rich without being arrogant—what would you say about someone like that?"

The Master answered, "That is acceptable, but it is still not as good as being poor and yet joyful, rich and yet loving ritual."

Zigong said, "An ode says,

'As if cut, as if polished;
As if carved, as if ground.'

Is this not what you have in mind?"

The Master said, "Zigong, you are precisely the kind of person with whom one can begin to discuss the *Odes*. Informed as to what has gone before, you know what is to come."

BOOK TWO

In this book, we see elaborations of a theme suggested in 1.2: political order is not obtained by means of force or government regulations, but rather by the noncoercive influence of the morally perfected person. Several descriptions of such wu-wei perfection appear in this book (including Confucius' famous spiritual autobiography in 2.4), and we also find an extended discussion of the "root" virtue of filial piety that emphasizes the importance of having the proper internal dispositions.

2.1 The Master said, "One who rules through the power of Virtue is analogous to the Pole Star: it simply remains in its place and receives the homage of the myriad lesser stars."

2.2 The Master said, "The *Odes* number several hundred, and yet can be judged with a single phrase: 'Oh, they will not lead you astray.'"

2.3 The Master said, "If you try to guide the common people with coercive regulations [*zheng* 政] and keep them in line with punishments, the common people will become evasive and will have no sense of shame. If, however, you guide them with Virtue, and keep them in line by means of ritual, the people will have a sense of shame and will rectify themselves."

2.4 The Master said, "At fifteen, I set my mind upon learning; at thirty, I took my place in society;[1] at forty, I became free of doubts;[2] at fifty, I understood Heaven's Mandate;[3] at sixty, my ear was attuned; and at seventy, I could follow my heart's desires without overstepping the bounds of propriety."

---

[1] That is, through mastery of the rites; cf. 8.8, 16.13, and 20.3.
[2] Cf. 9.29.
[3] Cf. 16.8, 20.3.

2.7 Ziyou asked about filial piety. The Master said, "Nowadays 'filial' means simply being able to provide one's parents with nourishment. But even dogs and horses are provided with nourishment. If you are not respectful, wherein lies the difference?"

2.8 Zixia asked about filial piety. The Master said, "It is the demeanor that is difficult. If there is work to be done, disciples shoulder the burden, and when wine and food are served, elders are given precedence, but surely filial piety consists of more than this."

2.9 The Master said, "I can talk all day long with Yan Hui without him once disagreeing with me. In this way, he seems a bit stupid. And yet when we retire and I observe his private behavior, I see that it is in fact worthy to serve as an illustration of what I have taught. Hui is not stupid at all."

2.10 The Master said, "Look at the means a man employs, observe the basis from which he acts, and discover where it is that he feels at ease. Where can he hide? Where can he hide?"

2.11 The Master said, "Both keeping past teachings alive and understanding the present—someone able to do this is worthy of being a teacher."

2.12 The Master said, "The gentleman is not a vessel."

2.15 The Master said, "If you learn without thinking about what you have learned, you will be lost. If you think without learning, however, you will fall into danger."

2.19 Duke Ai asked, "What can I do to induce the common people to be obedient?"

Confucius replied, "Raise up the straight and apply them to the crooked, and the people will submit to you. If you raise up the crooked and apply them to the straight, the people will never submit."

2.21 Some people said of Confucius, "Why is it that he is not participating in government?"[4]

---

[4]Lit. "doing government" (*weizheng* 為政). The reference is to Confucius' lack of an official position.

[Upon being informed of this,] the Master remarked, "The *Book of Documents* says,

> 'Filial, oh so filial,
> Friendly to one's elders and juniors;
> [In this way] exerting an influence upon those who govern.'

Thus, in being a filial son and good brother one is already taking part in government. What need is there, then, to speak of 'participating in government'?"

BOOK THREE

Much of this book consists of criticisms (direct or indirect) of the ritual improprieties of the Three Families that also tell us much about ritual in general. A related theme is the need for cultural refinement (wen 文) to be accompanied by native substance (zhi 質)—that is, traditional practices must be informed by genuine feeling if they are to be more than mere empty gestures. The problem with Confucius' contemporaries is not only that they flouted proper ritual forms (cf. 3.1, 3.11, 3.17, 3.18), but also that even when they observed them they did so insincerely (cf. 3.3, 3.4, 3.12). They are thus lacking when it comes to both cultural refinement and native substance.

3.1 Confucius said of the Ji Family, "They have eight rows of dancers performing in their courtyard. If they can condone this, what are they *not* capable of?"

3.3 The Master said, "A man who is not Good—what has he to do with ritual? A man who is not Good—what has he to do with music?"

3.4 Lin Fang asked about the roots of ritual.

The Master exclaimed, "What a noble question! When it comes to ritual, it is better to be sparse than extravagant. When it comes to mourning, it is better to be excessively sorrowful than fastidious."

3.8 Zixia asked, "[An ode says,]

> 'Her artful smile, with its alluring dimples,
> Her beautiful eyes, so clear,
> The unadorned upon which to paint.'

What does this mean?"

The Master said, "The application of colors comes only after a suitable unadorned background is present."

Zixia said, "So it is the rites that come after?"

7

The Master said, "It is you, Zixia, who has awakened me to the meaning of these lines! It is only with someone like you that I can begin to discuss the *Odes*."

3.11 Someone asked for an explanation of the *di* sacrifice. The Master said, "I do not understand it. One who understood it could handle the world as if he had it right here," and he pointed to the palm of his hand.

3.12 "Sacrifice as if [they were] present" means that, when sacrificing to the spirits, you should comport yourself as if the spirits were present.

The Master said, "If I am not fully present at the sacrifice, it is as if I did not sacrifice at all."

3.17 Zigong wanted to do away with the practice of sacrificing a lamb to announce the beginning of the month.

The Master said, "Zigong! You regret the loss of the lamb, whereas I regret the loss of the rite."

3.18 The Master said, "If in serving your lord you are careful to observe every detail of ritual propriety, people will [wrongly] think you obsequious."

3.19 Duke Ding asked, "How should a lord employ his ministers? How should a minister serve his lord?"

Confucius replied, "A lord should employ his ministers with ritual, and ministers should serve their lord with dutifulness."

3.20 That Master said, "The 'Cry of the Osprey' expresses joy without becoming licentious, and expresses sorrow without falling into excessive pathos."

3.23 The Master was discussing music with the Grand Music Master of Lu. He said, "What can be known about music is this: when it first begins, it resounds with a confusing variety of notes, but as it unfolds, these notes are reconciled by means of harmony, brought into tension by means of counterpoint, and finally woven together into a seamless whole. It is in this way that music reaches its perfection."

3.24 A border official from the town of Yi¹ requested an audience with the Master, saying, "I have never failed to obtain an audience with the gentlemen who have passed this way." Confucius' followers thereupon presented him.

After emerging from the audience, the border official remarked, "You disciples, why should you be concerned about your Master's loss of office? The world has been without the Way for a long time now, and Heaven intends to use your Master like the wooden clapper for a bell."

---

¹In the state of Wei, on the border with Lu.

BOOK FOUR

Many of the passages in this book concern the supreme virtue of Goodness. Those who are truly Good love the Confucian Way and embody it in a wu-wei fashion—completely unself-consciously and effortlessly—as opposed to those who pursue the Way because of ulterior motives. Such true gentlemen require nothing from the world but the genuine joy and satisfaction they derive from virtue, as opposed to "petty people" who are motivated by considerations of profit or other external goods. This book also contains a series of statements (4.19 and 4.21) on filial piety that flesh out the treatment in Book One.

4.1 The Master said, "To live in the neighborhood of the Good is fine. If one does not choose to dwell among those who are Good, how will one obtain wisdom?"

4.2 The Master said, "Without Goodness, one cannot remain constant in adversity and cannot enjoy enduring happiness.

"Those who are Good feel at home in Goodness, whereas those who are clever follow Goodness because they feel that they will profit [*li* 利] from it."

4.3 The Master said, "Only one who is Good is able to truly love others or despise others."

4.4 The Master said, "Merely set your heart sincerely upon Goodness and you will be free of bad intentions."

4.5 The Master said, "Wealth and social eminence are things that all people desire, and yet unless they are acquired in the proper way I will not abide them. Poverty and disgrace are things that all people hate, and yet unless they are avoided in the proper way I will not despise them.

"If the gentleman abandons Goodness, how can he merit the name? The gentleman does not go against Goodness even for the amount of

10

time required to finish a meal. Even in times of urgency or distress, he necessarily accords with it."

4.6 The Master said, "I have yet to meet a person who truly loved Goodness or hated a lack of Goodness. One who truly loved Goodness could not be surpassed, while one who truly hated a lack of Goodness would at least be able to act in a Good fashion, as he would not tolerate that which is not Good being associated with his person.

"Is there a person who can, for the space of a single day, simply devote his efforts to Goodness? I have never met anyone whose strength was insufficient for this task. Perhaps such a person exists, but I have yet to meet him."

4.7 The Master said, "People are true to type with regard to what sort of mistakes they make. Observe closely the sort of mistakes a person makes—then you will know his character."

4.8 The Master said, "Having in the morning heard that the Way was being put into practice, I could die that evening without regret."

4.9 The Master said, "A scholar-official who has set his heart upon the Way but who is still ashamed of having shabby clothing or meager rations is not worth engaging in discussion."

4.10 The Master said, "With regard to the world, the gentleman has no predispositions for or against any person. He merely associates with those he considers right."

4.12 The Master said, "If in your affairs you abandon yourself to the pursuit of profit, you will arouse much resentment."

4.13 The Master said, "If a person is able to govern the state by means of ritual propriety and deference, what difficulties will he encounter? If, on the other hand, a person is not able to govern the state through ritual propriety and deference, of what use are the rites to him?"

4.14 The Master said, "Do not be concerned that you lack an official position, but rather concern yourself with the means by which you might become established. Do not be concerned that no one has heard of you, but rather strive to become a person worthy of being known."

4.15 The Master said, "Master Zeng! All that I teach can be strung together on a single thread."

"Yes, sir," Master Zeng responded.

After the Master left, the disciples asked, "What did he mean by that?"

Master Zeng said, "All that the Master teaches amounts to nothing more than dutifulness [*zhong* 忠] tempered by understanding [*shu* 恕]."

4.16 The Master said, "The gentleman understands rightness, whereas the petty person understands profit."

4.17 The Master said, "When you see someone who is worthy, concentrate upon becoming their equal; when you see someone who is unworthy, use this as an opportunity to look within yourself."

4.18 The Master said, "In serving your parents you may gently remonstrate with them. However, once it becomes apparent that they have not taken your criticism to heart you should be respectful and not oppose them, and follow their lead diligently without resentment."

4.19 The Master said, "While your parents are alive, you should not travel far, and when you do travel you must keep to a fixed itinerary."

4.21 The Master said, "You must always be aware of the age of your parents. On the one hand, it is a cause for rejoicing, on the other a source of anxiety."

4.22 The Master said, "People in ancient times were not eager to speak, because they would be ashamed if their actions did not measure up to their words."

4.24 The Master said, "The gentleman wishes to be slow to speak, but quick to act."

4.25 The Master said, "Virtue is never solitary; it always has neighbors."

BOOK FIVE

Much of the book is dedicated to discussions of the various virtues that characterize the perfected Confucian gentleman, and it is therefore no surprise that most of the passages consist of descriptions of the behavior of historical or contemporary individuals, usually coupled with moral judgments delivered by Confucius. This sort of teaching by means of moral models is a crucial component of any virtue ethic: positive exemplars teach one about the virtues and provide behavioral models for the student to emulate, while negative examples teach one about vice and serve as cautionary tales.

5.1 The Master said of Gongye Chang, "He is marriageable. Although he was once imprisoned as a criminal, he was in fact innocent of any crime." The Master gave him his daughter in marriage.

5.4 Zigong asked, "What do you think of me?"
The Master replied, "You are a vessel."
"What sort of vessel?"
"A *hu* [瑚] or *lian* [璉] vessel."

5.8 Meng Wubo asked, "Is Zilu Good?"
The Master replied, "I do not know."
Meng Wubo repeated his question.
The Master said, "In a state of one thousand chariots, Zilu could be employed to organize the collection of military taxes, but I do not know whether or not he is Good."
"What about Ran Qiu?"
"In a town of one thousand households, or an aristocratic family of one hundred chariots, Ran Qiu could be employed as a steward, but I do not know whether or not he is Good."
"What about Zihua?"
"Standing in his proper place at court with his sash tied, Zihua could be employed to converse with guests and visitors, but I do not know whether or not he is Good."

13

5.9 The Master said to Zigong, "Who is better, you or Yan Hui?"

Zigong answered, "How dare I even think of comparing myself to Hui? Hui learns one thing and thereby understands ten. I learn one thing and thereby understand two."

The Master said, "No, you are not as good as Hui. Neither of us is as good as Hui."

5.10 Zai Wo was sleeping during the daytime. The Master said, "Rotten wood cannot be carved, and a wall of dung cannot be plastered. As for Zai Wo, what would be the use of reprimanding him?"

The Master added, "At first, when evaluating people, I would listen to their words and then simply trust that the corresponding conduct would follow. Now when I evaluate people I listen to their words but then closely observe their conduct. It is my experience with Zai Wo that has brought about this change."

5.12 Zigong said, "What I do not wish others to do unto me, I also wish not to do unto others."

The Master said, "Ah, Zigong! That is something quite beyond you."

5.13 Zigong said, "The Master's cultural brilliance is something that is readily heard about, whereas one does not get to hear the Master expounding upon the subjects of human nature or the Way of Heaven."

5.19 Zizhang said, "Prime Minister Ziwen was given three times the post of prime minister, and yet he never showed a sign of pleasure; he was removed from this office three times, and yet never showed a sign of resentment. When the incoming prime minister took over, he invariably provided him with a complete account of the official state of affairs. What do you make of Prime Minister Ziwen?"

The Master said, "He certainly was dutiful."

"Was he not Good?"

"I do not know about that—what makes you think he deserves to be called Good?"

"When Cuizi assassinated the Lord of Qi, Chen Wenzi—whose estate amounted to ten teams of horses—abandoned all that he possessed and left the state. Upon reaching another state, he said, 'The officials here are as bad as our Great Officer Cuizi,' and thereupon left that state. Again, after going to another state, he said, 'The officials here are as bad as our Great Officer Cuizi,' and thereupon left that state as well. What do you make of Chen Wenzi?"

The Master said, "He certainly was pure."

"Was he not Good?"

"I do not know about that—what makes you think he deserves to be called Good?"

5.22 When the Master was in the state of Chen, he sighed, "Oh, let us go home! Let us go home! Our young followers back in Lu are wild and ambitious—they put on a great show of brilliant culture, but they lack the means to prune and shape it."

5.26 Yan Hui and Zilu were in attendance. The Master said to them, "Why do you not each speak to me of your aspirations?"

Zilu answered, "I would like to be able to share my carts and horses, clothing and fur with my fellow students and friends, without feeling regret."

Yan Hui answered, "I would like to avoid being boastful about my own abilities or exaggerating my accomplishments."

Zilu then said, "I would like to hear of the Master's aspirations."

The Master said, "To bring comfort to the aged, to inspire trust in my friends, and be cherished by the youth."[1]

5.27 The Master said, "I should just give up! I have yet to meet someone who is able to perceive his own faults and then take himself to task inwardly."

5.28 The Master said, "In any village of ten households there are surely those who are as dutiful or trustworthy as I am, but there is no one who matches my love for learning."

---

[1] Alternately, "To comfort the aged, trust my friends, and cherish the young."

BOOK SIX

This book focuses on judgments of disciples, other contemporaries, and historical figures, all of whom function as case studies of either the Confucian virtues being put into practice or the vices an aspiring gentleman is to avoid. Since Confucius' pedagogical goal is to instill virtuous dispositions rather than impart abstract principles, this sort of education by example is a primary strategy.

6.3 Duke Ai asked, "Who among your disciples might be said to love learning?"

Confucius answered, "There was one named Yan Hui who loved learning. He never misdirected his anger and never made the same mistake twice. Unfortunately, his allotted life span was short, and he has passed away. Now that he is gone, there are none who really love learning—at least, I have yet to hear of one."

6.5 When Yuan Si was serving as steward, he was offered a salary of nine hundred measures of millet,[1] but he declined it.

The Master said, "Do not decline it! [If you do not need it yourself,] could you not use it to aid the households in your neighborhood?"

6.7 The Master said, "Ah, Yan Hui! For three months at a time his heart did <u>not stray from Goodness</u>. The rest could only sporadically maintain such a state."

6.10 Boniu fell ill, and the Master went to ask after his health. Grasping his hand through the window, the Master sighed, "That we are going to lose him must be due to fate! How else could such a man be afflicted with such an illness [and we left with nothing we can do]?[2] How else could such a man be afflicted with such an illness?"

---

[1] Or, alternately, the harvest from 900 square *li* of fields; the unit of measure is not specified in the passage.

[2] The latter half of the sentence is present in the Dingzhou version, and is also part of the *Record of the Historian* version of this story.

6.11 The Master said, "What a worthy man was Yan Hui! Living in a narrow alley, subsisting on a basket of grain and gourd full of water—other people could not have born such hardship, yet it never spoiled Hui's joy. What a worthy man was Hui!"

6.12 Ran Qiu said, "It is not that I do not delight in your Way, Master, it is simply that my strength is insufficient."

The Master said, "Someone whose strength is genuinely insufficient collapses somewhere along the Way. As for you, you deliberately draw the line."

6.13 The Master said to Zixia, "Be a gentlemanly *ru*. Do not be a petty *ru*."

6.17 The Master said, "Who is able to leave a room without going out through the door? How is it, then, that no one follows this Way?"

6.18 The Master said, "When native substance overwhelms cultural refinement, the result is a crude rustic. When cultural refinement overwhelms native substance, the result is a foppish pedant. Only when culture and native substance are perfectly mixed and balanced do you have a gentleman."

6.20 The Master said, "One who knows it is not the equal of one who loves it, and one who loves it is not the equal of one who takes joy in it."

6.21 The Master said, "You can discuss the loftiest matters with those who are above average, but not with those who are below average."

6.22 Fan Chi asked about wisdom.

The Master said, "Working to ensure social harmony among the common people, respecting the ghosts and spirits while keeping them at a distance—this might be called wisdom."

He then asked about Goodness.

The Master said, "One who is Good sees as his first priority the hardship of self-cultivation, and only after thinks about results or rewards. Yes, this is what we might call Goodness."

6.23 The Master said, "The wise take joy in rivers, while the Good take joy in mountains. The wise are active, while the Good are still. The wise are joyful, while the Good are long-lived."

6.25 The Master said, "A *gu* [觚] that is not a proper *gu*—is it really a *gu*? Is it really a *gu*?"

6.27 The Master said, "Someone who is broadly learned with regard to culture, and whose conduct is restrained by the rites, can be counted upon to not go astray."

6.28 The Master had an audience with Nanzi, and Zilu was not pleased. The Master swore an oath, saying, "If I have done anything wrong, may Heaven punish me! May Heaven punish me!"

6.29 The Master said, "Acquiring Virtue by applying the mean—is this not best? And yet among the common people few are able to practice this virtue for long."

6.30 Zigong said, "If there were one able to broadly extend his benevolence to the common people and bring succor to the multitudes, what would you make of him? Could such a person be called Good?"

The Master said, "Why stop at Good? Such a person should surely be called a sage! Even someone like Yao or Shun would find such a task daunting. Desiring to take his stand, one who is Good helps others to take their stand; wanting to realize himself, he helps others to realize themselves. Being able to take what is near at hand as an analogy could perhaps be called the method of Goodness."

BOOK SEVEN

A discernable common theme in this book is the importance of a properly directed and sufficiently intense will or intention, which requires a focus on the goods internal to Confucian practice. Such a focus leads to a sense of joy that renders one immune to the allure of externalities.

7.1 The Master said, "I transmit rather than innovate. I trust in and love the ancient ways. I might thus humbly compare myself to Old Peng."

7.2 The Master said, "Remaining silent and yet comprehending, learning and yet never becoming tired, encouraging others and never growing weary—these are tasks that present me with no difficulty."

7.3 The Master said, "That I fail to cultivate Virtue, that I fail to inquire more deeply into that which I have learned, that upon hearing what is right I remain unable to move myself to do it, and that I prove unable to reform when I have done something wrong—such potential failings are a source of constant worry to me."

7.4 In his leisure moments, the Master was composed and yet fully at ease.

7.5 The Master said, "How seriously I have declined! It has been so long since I last dreamed of meeting the Duke of Zhou."

7.6 The Master said, "Set your heart upon the Way, rely upon Virtue, lean upon Goodness, and explore widely in your cultivation of the arts."

7.7 The Master said, "I have never denied instruction to anyone who, of their own accord, offered up as little as a bundle of silk or a bit of cured meat."

7.8 The Master said, "I will not open the door for a mind that is not already striving to understand, nor will I provide words to a tongue that is not already struggling to speak. If I hold up one corner of a problem, and the student cannot come back to me with the other three, I will not attempt to instruct him again."

7.9 When the Master dined in the company of one who was in mourning, he never ate his fill.

7.10 The Master would never sing on a day when he had wept.

7.12 The Master said, "If wealth were something worth pursuing, then I would pursue it, even if that meant serving as an officer holding a whip at the entrance to the marketplace. Since it is not worth pursuing, however, I prefer to follow that which I love."

7.14 When the Master was in the state of Qi, he heard the Shao music, and for three months after did not even notice the taste of meat. He said, "I never imagined that music could be so sublime."

7.16 The Master said, "Eating plain food and drinking water, having only your bent arm as a pillow—certainly there is joy to be found in this! Wealth and eminence attained improperly[1] concern me no more than the floating clouds."

7.17 The Master said, "If I were granted many more years, and could devote fifty of them to learning, surely I would be able to be free of major faults."

7.18 The Master used the classical pronunciation when reciting the *Odes* and the *History*, and when conducting ritual. In all of these cases, he used the classical pronunciation.

7.19 The Duke of She asked Zilu about Confucius. Zilu had no reply.
[Upon Zilu's return,] the Master said, "Why did you not just say: 'He is the type of person who is so passionate that he forgets to eat, whose

---

[1] Lit. in a "not right [*yi*]" fashion.

joy renders him free of worries, and who grows old without noticing the passage of the years'?"

7.20 The Master said, "I am not someone who was born with knowledge. I simply love antiquity, and diligently look there for knowledge."

7.22 The Master said, "When walking with two other people, I will always find a teacher among them. I focus on those who are good and seek to emulate them, and focus on those who are bad in order to be reminded of what needs to be changed in myself."

7.23 The Master said, "It is Heaven itself that has endowed me with virtue. What have I to fear from the likes of Huan Tui?"

7.24 The Master said, "Do you disciples imagine that I am being secretive? I hide nothing from you. I take no action, I make no move, without sharing it with you. This is the kind of person that I am."

7.28 The Master said, "No doubt there are those who try to innovate without acquiring knowledge, but this is a fault that I do not possess. I listen widely, and then pick out that which is excellent in order to follow it; I see many things, and then remember them. This constitutes a second-best sort of knowledge."

7.30 The Master said, "Is Goodness really so far away? If I simply desire Goodness, I will find that it is already here."

7.32 Whenever the Master was singing in a group and heard something that he liked, he inevitably asked to have it sung again, and only then would harmonize with it.

7.33 The Master said, "There is no one who is my equal when it comes to cultural refinement, but as for actually becoming a gentleman in practice, this is something that I have not yet been able to achieve."

7.34 The Master said, "How could I dare to lay claim to either sageliness or Goodness? What can be said about me is no more than this: I work at it without growing tired and encourage others without growing weary."

Gong Xihua observed, "This is precisely what we disciples are unable to learn."

7.35 The Master was seriously ill, and Zilu asked permission to offer a prayer.

The Master said, "Is such a thing done?"

Zilu said, "It is. The *Eulogy* reads, 'We pray for you above and below, to the spirits of Heaven and of Earth.'"

The Master said, "In that case, I have already been offering up my prayers for some time now."

7.37 The Master said, "The gentleman is self-possessed and relaxed, while the petty man is perpetually full of worry."

7.38 The Master was affable yet firm, awe-inspiring without being severe, simultaneously respectful and relaxed.

BOOK EIGHT

This book does not seem to have a clear thematic focus.

8.2 The Master said, "If you are respectful but lack ritual you will become exasperating; if you are careful but lack ritual you will become timid; if you are courageous but lack ritual you will become unruly; and if you are upright but lack ritual you will become inflexible.

"If the gentleman is kind to his relatives, the common people will be inspired toward goodness; if he does not neglect his old acquaintances, the people will honor their obligations to others."

8.7 Master Zeng said, "A scholar-official must be strong and resolute, for his burden is heavy and his way [*dao* 道] is long. He takes up Goodness as his own personal burden—is it not heavy? His way ends only with death—is it not long?"

8.8 The Master said, "Find inspiration in the *Odes*, take your place through ritual, and achieve perfection with music."

8.9 The Master said, "The common people can be made to follow it, but they cannot be made to understand it."

8.12 The Master said, "It is not easy to find someone who is able to learn for even the space of three years without a thought given to official salary."

8.13 The Master said, "Be sincerely trustworthy and love learning, and hold fast to the good Way until death. Do not enter a state that is endangered, and do not reside in a state that is disordered. If the Way is being realized in the world then show yourself; if it is not, then go into reclusion. In a state that has the Way, to be poor and of low status is a cause for shame; in a state that is without the Way, to be wealthy and honored is equally a cause for shame."

8.19 The Master said, "How great was Yao as a ruler! So majestic! It is Heaven that is great, and it was Yao who modeled himself upon it. So vast! Among the common people there were none who were able to find words to describe him. How majestic in his accomplishments, and glorious in cultural splendor!"

BOOK NINE

Most of the passages in this book consist of the Master's pronouncements concerning the importance of focus, sincerity, and perseverance in the pursuit of learning and virtue. In contrast are other passages where Confucius expresses his frustration with his contemporaries for failing to embrace the Way that he has been fated by Heaven to proclaim to the world.

9.2 A villager from Daxiang remarked sarcastically, "How great is Confucius! He is so broadly learned, and yet has failed to make a name for himself in any particular endeavor."

When the Master was told of this, he said to his disciples, "What art, then, should I take up? Charioteering? Archery? I think I shall take up charioteering."

9.3 The Master said, "A ceremonial cap made of linen is prescribed by the rites, but these days people use silk. This is frugal, and I follow the majority. To bow before ascending the stairs is what is prescribed by the rites, but these days people bow after ascending. This is arrogant, and—though it goes against the majority—I continue to bow before ascending."

9.5 The Master was surrounded in Kuang. He said, "Now that King Wen [文] is gone, is not culture [*wen* 文] now invested here in me? If Heaven intended this culture to perish, it would not have given it to those of us who live after King Wen's death. Since Heaven did not intend that this culture should perish, what can the people of Kuang do to me?"

9.10 Whenever the Master saw someone who was wearing mourning clothes, was garbed in full official dress, or was blind, he would always rise to his feet, even if the person was his junior. When passing such a person, he would always hasten his step.

9.11 With a great sigh Yan Hui lamented, "The more I look up at it the higher it seems; the more I delve into it, the harder it becomes. Catching a glimpse of it before me, I then find it suddenly at my back.

"The Master is skilled at gradually leading me on, step by step. He broadens me with culture and restrains me with the rites, so that even if I wanted to give up I could not. Having exhausted all of my strength, it seems as if there is still something left, looming up ahead of me. Though I desire to follow it, there seems to be no way through."

9.12 The Master was gravely ill, and Zilu instructed his fellow disciples to attend Confucius as if the disciples were his ministers.

During a remission in his illness, the Master [became aware of what was happening and] rebuked Zilu, saying, "It has been quite some time now, has it not, that you have been carrying out this charade! If I have no ministers and yet you act as if I have, who do you think I am going to fool? Am I going to fool Heaven? Moreover, would I not rather die in the arms of a few of my disciples than in the arms of ministers? Even if I do not merit a grand funeral, it is not as if I would be left to die by the side of the road!"

9.13 Zigong said, "If you possessed a piece of beautiful jade, would you hide it away in a locked box, or would you try to sell it at a good price?"

The Master responded, "Oh, I would sell it! I would sell it! I am just waiting for the right offer."

9.14 The Master expressed a desire to go and live among the Nine Yi Barbarian tribes. Someone asked him, "How could you bear their uncouthness?"

The Master replied, "If a gentleman were to dwell among them, what uncouthness would there be?"

9.17 Standing on the bank of a river, the Master said, "Look at how it flows on like this, never stopping day or night!"

9.18 The Master said, "I have yet to meet a man who loves Virtue as much as he loves female beauty."

9.19 The Master said, "[The task of self-cultivation] might be compared to the task of building up a mountain: if I stop even one basketful of earth short of completion, then I have stopped completely. It might also be compared to the task of leveling ground: even if I have only dumped a single basketful of earth, at least I am moving forward."

9.22 The Master said, "Surely there are some sprouts that fail to flower, just as surely as there are some flowers that fail to bear fruit!"

9.23 The Master said, "We should look upon the younger generation with awe because how are we to know that those who come after us will not prove our equals? Once, however, a man reaches the age of forty or fifty without having learned anything, we can conclude from this fact alone that he is not worthy of being held in awe."

9.24 The Master said, "When a man is rebuked with exemplary words after having made a mistake, he cannot help but agree with them. However, what is important is that he change himself in order to *accord* with them. When a man is praised with words of respect, he cannot help but be pleased with them. However, what is important is that he actually *live up* to them. A person who finds respectful words pleasing but does not live up to them, or agrees with others' reproaches and yet does not change—there is nothing I can do with one such as this."

9.28 The Master said, "Only after Winter comes do we know that the pine and cypress are the last to fade."

9.29 The Master said, "The wise are not confused, the Good do not worry, and the courageous do not fear."

BOOK TEN

Based on their style, lack of explicit subject, and parallels to be found in other early ritual texts such as the Record of Ritual or Book of Etiquette and Ritual, scholars have concluded that most of the passages in this book were probably culled from a lost ritual text that provided anonymous guidelines and injunctions for the aspiring gentleman. From earliest times, however, this book has been viewed by commentators as an extended description of the ritual behavior of Confucius in particular, and it was probably intended by the editors of the earliest stratum of the Analects *(Books One through Ten) to be understood that way. The translation and commentary will reflect this understanding of the text, rendering it as descriptive rather than injunctive, and understanding Confucius as the implicit subject, although he is only explicitly mentioned in a few passages. Seen as an actual description of the Master's behavior rather than a set of impersonal ritual guidelines, Book Ten serves as a sort of capstone for the first stratum, providing a series of descriptions of the Master effortlessly embodying in his words, behavior, and countenance the lessons imparted throughout the rest of the text. What is being emphasized in this book is the ease and grace with which the Master embodies the spirit of the rites in every aspect of his life—no matter how trivial—and accords with this spirit in adapting to new and necessarily unforeseeable circumstances. The final passage, 10.27, identifies this ability as the virtue of "timeliness" (shi 時)—that is, always according perfectly with the demands of the situation at hand. This is Confucius' forte, and he is in fact known to posterity (through the efforts of Mencius) as the "timely sage": the one whose ritual responses were always effortlessly and unself-consciously appropriate (Mencius 5:B:1).*

10.2 At court, when speaking with officers of lower rank, he was pleasant and affable; when speaking with officers of upper rank, he was formal and proper. When his lord was present, he combined an attitude of cautious respect with graceful ease.

10.3 When called on by his lord to receive a guest, his countenance would become alert and serious, and he would hasten his steps. When he saluted those in attendance beside him—extending his clasped hands to the left or right, as their position required—his robes remained perfectly arrayed, both front and back. Hastening forward, he moved smoothly, as though gliding upon wings. Once the guest had left, he would always return to report, "The guest is no longer looking back."

10.10 He would not instruct while eating, nor continue to converse once hc had retired to bed.

10.11 Even though a meal was only of coarse grain or vegetable broth, he invariably gave some as a sacrificial offering, and would do so in a grave and respectful manner.

10.12 He would not sit unless his mat was straight [*zheng* 正].

10.17 One day the stables burned. When the Master returned from court, he asked, "Was anyone hurt?" He did not ask about the horses.

10.19 When he was sick, and his lord came to visit him, he would lay with his head to the east, draped in his court robes, with his ceremonial sash fastened about him.

10.20 When summoned by his lord, he would set off on foot, without waiting for his horses to be hitched to the carriage.

10.23 When receiving a gift from a friend—even something as valuable as a cart or a horse—he did not bow unless it was a gift of sacrificial meat.

10.25 When he saw someone fasting or mourning, he invariably assumed a changed expression, even if they were an intimate acquaintance. When he saw someone wearing a ritual cap or a blind person, he would invariably display a respectful countenance, even if they were of low birth [*xie* 褻].

When riding past someone dressed in funeral garb, he would bow down and grasp the crossbar of his carriage. He would do so even if the mourner was a lowly peddler.

When presented food with full ritual propriety, he would invariably assume a solemn expression and rise from his seat.

He would also assume a solemn expression upon hearing a sudden clap of thunder or observing a fierce wind.

10.27 Startled by their arrival, a bird arose and circled several times before alighting upon a branch. [The Master] said, "This pheasant upon the mountain bridge—how timely it is! How timely it is!" Zilu saluted the bird, and it cried out three times before flying away.

BOOK ELEVEN

As Liu Baonan notes, "This entire chapter is devoted to the words and actions of the disciples." Most of the passages consist of evaluations of the characters of various disciples that serve to illustrate general points about virtue and self-cultivation.

11.4 The Master said, "Yan Hui is of no help to me—he is pleased with everything that I say."

11.8 When Yan Hui died, Yan Lu, his father, requested the Master's carriage, so that it could be used for Yan Hui's coffin enclosure.

The Master replied, "Everyone recognizes his own son, whether he is talented or not. When Bo Yu, my own son, passed away, he had a coffin, but no enclosure. I did not go on foot in order to provide him with an enclosure. Having held rank below the ministers, it is not permissible for me to go on foot."

11.9 When Yan Hui passed away, the Master lamented, "Oh! Heaven has bereft me! Heaven has bereft me!"

11.12 Zilu asked about serving ghosts and spirits. The Master said, "You are not yet able to serve people—how could you be able to serve ghosts and spirits?"

"May I inquire about death?"

"You do not yet understand life—how could you possibly understand death?"

11.17 The Master said, "The head of the Ji Family is wealthier than even the Duke of Zhou ever was, and yet Ran Qiu collects taxes on his behalf to further increase his already excessive wealth. Ran Qiu is no disciple of mine. If you disciples were to sound the drums and attack him, I would not disapprove."

11.22 Zilu asked, "Upon learning of something that needs to be done, should one immediately take care of it?"

The Master replied, "As long as one's father and elder brothers are still alive, how could one possibly take care of it immediately?"

Zihua [having observed both exchanges] inquired, "When Zilu asked you whether or not one should immediately take care of something upon learning of it, you told him one should not, as long as one's father and elder brothers were still alive. When Ran Qiu asked the same question, however, you told him that one should immediately take care of it. I am confused, and humbly ask to have this explained to me."

The Master said, "Ran Qiu is overly cautious, and so I wished to urge him on. Zilu, on the other hand, is too impetuous, and so I sought to hold him back."

11.26 Zilu, Zengxi, Ran Qiu, and Zihua were seated in attendance. The Master said to them, "Because I am older than any of you, no one is willing to employ me. Yet you, too, often complain, 'No one appreciates me.' Well, if someone were to appreciate you, what would you do?"

Zilu spoke up immediately. "If I were given charge of a state of a thousand chariots—even one hemmed in between powerful states, suffering from armed invasions and afflicted by famine—before three years were up I could infuse its people with courage and a sense of what is right."

The Master smiled at him.

He then turned to Ran Qiu. "You, Ran Qiu!" he said, "What would you do?"

Ran Qiu answered, "If I were given charge of a state sixty or seventy—or even fifty or sixty—square *li* in area, before three years were up I could see that the people would have all that they needed. As for instructing its people in ritual practice and music, this is a task that would have to await the arrival of a gentleman."

The Master then turned to Zihua. "You, Zihua! What would you do?"

Zihua answered, "I am not saying that I would actually be able to do it, but my wish, at least, would be to learn it. I would like to serve as a minor functionary—properly clad in ceremonial cap and gown—in ceremonies at the ancestral temple, or at diplomatic gatherings."

The Master then turned to Zengxi. "You, Zengxi! What would you do?"

Zengxi stopped strumming his zither, and as the last notes faded away he set the instrument aside and rose to his feet. "I would choose to do something quite different from any of the other three."

"What harm is there in that?" the Master said. "We are all just talking about our aspirations."

Zengxi then said, "In the third month of Spring, once the Spring garments have been completed, I should like to assemble a company of five or six young men and six or seven boys to go bathe in the Yi River and enjoy the breeze upon the Rain Dance Altar, and then return singing to the Master's house."

The Master sighed deeply, saying, "I am with Zengxi!"

The other three disciples left, but Master Zeng stayed behind. He asked, "What did you think of what the other disciples said?"

"Each of them was simply talking about his aspirations."

"Then why, Master, did you smile at Zilu?"

"One governs a state by means of ritual. His words failed to express the proper sense of deference, and that is why I smiled at him."

"Was Ran Qiu, then, not concerned with statecraft?"

"Since when did something sixty or seventy—even fifty or sixty—square *li* in area not constitute a state?"

"Was Zihua, then, not concerned with statecraft?"

"If ancestral temples and diplomatic gatherings are not the business of the feudal lords, what then are they? If Zihua's aspiration is a minor one, then what would be considered a major one?"

BOOK TWELVE

As Legge observes, this book conveys "lessons on perfect virtue [ren], government, and other questions of morality, addressed in conversation by Confucius chiefly to his disciples. The different answers, given about the same subject to different questioners, show well how the sage suited his instruction to the characters and capacities of the parties with whom he had to do" (1991a: 250). A prominent theme is the contrast between Confucian rule by Virtue and personal example as opposed to rule by force or coercive laws.

12.1 Yan Hui asked about Goodness.

The Master said, "Restraining yourself and returning to the rites [*keji fuli* 克己復禮] constitutes Goodness. If for one day you managed to restrain yourself and return to the rites, in this way you could lead the entire world back to Goodness. The key to achieving Goodness lies within yourself—how could it come from others?"

Yan Hui asked, "May I inquire as to the specifics?"

The Master said, "Do not look unless it is in accordance with ritual; do not listen unless it is in accordance with ritual; do not speak unless it is in accordance with ritual; do not move unless it is in accordance with ritual."

Yan Hui replied, "Although I am not quick to understand, I ask permission to devote myself to this teaching."

12.5 Anxiously, Sima Niu remarked, "Everyone has brothers, I alone have none."

Zixia replied, "I have heard it said, 'Life and death are governed by fate; wealth and honor are determined by Heaven.' A gentleman is respectful and free of errors. He is reverent and ritually proper in his dealings with others. In this way, everyone within the Four Seas[1] is his brother. How could a gentleman be concerned about not having brothers?"

---

[1] I.e., the entire world; China was viewed as being surrounded on all sides by oceans.

12.7 Zigong asked about governing.

The Master said, "Simply make sure there is sufficient food, sufficient armaments, and that you have the confidence of the common people."

Zigong said, "If sacrificing one of these three things became unavoidable, which would you sacrifice first?"

The Master replied, "I would sacrifice the armaments."

Zigong said, "If sacrificing one of the two remaining things became unavoidable, which would you sacrifice next?"

The Master replied, "I would sacrifice the food. Death has always been with us, but a state cannot stand once it has lost the confidence of the people."

12.8 Ji Zicheng said, "Being a gentleman is simply a matter of having the right native substance, and nothing else. Why must one engage in cultural refinement?"

Zigong replied, "It is regrettable, Sir, that you should speak of the gentleman in this way—as they say, 'A team of horses cannot overtake your tongue.'

"A gentleman's cultural refinement resembles his native substance, and his native substance resembles his cultural refinement. The skin of a tiger or leopard, shorn of its fur, is no different from the skin of a dog or sheep."

12.9 Duke Ai said to Master You, "The harvest was poor and I cannot satisfy my needs. What should I do?"

Master You said, "Why do you not try taxing the people one part in ten?"

"I am currently taxing them two parts in ten, and even so I cannot satisfy my needs. How could reducing the tax to one part in ten help?"

Master You answered, "If the common people's needs are satisfied, how could their lord be lacking? If the common people's needs are not satisfied, how can their lord be content?"

12.11 Duke Jing of Qi asked Confucius about governing.

Confucius responded, "Let the lord be a true lord, the ministers true ministers, the fathers true fathers, and the sons true sons."

The Duke replied, "Well put! Certainly if the lord is not a true lord, the ministers not true ministers, the fathers not true fathers, and the sons not true sons, even if there is sufficient grain, will I ever get to eat it?"

12.13 The Master said, "When it comes to hearing civil litigation, I am as good as anyone else. What is necessary, though, is to bring it about that there is no civil litigation at all."

12.17 Ji Kangzi asked Confucius about governing.

Confucius responded, "To 'govern' [*zheng* 政] means to be 'correct' [*zheng* 正]. If you set an example by being correct yourself, who will dare to be incorrect?"

12.18 Ji Kangzi was concerned about the prevalence of robbers in Lu and asked Confucius about how to deal with this problem.

Confucius said, "If you could just get rid of your own excessive desires, the people would not steal even if you rewarded them for it."

12.19 Ji Kangzi asked Confucius about governing, saying, "If I were to execute those who lacked the Way in order to advance those who possessed the Way, how would that be?"

Confucius responded, "In your governing, Sir, what need is there for executions? If you desire goodness, then the common people will be good. The Virtue of a gentleman is like the wind, and the Virtue of a petty person is like the grass—when the wind moves over the grass, the grass is sure to bend."

12.22 Fan Chi asked about Goodness.

The Master replied, "Care for others."

He then asked about wisdom.

The Master replied, "Know others."

Fan Chi still did not understand, so the Master elaborated: "Raise up the straight and apply them to the crooked, and the crooked will be made straight."

Fan Chi retired from the Master's presence. Seeing Zixia, he said, "Just before I asked the Master about wisdom, and he replied, 'Raise up the straight and apply them to the crooked, and the crooked will be made straight.' What did he mean by that?"

Zixia answered, "What a wealth of instruction you have received! When Shun ruled the world, he selected from amongst the multitude, raising up Gao Yao, and those who were not Good then kept their distance. When Tang ruled the world, he selected from amongst the multitude, raising up Yi Yin, and those who were not Good then kept their distance."

12.24 Master Zeng said, "The gentleman acquires friends by means of cultural refinement, and then relies upon his friends for support in becoming Good."

BOOK THIRTEEN

As in Book Twelve, many of the passages in this book focus on the theme of governing by personal example and the gentle power of <u>Virtue</u> rather than by means of laws or coercion. The importance of superiors knowing others so that they can employ them fairly and effectively is emphasized, as is the importance of inferiors being forthright and courageous, unafraid to contradict their lord or incur the disfavor of their colleagues. Several passages explicitly contrast the gentleman and petty person, and many others do so implicitly: the gentleman is flexible and context sensitive, while lesser people are rigid and prone to both flattering and being flattered. Related to this theme is a suspicion of public opinion and concern about appearance and actuality, especially the danger of petty people assuming the semblance of virtue.

13.3 Zilu asked, "If the Duke of Wei were to employ you to serve in the government of his state, what would be your first priority?"

The Master answered, "It would, of course, be the rectification of names [*zhengming* 正名]."

Zilu said, "Could you, Master, really be so far off the mark? Why worry about rectifying names?"

The Master replied, "How boorish you are, Zilu! When it comes to matters that he does not understand, the gentleman should remain silent.

"If names are not rectified, speech will not accord with reality; when speech does not accord with reality, things will not be successfully accomplished. When things are not successfully accomplished, ritual practice and music will fail to flourish; when ritual and music fail to flourish, punishments and penalties will miss the mark. And when punishments and penalties miss the mark, the common people will be at a loss as to what to do with themselves. This is why the gentleman only applies names that can be properly spoken and assures that what he says can be properly put into action. The gentleman simply guards against arbitrariness in his speech. That is all there is to it."

13.4 Fan Chi asked to learn about plowing and growing grain [from Confucius].

The Master said, "When it comes to that, any old farmer would be a better teacher than I."

He asked to learn about growing fruits and vegetables.

The Master said, "When it comes to that, any old gardener would be a better teacher than I."

Fan Chi then left. The Master remarked, "What a common fellow [*xiaoren* 小人] that Fan Chi is! When a ruler loves ritual propriety, then none among his people will dare to be disrespectful. When a ruler loves rightness, then none among his people will dare not to obey. When a ruler loves trustworthiness, then none of his people will dare to not be honest. The mere existence of such a ruler would cause the common people throughout the world to bundle their children on their backs and seek him out. Of what use, then, is the study of agriculture?"

13.5 The Master said, "Imagine a person who can recite the several hundred odes by heart but, when delegated a governmental task, is unable to carry it out, or when sent abroad as an envoy, is unable to engage in repartee. No matter how many odes he might have memorized, of what use are they to him?"

13.6 The Master said, "When the ruler is correct, his will is put into effect without the need for official orders. When the ruler's person is not correct, he will not be obeyed no matter how many orders he issues."

13.16 The Duke of She asked about governing.

The Master said, "[Act so that] those near to you are pleased, and those who are far from you are drawn closer."

13.18 The Duke of She said to Confucius, "Among my people there is one we call 'Upright Gong.' When his father stole a sheep, he reported him to the authorities."

Confucius replied, "Among my people, those who we consider 'upright' are different from this: fathers cover up for their sons, and sons cover up for their fathers. 'Uprightness' is to be found in this."

13.20 Zigong asked, "What does a person have to be like before he could be called a true scholar-official?"

The Master said, "Conducting himself with a sense of shame, and not dishonoring his ruler's mandate when sent abroad as a diplomat— such a person could be called a scholar-official."

"May I ask what the next best type of person is like?"

"His lineage and clan consider him filial, and his fellow villagers consider him respectful to his elders."

"And the next best?"

"In his speech, he insists on being trustworthy, and with regard to his actions, he insists that they bear fruit. What a narrow, rigid little man he is! And yet he might still be considered the next best."

"How about those who today are involved in government?"

The Master exclaimed, "Oh! Those petty functionaries are not even worth considering."

13.21 The Master said, "If you cannot manage to find a person of perfectly balanced conduct to associate with, I suppose you must settle for the wild or the fastidious. In their pursuit of the Way, the wild plunge right in, while the fastidious are always careful not to get their hands dirty."

13.24 Zigong asked, "What would you make of a person whom everyone in the village likes?"

The Master said, "I would not know what to make of him."

"What about someone whom everyone in the village hates?"

"I would still not know. Better this way: those in the village who are good like him, and those who are not good hate him."

BOOK FOURTEEN

Most of the passages in this book concern themselves in some way with the respective duties of ruler and minister. Here the key to rulership is presented as employing people correctly, which requires that one be a good judge of character—a potentially difficult task, since often a person's outward presentation does not always match their inner character or actual behavior. A large portion of the book is dedicated to case examples of how one would go about judging the character of others, with the Master evaluating the behavior of various historical figures, noting both their strengths and weaknesses, and thereby illustrating the perceptive powers of a gentleman. On the minister's side, one must be dedicated to the Way and not to the pursuit of salary, honest with oneself and others, and courageous in remonstrating with one's ruler when it comes to matters of rightness.

14.1 Yuan Si asked about shame.

The Master said, "When the state has the Way, accept a salary; when the state is without the Way, to accept a salary is shameful."

"To refrain from competitiveness, boastfulness, envy, and greed—can this be considered Goodness?"

The Master said, "This can be considered difficult, but as for its being Good, that I do not know."

14.4 The Master said, "Those who possess Virtue will inevitably have something to say, whereas those who have something to say do not necessarily possess Virtue. Those who are Good will necessarily display courage, but those who display courage are not necessarily Good."

14.5 Nangong Kuo said to Confucius, "Yi was a skillful archer, and Ao was a powerful naval commander, and yet neither of them met a natural death. Yu and Hou Ji, on the other hand, did nothing but personally tend to the land, and yet they both ended up with possession of the world."

41

The Master did not answer.

After Nangong Kuo left, the Master sighed, "What a gentlemanly person that man is! How he reveres Virtue!"

14.12 Zilu asked about the complete person.

The Master said, "Take a person as wise as Zang Wuzhong, as free of desire as Gongchuo, as courageous as Zhuangzi of Bian, and as accomplished in the arts as Ran Qiu, and then acculturate them by means of ritual and music—such a man might be called a complete person."

He continued: "But must a complete person today be exactly like this? When seeing a chance for profit he thinks of what is right; when confronting danger he is ready to take his life into his own hands; when enduring an extended period of hardship he does not forget what he had professed in more fortunate times—such a man might also be called a complete person."

14.13 The Master asked Gongming Jia about Gongshu Wenzi, saying, "Is it really true that your master did not speak, did not laugh, and did not take?"

Gongming Jia answered, "Whoever told you that was exaggerating. My master only spoke when the time was right, and so people never grew impatient listening to him. He only laughed when he was genuinely full of joy, and so people never tired of hearing him laugh. He only took what was rightfully his, and so people never resented his taking of things."

The Master said, "Was he really that good? Could he really have been that good?"

14.24 The Master said, "In ancient times scholars learned for their own sake; these days they learn for the sake of others."

14.25 Qu Boyu sent a messenger to Confucius. Confucius sat down beside him and asked, "How are things with your Master?"

The messenger replied, "My Master wishes to reduce his faults, but has not yet been able to do so."

After the messenger left, the Master said, "Now that is a messenger! That is a messenger!"

14.27 The Master said, "The gentleman is ashamed to have his words exceed his actions."

14.29 Zigong was given to criticizing others.

The Master remarked sarcastically, "What a worthy man that Zigong must be! As for me, I hardly have the time for this."

14.30 The Master said, "Do not worry that you are not recognized by others; worry rather that you yourself lack ability."

14.34 Someone asked, "What do you think of the saying, 'Requite injury with kindness [*de* 德]'?"

The Master replied, "With what, then, would one requite kindness? Requite injury with uprightness, and kindness with kindness."

14.35 The Master sighed, "Alas! No one understands me."

Zigong replied, "How can you say that no one understands you, Master?"

"I am not bitter toward Heaven, nor do I blame others. I study what is below in order to comprehend what is above. If there is anyone who could understand me, perhaps it is Heaven."

14.36 Gongbo Liao submitted an accusation against Zilu to the head of the Ji Family. Zifu Jingbo reported this to Confucius, adding, "That master [i.e., Ji Kangzi] has certainly been led astray by Gongbo Liao, but my influence with him is still sufficient to see to it that Gongbo Liao's corpse is displayed at court or in the marketplace."

The Master said, "Whether or not the Way is to be put into action is a matter of fate. Whether or not the Way is to be discarded is also a matter of fate. What power does Gongbo Liao have to affect fate?"

14.38 Zilu spent the night at Stone Gate. The next morning, the gate-keeper asked him, "Where have you come from?"

Zilu answered, "From the house of Confucius."

"Isn't he the one who knows that what he does is impossible and yet persists anyway?"

BOOK FIFTEEN

Like Book Seventeen, this book is a lengthy collection of generally short passages without any clear unifying theme.

15.1 Duke Ling of Wei asked Confucius about military formations [*chen* 陳].

Confucius replied, "I know something about the arrangement of ceremonial stands and dishes for ritual offerings, but I have never learned about the arrangement of battalions and divisions."

He left the next day.

15.2 [When Confucius was besieged] in the state of Chen, all of the provisions were exhausted, and his followers were so weak from hunger that they could not even stand. Upset, Zilu appeared before the Master and said, "Does even the gentleman encounter hardship?"

The Master said, "Of course the gentleman encounters hardship. The difference is that the petty man, encountering hardship, is overwhelmed by it."

15.5 The Master said, "Is Shun not an example of someone who ruled by means of wu-wei? What did he do? He made himself reverent and took his proper [ritual] position facing south, that is all."

15.9 The Master said, "No scholar-official of noble intention or Good person would ever pursue life at the expense of Goodness, and in fact some may be called upon to give up their lives in order to fulfill Goodness."

15.11 Yan Hui asked about running a state.

The Master said, "Follow the calendar of the Xia, travel in the carriages of the Shang, and clothe yourself in the ceremonial caps of the Zhou."

"As for music, listen only to the Shao and Wu. Prohibit the tunes of Zheng, and keep glib people at a distance—for the tunes of Zheng are licentious, and glib people are dangerous."

15.16 The Master said, "I have never been able to do anything for a person who is not himself constantly asking, 'What should I do? What should I do?'"

15.18 The Master said, "The gentleman takes rightness as his substance, puts it into practice by means of ritual, gives it expression through modesty, and perfects it by being trustworthy. Now that is a gentleman!"

15.24 Zigong asked, "Is there one word that can serve as a guide for one's entire life?"

The Master answered, "Is it not 'understanding' [*shu* 恕]? Do not impose on others what you yourself do not desire."

15.28 The Master said, "When the multitude hates a person, you must examine them and judge for yourself. The same holds true for someone whom the multitude love."

15.29 The Master said, "Human beings can broaden the Way—it is not the Way that broadens human beings."

15.30 The Master said, "To make a mistake and yet to not change your ways—this is what is called truly making a mistake."

15.31 The Master said, "I once engaged in thought for an entire day without eating and an entire night without sleeping, but it did no good. It would have been better for me to have spent that time in learning."

15.36 The Master said, "When it comes to being Good, defer to no one, not even your teacher."

15.37 The Master said, "The gentleman is true, but not rigidly trustworthy."

15.39 The Master said, "In education, there are no differences in kind."

15.41 The Master said, "Words should convey their point, and leave it at that."

15.42 The Music Master Mian came to see Confucius.

When they came to the steps, the Master said, "Here are the steps." When they reached his seat, the Master said, "Here is your seat." After everyone was seated, the Master informed him as to who was present, saying, "So-and-so is seated here, and So-and-so is seated over there."

When the Music Master left, Zizhang asked, "Is this the way to converse with a Music Master?"

The Master replied, "Yes, this is indeed the way to assist a Music Master."

BOOK SIXTEEN

This is a stylistically somewhat strange book, and it is here that one begins to find the sort of anomalies—fragmentary passages, unusually long narratives, concern with numbers, Confucius being referred to as "Kongzi" rather than "the Master"—that mark Books Sixteen through Twenty as belonging to the latest stratum of the text.

16.4 Confucius said, "Beneficial types of friendship number three, as do harmful types of friendship. Befriending the upright, those who are true to their word,[1] or those of broad learning—these are the beneficial types of friendship. Befriending clever flatterers, skillful dissemblers, or the smoothly glib—these are the harmful types of friendship."

16.5 Confucius said, "Beneficial types of joy number three, as do harmful types of joy. Taking joy in regulating yourself through the rites and music,[2] in commending the excellence of others, or in possessing many worthy friends—these are the beneficial types of joy. Taking joy in arrogant behavior, idle amusements, or decadent licentiousness—these are the harmful types of joys."

16.7 Confucius said, "The gentleman guards against three things: when he is young, and his blood and vital essence are still unstable, he guards against the temptation of female beauty; when he reaches his prime, and his blood and vital essence have become unyielding, he guards against being contentious; when he reaches old age, and his blood and vital essence have begun to decline, he guards against being acquisitive."

16.8 The Master said, "The gentleman stands in awe of three things: the Mandate of Heaven, great men, and the teachings of the sages. The

---

[1] *Liang* 諒 has had a negative connotation ("rigidly trustworthy") in a previous passage (15.36), but clearly has a positive sense here.

[2] The Dingzhou text has only "the rites" here.

petty person does not understand the Mandate of Heaven, and thus does not regard it with awe; he shows disrespect to great men, and ridicules the teachings of the sages."

16.9 Confucius said, "Those who are born understanding it are the best; those who come to understand it through learning are second. Those who find it difficult to understand and yet persist in their studies come next. People who find it difficult to understand but do not even try to learn are the worst of all."

16.13 Ziqin asked Boyu, "Have you acquired any esoteric learning?"

Boyu replied, "I have not. My father was once standing by himself in the courtyard, and as I hurried by with quickened steps,[3] he asked, 'Have you learned the *Odes*?' I replied, 'Not yet.' He said, 'If you do not learn the *Odes*, you will lack the means to speak.' I then retired and learned the *Odes*.

"On another day, my father was once again standing by himself in the courtyard and, as I hurried by with quickened steps, he asked, 'Have you learned ritual?'[4] I replied, 'Not yet.' He said, 'If you do not learn ritual, you will lack the means to take your place.' I then retired and learned ritual.

"These two things are what I have been taught."

Ziqin retired and, smiling to himself, remarked, "I asked one question and got three answers: I learned about the *Odes*, I learned about ritual, and I learned how the gentleman keeps his son at a distance."

---

[3] A sign of respect; cf. 10.3.

[4] Some commentators suggest that *li* 禮 is meant as the title of a text ("the *Rites*"), which would indicate the existence of formal ritual texts—such as the *Record of Ritual*—at the time 16.13 was recorded. This, in turn, would be a sign of a quite late date for this passage.

BOOK SEVENTEEN

This book contains a mixture of general observations and historical accounts.

17.2 The Master said, "By nature people are similar; they diverge as the result of practice."

17.3 The Master said, "Only the very wise and the very stupid do not change."

17.8 The Master said, "Zilu! Have you heard about the six [virtuous] words and their six corresponding vices?"

Zilu replied, "I have not."

"Sit! I will tell you about them.

"Loving Goodness without balancing it with a love for learning will result in the vice of foolishness. Loving wisdom without balancing it with a love for learning will result in the vice of deviance. Loving trustworthiness without balancing it with a love for learning will result in the vice of harmful rigidity. Loving uprightness without balancing it with a love for learning will result in the vice of intolerance. Loving courage without balancing it with a love for learning will result in the vice of unruliness. Loving resoluteness without balancing it with a love for learning will result in the vice of willfulness."

17.9 The Master said, "Little Ones, why do none of you learn the *Odes*? The *Odes* can be a source of inspiration and a basis for evaluation; they can help you to come together with others, as well as to properly express complaints. In the home, they teach you about how to serve your father, and in public life they teach you about how to serve your lord. They also broadly acquaint you with the names of various birds, beasts, plants, and trees."

17.10 The Master said to Boyu, "Have you mastered the *Odes* from the 'South of Zhou' and the 'South of Shao'? A man who has not mastered the 'South of Zhou' and the 'South of Shao' is like someone standing with his face to the wall, is he not?"

17.11 The Master said, "When we say, 'the rites, the rites,' are we speaking merely of jade and silk? When we say, 'music, music,' are we speaking merely of bells and drums?"

17.13 The Master said, "The village worthy is the thief of virtue."

17.18 The Master said, "I hate that purple has usurped the place of vermillion, that the tunes of Zheng have been confused with classical music, and that the clever of tongue have undermined both state and family."

17.19 The Master sighed, "Would that I did not have to speak!"

Zigong said, "If the Master did not speak, then how would we little ones receive guidance from you?"

The Master replied, "What does Heaven ever say? Yet the four seasons are put in motion by it, and the myriad creatures receive their life from it. What does Heaven ever say?"

17.21 Zai Wo asked about the three-year mourning period, saying, "Surely one year is long enough. If the gentleman refrains from practicing ritual for three years, the rites will surely fall into ruin; if he refrains from music for three years, this will surely be disastrous for music. After the lapse of a year the old grain has been used up, while the new grain has ripened, and the four different types of tinder have all been drilled in order to rekindle the fire. One year is surely long enough."

The Master asked, "Would you feel comfortable then eating your sweet rice and wearing your brocade gowns?"

"I would."

The Master replied, "Well, if you would feel comfortable doing so, then by all means you should do it. When the gentleman is in mourning, he gets no pleasure from eating sweet foods, finds no joy in listening to music, and feels no comfort in his place of dwelling. This is why he gives up these things. But if you would feel comfortable doing them, then by all means you should!"

After Zai Wo left, the Master remarked, "This shows how lacking in Goodness this Zai Wo is! A child is completely dependent upon the care of his parents for the first three years of his life—this is why the three-year mourning period is common practice throughout the world. Did Zai Wo not receive three years of care from his parents?"

17.23 Zilu asked, "Does the gentleman admire courage?"

The Master said, "The gentleman admires rightness above all. A gentleman who possessed courage but lacked a sense of rightness would create political disorder, while a common person who possessed courage but lacked a sense of rightness would become a bandit."

17.25 The Master said, "Women and servants are particularly hard to manage: if you are too familiar with them, they grow insolent, but if you are too distant, they grow resentful."

BOOK EIGHTEEN

This book consists primarily of accounts of historical figures and encounters between Confucius and contemporary recluses—both primitivists who reject society altogether and principled recluses disgusted with the present age. The main themes seem to be timeliness and balance: both the ancients and Confucius knew how to respond to the age, and they are contrasted with rigid, overly purist recluses, who in clinging to virtue and avoiding the complexities of negotiating their contemporary world lose some of their humanity.

18.6 Confucius passed Chang Ju and Jie Ni, who were yoked together pulling a plow through a field. He sent Zilu to ask them where the ford was to be found.

Chang Ju inquired, "That fellow holding the reins there—who is he?"

Zilu answered, "That is Confucius."

"Do you mean Confucius of Lu?"

"The same."

"Then *he* should know where the ford is."

Zilu then asked Jie Ni.

Jie Ni also replied with a question: "Who are you?"

"I am Zilu."

"The disciple of Confucius of Lu?"

"Yes."

"The whole world is as if engulfed in a great flood, and who can change it? Given this, instead of following a scholar who merely avoids the bad people [of this age], wouldn't it be better for you to follow scholars like us, who avoid the age itself?" He then proceeded to cover up his seeds with dirt and did not pause again.

Zilu returned and reported this conversation to Confucius. The Master was lost in thought for a moment, and then remarked, "A person cannot flock together with the birds and the beasts. If I do not associate with the followers of men, then with whom would I associate? If the Way were realized in the world, then I would not need to change anything."

18.7 Zilu was traveling with Confucius, but had fallen behind. He encountered an old man carrying a wicker basket suspended from his staff. Zilu asked, "Have you seen my Master?"

The old man answered,

> "'Won't soil his dainty hands
> Can't tell millet from corn.'
> Who, then, might your master be?"

He then planted his staff in the ground and began weeding.

[Not knowing how to reply] Zilu simply remained standing with his hands clasped as a sign of respect.

The old man subsequently invited Zilu back to his house to stay the night. After killing a chicken and preparing some millet for Zilu to eat, he presented his two sons to him. The next day, Zilu caught up with Confucius and told him what had happened.

"He must be a scholar recluse," the Master said. He sent Zilu back to the old farmer's house to meet with him again, but by the time Zilu got there the man had already disappeared. Zilu then remarked, "To avoid public service is to be without a sense of what is right. Proper relations between elders and juniors cannot be discarded—how, then, can one discard the rightness that obtains between ruler and minister? To do so is to wish to keep one's hands from getting dirty at the expense of throwing the great social order into chaos. The gentleman takes office in order to do what is right, even though he already knows that the Way will not be realized."

BOOK NINETEEN

This book consists entirely of sayings from the disciples, many of which are summaries or elaborations of themes already seen in earlier books. A number of uncharacteristic features emerge in this book, especially in the second half, and this is probably indicative of a fairly late date.

19.6 Zixia said, "Learning broadly and firmly retaining what one has learned, being incisive in one's questioning and able to reflect upon what is near at hand—Goodness is to be found in this."

19.7 Zixia said, "The various artisans dwell in their workshops in order to perfect their crafts, just as the gentleman learns in order to reach the end of his Way."

19.11 Zixia said, "As long as one does not transgress the bounds when it comes to important Virtues, it is permissible to cross the line here and there when it comes to minor Virtues."

19.12 Ziyou said, "Among the disciples of Zixia, the younger ones are fairly competent when it comes to tasks such as mopping and sweeping, answering summons, and entering and retiring from formal company, but these are all superficialities.[1] They are completely at a loss when it comes to mastering the basics. Why is this?"

When Zixia heard of this, he remarked, "Alas! Ziyou seems to have missed the point. Whose disciples will be the first to be taught the Way of the gentleman, and then in the end grow tired of it? It is like the grass and the trees: you make distinctions between them according to their kind. The Way of the gentleman, how can it be slandered so? Starting at the beginning and working through to the end—surely this describes none other than the sage!"

---

[1] Lit. "the branches" (*mo* 末), contrasted with the "basics"—lit. the "root" (*ben* 本).

19.14 Ziyou said, "Mourning should fully express grief and then stop at that."

19.21 Zigong said, "A gentleman's errors are like an eclipse of the sun or the moon: when he errs, everyone notices it, but when he makes amends, everyone looks up to him."

BOOK TWENTY

This book consists of only three passages, of which the first two are exceptionally long, and strikes one as a somewhat random collection of passages that, for whatever reason, were not fitted into other books.

20.3 Confucius said, "One who does not understand fate lacks the means to become a gentleman. One who does not understand ritual lacks the means to take his place. One who does not understand words lacks the means to evaluate others."

APPENDIX 1

COMMENTARY

Book One Commentary

1.1 As Cheng Shude (following Mao Qiling) notes, "People today think of 'learning' as the pursuit of knowledge, whereas the ancients thought of 'learning' as cultivating the self." For evidence, he points to 6.3, where Confucius cites Yan Hui as the only one of his disciples who truly loved learning because he "never misdirected his anger and never repeated a mistake twice." We will see throughout the text that the sort of learning Confucius is interested in is a practical kind of "know-how" rather than abstract theoretical knowledge.

1.2 The line enclosed in quotation marks is probably a traditional saying. A comment upon this passage found in the *Garden of Persuasions* reads, "If the roots are not straight then the branches will necessarily be crooked, and if the beginning does not flourish then the end will necessarily wither. An ode says, 'The highlands and lowlands have been pacified/ The springs and streams have been made clear/ Once the roots are firmly established, the Way will grow.'" The quoted ode is a variant of the extant Ode 227. We see from the common Confucian theme that political order grows naturally out of the moral character formed within the context of family life.

1.3 This suspicion of glib speech and superficial appearance is found throughout the *Analects*. In 15.11 the danger presented by "glib people" (*ningren* 佞人) is compared to the derangement of morals brought about by the music of Zheng. David Nivison (1999: 751) has made a very interesting observation that may explain Confucius' hatred for these clever, ingratiating people: in archaic Chinese, *ning* was pronounced **nieng*[1] and is actually a graphic modification of its cognate *ren* 仁 (**nien*). The original meaning of *ren* was something like "noble in form," and it would appear that *ning* was its counterpart in the verbal realm: "attractive or noble in speech." In giving *ning* a negative meaning in the

---

[1] Generally the modern Mandarin pronunciation of Chinese characters will be given, the Mandarin dialect being the standard form of modern spoken Chinese. When relevant, however, the postulated archaic pronunciation—reconstructed indirectly by historians of phonetics, and denoted with an asterisks—will also be provided.

57

Analects, Confucius drives a wedge between the two qualities: *ren* now becomes "true" (i.e., inner) nobleness or Goodness, whereas *ning* represents the false, external counterfeit of *ren*.

1.4 Here again we find the emphasis on practice—actual social behavior—as opposed to academic, theoretical knowledge. The sort of incessant self-examination practiced by Master Zeng no doubt informs his observation in 8.7 that "the burden is heavy and the Way is long." For the importance of introspection, cf. 5.27.

1.6 There is some debate about how to understand the term *wen* ("writing," "culture") here, but it most likely refers to a set of cultural practices such as those later formalized as the so-called "six arts" of ritual, music, archery, charioteering, calligraphy, and mathematics in which any cultured person was trained (see 7.6). Liu Baonan notes that the purpose of this passage is to emphasize that "manifesting filial piety and respect for elders in one's behavior is the primary concern, while the study of the cultural arts is secondary."

1.9 The target audience for this saying seems to be rulers or potential rulers, the message being that the key to ordering the state is paying attention to one's own behavior (a theme often repeated in Books Twelve and Thirteen).

1.10 Huang Kan believes the point of this passage to be that the quality of rulership in a state is revealed in the sentiment of the common people, to which Confucius was particularly sensitive because of his virtuous nature. Rulers thus "give away" this information inadvertently to one as attuned as Confucius, who therefore does not have to make inquiries in the ordinary fashion. Zhu Xi believes that it is the rulers who, drawn by the power of the Master's virtue, actively seek out Confucius to discuss the problems of governance. In any case, the point seems to be that Confucius "sought it in himself, not in others" (15.21), or that (as Lu Longqi puts it) "the sage seeks things by means of virtue, unlike ordinary people who seek things with their minds." That is, while ordinary people consciously and deliberately pursue external goals, the sage focuses his attention upon his own inner virtue and allows external things to come to him naturally.

1.11 Three years (usually understood as into the third year, or twenty-five months) is the standard mourning period for a parent. As Kong Anguo explains, "When his father is still alive, the son is not able to act as he wants [because he must obey the father's commands], so one can only observe his intentions in order to judge his character. It is only once his father has passed away that the son can learn about his character by observing his own actions. As long as the filial son is in mourning, his sorrow and longing is such that it is as if the father were still present, and this is why he does not alter the ways of his father." In this passage, we see hints of the priority given to familial affection and loyalty over considerations of what is more abstractly "right" that is expressed more starkly in 13.18.

1.12 What it means to practice ritual with "harmonious ease" (i.e., in a wu-wei fashion) is illustrated in the description of Confucius' ritual behavior in Book Ten. Ritual behavior must be accompanied by such easy joy and harmony if it is to be truly valued. On the other hand, such "ease" involves more than simply indulging one's innate emotions: the innate emotions must be properly shaped by ritual forms before they can become truly "harmonious." The message here is related to the theme of possessing both "native substance" (*zhi* 質) and "cultural refinement" (*wen* 文) in their proper balance (cf. 3.8, 6.18).

1.15 "Cutting and polishing" refer to the working of bone and ivory, while "carving and grinding" refer to jade work: cutting and carving being the initial rough stages, and polishing and grinding the finishing touches. Here the task of self-cultivation is understood metaphorically in terms of the arduous process of roughly shaping and then laboriously finishing recalcitrant materials. Zigong's quotation of this ode shows that he has instantly grasped Confucius' point.

This instant grasping of the larger point to be taught is an excellent example of a student "being given three corners of a square and coming up with the fourth" (7.8).

Book Two Commentary

2.1 The point of this passage is that the spontaneous harmony brought about by Heaven in the natural world is to be a model for the human ruler, who—in a wu-wei fashion—will bring the world to order silently, inevitably, and unself-consciously through the power of his perfected moral Virtue. As Bao Xian notes, "One who possesses Virtue is wu-wei, and—like the Pole Star—does not move yet receives the homage of the myriad lesser stars." Cf. 2.3, 2.21, 12.17, 12.19, and especially 15.5.

2.2 The quoted phrase is from Ode 297. The original reference is to powerful war horses bred to pull chariots and trained not to swerve from the desired path.

The metaphorical meaning is that one committed through study to the *Odes*—"yoked" to them, as it were—will not be led astray from the Confucian Way.

2.3 This passage represents another expression of the theme of ruling through the power of Virtue (wu-wei) rather than force. As Guo Xiang notes, "If you employ governmental regulations you may correct people's outer behavior, but in their hearts, they will not have submitted. Concerned only with expediency and evasion, they will behave shamelessly toward things. Is this not a superficial way of transforming people?" Zhu Xi adds, "Although they will probably not dare to do anything bad, the tendency to do bad will never leave them." Cf. 8.9.

2.4 We have here Confucius' spiritual autobiography. We can see his evolution as encompassing three pairs of stages. In the first pair (stages one and two), the aspiring gentleman commits himself to the Confucian Way, submitting to the rigors of study and ritual practice until these traditional forms have been internalized to the point where he is able to "take his place" among others. In the second pair, the practitioner begins to feel truly at ease with this new manner of being, and is able to understand how the Confucian Way fits into the order of things and complies with the will of Heaven.[1] The clarity and sense of ease this brings with it leads to the final two stages, where one's dispositions have been so thoroughly harmonized with the dictates of normative culture that one accords with them spontaneously—that is, the state of wu-wei. Some interpretations take the ear being "attuned" to mean that Confucius at this point immediately apprehends the subtle content of the teachings he hears (Zheng Xuan), some that there is no conflict between his inner dispositions and the teachings of the sages (Wang Bi), and some both of these things. As Li Chong explains, "'Having an attuned ear' means that, upon hearing the exemplary teachings of the Former Kings, one immediately apprehended their virtuous conduct, and 'following the models of the Lord' (a reference to King Wen in Ode 241), nothing goes against the tendencies of one's heart." Or, as Zhu Xi explains it, "Being able to follow one's heart's desires without transgressing exemplary standards means that one acts with ease, hitting the mean without forcing it."

2.7 The focus here is upon the importance of internal involvement when it comes to virtuous behavior, "respect" (*jing* 敬) encompassing both a manner of behaving and an emotional attitude.

---

[1] The link between these two stages—being without doubts and understanding the Mandate of Heaven—is also suggested by the line from 9.29, "One who understands does not doubt."

2.8 A convincing way of understanding this passage is to see it as building on and clarifying 2.7, in which case "demeanor" (*se* 色) should be understood as referring to one's internal emotional state as revealed in one's features. As Zhai Hao puts it, "The point of this passage is that even respect does not constitute filial piety unless it is accompanied by affection. Taking on the burden of work to be done and offering sustenance are the sorts of things disciples or students do to show reverence for their elders. Serving one's parents, on the other hand, involves in addition deep affection, a harmonious disposition, and a willing heart." True filial piety involves not only the respect due to any elder family member, but in addition a kind of spontaneous, profoundly affectionate bond.

2.9 Here, in our first mention of Confucius' favorite disciple, Yan Hui, in the text, we get a clear indication that there is something special about him. Some commentaries (particularly the early ones) assume that the "private behavior" that Confucius observes is Yan Hui engaged in informal conversation with other disciples, while other commentaries believe that Confucius is observing Yan Hui's behavior when he is alone, in solitary repose. Line three of the following passage ("discover where it is that he feels at ease") suggests that latter reading. In any case, the point is that Hui does not disagree or ask questions because he immediately comprehends everything that he is taught, suggesting that he might be one of those superior few who are "born knowing it" (16.9), unlike those such as Confucius who must learn in order to know the Way (7.20). Cf. 5.9 and 6.7.

2.10 That is, how can his true character remain hidden? A person's character is not properly judged by his words or his public reputation, but is rather revealed to one who carefully observes his actual behavior, comes to know something about his motivations, and discovers what he is like in private. It is in the details of one's daily behavior that true virtue is manifested. Cf. 4.2, "The Good person feels at home in Goodness."

2.11 There is commentarial disagreement over whether this passage refers to keeping ancient teachings alive, or to keeping what one has previously learned in a lifetime current in one's mind so that one knows what to expect in the future. The role of the teacher would suggest the former. Li Ao points out, however, that passages such as 1.15 ("Informed as to what has gone before, you know what is to come") seem congruent with the latter interpretation.

2.12 *Qi* 器, lit. a ritual vessel or implement designed to serve a particular function, is also used metaphorically to refer to people who are specialized in one particular task. Although some commentators take this passage to mean that the gentleman is universally—rather than narrowly—skilled, the point seems rather that the gentleman is not a specialist (cf. 6.13, 9.2, 13.4, and 19.7).

2.15 As Bao Xian notes, "If one learns but does not reflectively seek out the meaning of what is being taught, one will be lost and will have gained nothing from it." Some commentators, such as He Yan, take *dai* 殆 ("danger") in its alternate sense of exhaustion: "If one thinks without studying, one will achieve nothing in the end, and will have merely exhausted one's intellectual energy for nothing." Learning requires the active participation of the student (cf. 5.27, 7.8, and 15.16), but also imposes essential structure on the student's activities (17.10 and especially 15.31).

2.19 The metaphor for the virtuous influence of superiors found here and in 12.22 recalls the image of the "press-frame" for straightening out crooked wood that became a favorite of Xunzi's for describing the process of self-cultivation. The reference is to the salutary effect of moral officials upon the Virtue of the common people; cf. the "wind and grass" metaphor in 12.19. Duke Ai was the nominal ruler of Confucius' native state of Lu. As Jiang Xi comments:

> Duke Ai was presented with a once-in-a-lifetime opportunity, and sagely worthies filled his state. If he had simply raised them up and employed them, he could have become the true King of Lu. Unfortunately, he cared only for sensual pleasures and left control of the administration to a flock of evil-doers. As a result, the hearts of the people were filled with resentment. Duke Ai was troubled by this state of affairs, and so asked this question of Confucius.

2.21 There are probably two layers of meaning here. The more general point is that one should "do government" through "not doing" (wu-wei): that is, by perfecting oneself—as Master You puts it in 1.2, establishing the "root" of virtue—and letting the rest follow naturally through the power of one's personal example and Virtue. Some commentators also see here an indirect criticism of the Ji Family, whose usurpation of power in Lu involved shocking mistreatment of parents and brothers. Cf. 12.11 and 13.3.

Book Three Commentary

3.1 According to later ritual texts, different ranks in society were allowed different numbers of dancers to perform outside the ancestral hall during ceremonial occasions: the Son of Heaven allowed eight rows of eight dancers, feudal lords six rows, ministers four rows, and officials two rows. Although he was de facto ruler of Lu, the head of the Ji Family officially held only the position of minister, and his use of eight dancers thus represented an outrageous usurpation of the ritual prerogatives of the Zhou king.

3.3 Although it serves as a general statement concerning the relationship of internal disposition to Confucian practice (cf. 3.12 and 17.11), this comment is probably more specifically directed at the head of the Ji Family and the other leading families of Lu criticized in 3.1. A passage in the *History of the Han*, after quoting this line, explains,

> The point is that a person who is not Good does not have the means to apply himself . . . not having the means to apply himself, he is unable to practice ritual and music. Even if he has many other talents, they will only be used to do no good. During the Master's age, ritual and music were under attack by the ministers [of Lu], who greedily usurped the prerogatives of the king and mutually followed the established habits of corruption, and practiced wrongness so that it triumphed over what was right.

3.4 Lin Fang is usually identified as a man of Lu, and presumably shared Confucius' concern that his fellow citizens were neglecting the "roots" and attending to the superficial "branches" of ritual practice, which is why he is commended by Confucius for his question. When it comes to ritual it is harmony that is valued (1.12), but if one is to err, it should be on the side of the "roots"—that is, the emotions that ideally inform and motivate the ritual forms. Sparse ritual paraphernalia backed by genuine respect is better than empty ritual excess, and grief-induced lapses in ritual forms of mourning (e.g., Confucius' own excesses upon the death of Yan Hui) are more easily countenanced than cool, emotionless perfection. Zhu Xi is probably correct in linking this theme to the relationship of emotional substance over cultural form described in 6.18. Although here in Book Three the importance of substance over cultural form is emphasized by Confucius (cf. 3.3, 3.4, 3.8, 3.12), in other passages we see form being stressed over substance. Probably the desirability of both being balanced that is expressed in 6.18 is Confucius' ultimate position, and his favoring of one over another is merely a response to the pedagogical needs of the moment (11.22).

3.8 Again we have a disciple making the sort of conceptual leap that Confucius required of his students (cf. 1.15, 7.8). The point grasped by Zixia is that the adornment provided by the rites is meant to build upon appropriate native emotions or tendencies. Just as all of the cosmetics in the world are of no avail if the basic lines of the face are not pleasing, so is the refinement provided by ritual forms of no help to one lacking in native substance. Cf. 3.4, 5.10, and

6.18. An even stronger expression of the importance of substance is found in the *Record of Ritual*: "Just as that which is naturally sweet can be further harmonized through cooking, and just as colors may be applied to a white background, so a person who is dutiful and trustworthy can be allowed to learn the rites."[1] Here the virtues of dutifulness and trustworthiness are presented as native talents that are the prerequisites for moral education.

3.11 Of course the unspoken implication is that there is *no one* in Lu who really understands the *di*, especially the Three Families, who have been shamelessly performing it in gross violation of ritual norms. The ability of a properly performed ritual—especially those having to do with filial piety, such as the *di* sacrifice to one's ancestors—to order the entire world in a wu-wei fashion is expressed particularly strongly here, but has parallels in such passages as 1.2, 2.21, and 12.11.

3.12 To sacrifice "as if the spirits were present" means to do so with an attitude of reverence and awe. There is no attribution for the first line, and its form (cryptic text followed by an expanded, explanatory version) suggests that it might be a fragment from a lost ritual text interpolated by a later editor. Whether the Master's words or not, it nonetheless clearly harmonizes with the comment from Confucius that follows. Although some commentators take "being present" in the second line in its literal sense (i.e., being physically present at the sacrifice, not sending a proxy in one's stead), the sense of the first line suggests that what is at issue is psychological or inner presence.

3.17 According to commentators, this lamb sacrifice had originally been part of a larger ritual in the state of Lu to mark the official beginning of the new month, and which—according to the *Annals* (Legge 1991d: 243)—was discontinued during the reign of Duke Wen. According to Huang Kan, although the larger ritual itself was no longer being practiced by the rulers of Lu, the practice of sacrificing the lamb was being kept alive by traditionally-minded government functionaries. Zigong does not see the point of continuing this vestigial, materially wasteful practice in the absence of its original ritual context. Insisting upon the continuance of this practice, however, is Confucius' way of mourning the loss of the original rite and keeping its memory alive, which in his view is worth the cost of an occasional lamb. The valuing of ritual propriety over pragmatic or financial considerations links this passage to the fact that Lu—as the inheritor of Zhou culture—still preserved at least the forms of the ancient rites.

---

[1] Chapter 10 ("Rites in the Formation of Character"); Legge 1967, vol. 1: 414.

3.18 Ritual practice had so degenerated by Confucius' age that a proper ritual practitioner was viewed with suspicion or disdain. As many commentators note, an example of observing every detail of ritual propriety is found in 9.3, where Confucius stubbornly insists upon bowing before ascending the stairs to have an audience with a ruler, as ritual demands, rather than following the more casual contemporary practice of bowing after ascending the stairs. Such archaic manners were no doubt received by his contemporaries with precisely the sort of amusement or cynicism mentioned here.

3.19 Again we have a general observation about ritual and virtue that probably has a more specific target as well. As Jiao Hong explains, "In the *Annals of Master Yan* we read, 'Only by means of ritual can one govern a state.' Ritual is the tool employed by the Former Kings when they considered titles and social distinctions and thereby eliminated the seeds of disorder. Duke Ding was the kind of ruler who 'held the blade of the sword and offered the handle to his enemies,'[2] and therefore Confucius wants him to protect himself by means of ritual. The Three Families were the type of ministers of whom one might say, 'the tail is too big to wag,'[3] and therefore Confucius wishes to instruct them in the ways of dutifulness."

3.20 The "Cry of the Osprey" is the first of the *Odes*, and sometimes stands in metonymically for the *Odes* as a whole. There are two equally plausible interpretations of this passage, depending on whether one thinks that it is the text of Ode 1 in particular or the music of the ode (and possibly the *Odes* in general) that is being praised. The text describes a young gentleman longing for and passionately seeking out a beautiful, virtuous young woman. Although originally the young woman in question was probably the anonymous subject of a peasant folk song, in the commentarial tradition that grew up around the *Odes* she became associated with the royal consort of King Wen, and the poem thus came to be seen as a model of restrained, honorable relations between the sexes. Commentators such as Kong Anguo, on the other hand, understand this passage as referring to the music of the ode: "'Expressing joy without becoming licentious, expressing sorrow without falling into excessive pathos' refers to the perfect harmony [of the music]." In either case, we see in the *Odes* the perfect balance of emotion and restraint that characterizes the gentleman.

---

[2] A colloquial saying (lit. "to hold *tai'a* 太阿 [a famously sharp sword] backward") meaning essentially "to give someone the stick with which to beat you." The phrase first appeared in the *History of the Han*.

[3] That is, those in a normally inferior position have grown more powerful than those in a normally superior position—not too far in general meaning from the English saying, "The tail wagging the dog." The original reference is to the *Zuo Commentary* (Legge 1994d: 635).

3.23 Music thus serves as a model or metaphor for the process of self-cultivation: starting in confusion, passing through many phases and culminating in a state of wu-wei perfection.

3.24 Most commentators take this as a reference to Confucius' loss of the office of Criminal Judge in the state of Lu; this is presumably the reason that Confucius and his disciples are leaving the state. The ability of the border official to see Confucius' true mission is taken by many commentators as an indication that he is a sage in hiding: a virtuous man who has taken a lowly position in order to protect himself in chaotic and unvirtuous times. The bell referred to is (depending on which source one consults) the kind used either by itinerant collectors and transmitters of folk songs or functionaries who circulated around the countryside promulgating official announcements. In either case, the border official's point is thus that Heaven has deliberately caused Confucius to lose his official position so that he might wander throughout the realm, spreading the teachings of the Way and waking up the fallen world.

Book Four Commentary

4.1 There are two main interpretations of this passage—one literal, the other more metaphorical—and each is reflected in the two Warring States followers of Confucius. We see echoes of the more literal take in the *Xunzi*: "Therefore, when it comes to his residence, the gentleman is necessarily picky when choosing his village, and in his travels he seeks out the company of other scholars. He does so in order to guard against depravity and crudeness, and stay close to the right path of the mean."[1] Understood in this way, the focus of the passage is the importance of one's social environment for the development of one's character. A slightly different interpretation is found in *Mencius* 2:A:7, where a quotation of 4.1 is prefaced with the following:

> Is an arrow-maker not less benevolent [*ren*] than the armor-maker? The arrow-maker is concerned solely with harming others, while the armor-maker is concerned solely with making sure others are not harmed. With shaman-doctors and coffin-makers it is the same.[2] Therefore, one cannot but be careful in the choice of one's profession.

---

[1] Chapter 1 ("Encouraging Learning"); Knoblock 1988: 137.

[2] I.e., the same situation as that of the arrow-maker: they both profit from the misfortune or suffering of others.

Although here one's "dwelling place" is understood metaphorically as one's general sphere of activity, the general idea is similar: one must be careful when choosing one's environment.

4.2 Regarding the first half of this saying, Kong Anguo comments, "Some cannot remain constant in adversity because sustained adversity motivates them to do wrong, and cannot enjoy enduring happiness because they inevitably fall into arrogance and sloth." The second half is an explanation of the first: those who are truly Good are spontaneously and unself-consciously Good—they "feel at home" in virtue, having internalized it to the point where externalities no longer matter. Both Confucius (7.16, 7.19) and Yan Hui (6.7, 6.11) illustrate this quality.

4.3 Jiao Xun, elaborating upon Kong Anguo's commentary, explains, "The Good person loves what is really worthy of admiration in others and despises that which is genuinely despicable in them. This is why such a person is said to 'be able to love others and despise others.'" Only the Good person is an accurate and impartial judge of character, able to love virtue in others without envy and despise vice in others without malice.

4.4 There are at least two other ways to render the second half of this line: "free of hatred (reading 惡 in falling tone, as in 4.3) or "free of wrongdoing" (Zhu Xi). The first seems ruled out by the sense of 4.3: the Good person does in fact despise or hate when such an emotion is appropriate.

4.5 The true gentleman is dedicated to the Way as an end in itself, and does not pursue it for the sake of external goods (4.9, 7.12, 8.12). As a result, he embodies the Way unself-consciously and effortlessly, and derives a constant joy that renders him indifferent to externalities (7.16, 7.19, 9.29). Cf. the *Xunzi*: "Where there is Goodness there is no poverty or hardship, and where Goodness is lacking there is no wealth or honor."[3]

4.6 In 7.30 we read, "Is Goodness really so far away? If I merely desire Goodness, I will find that Goodness is already here." A bit of frustration is apparent in this passage: we all have the ability to be Good if we would simply love it as we should, but how can one instill this love in someone who does not already have it (or who loves the wrong things)? This problem comes again in 6.12, when the disappointing disciple Ran Qiu claims to love the Way but complains that he lacks the strength to pursue it. Confucius sharply rebukes him in words

---

[3]Chapter 23 ("Human Nature Is Bad"); Knoblock 1994: 161.

that echo 4.6: "Those for whom it is genuinely a problem of insufficient strength end up collapsing somewhere along the Way. As for you, you deliberately draw the line." This is the heart of a paradox that Confucius faced—we might refer to it as the "paradox of wu-wei," or problem of how to consciously develop in oneself or instill in others genuine unself-conscious spontaneity—that will come up again and again in the *Analects* (cf. 5.10, 7.34). We also see in this passage the hierarchy of moral attainment: positive, unself-conscious love of Goodness being superior to a mere aversion to immorality.

4.7 Understood in this way, the point of this passage is that it is in unpremeditated, unconscious actions that one's true character is revealed (cf. 2.9, 2.10), and this seems to fit well with the overall sense of Book Four. The pre-Tang commentators, however, take this passage as a comment on rulership and the need for understanding (*shu* 恕). Kong Anguo, for instance, remarks, "The fact that petty people are not able to act like gentlemen is not their fault, and so one should be understanding and not blame them. If you observe their mistakes, you can put both the worthies and the fools in their proper places, and this is what it means to be Good." The link between Goodness and understanding that we find elsewhere (6.30, 15.24) makes this a plausible reading, and it is reinforced by the fact that many pre-Tang versions of the text have *min* 民 "common people" as the subject of the first clause. Understood this way, the last part of the passage should be rendered something like, "this is what it means to understand Goodness."

4.8 The pre-Tang commentators take the passage in the manner reflected by the translation. He Yan's commentary reads, "The point is that [Confucius] is approaching death and has yet to hear that the world has adopted the Way."

Zhu Xi, on the other hand, understands the passage to mean: "Having in the morning learned the Way, one could die that evening without regret." He comments, "If one were able to hear the Way, one's life would flow easily and one's death would come peacefully, and there would be no more regrets." Both interpretations are plausible.

4.9 Li Chong comments, "Those who value what lies within forget about what lies without. This is why in past ages those who possessed the Way were able to put it into action, caused their family members to forget about their poverty, and caused kings and dukes to forget about glory—how much less would they have worried about clothing and food?"

4.10 The verbs of this passage all have to do with social associations, but it can be (and often is) understood more metaphorically and abstractly: "the gentleman has no predispositions for or against anything, and merely seeks to be on the side of the right." In either case, we see here an indication of the situational responsiveness of the gentleman, who relies upon his internal moral sense—rather than conventional social prejudice—when judging people or affairs. Confucius' approval of his conventionally tabooed son-in-law in 5.1 and his suspicion of unexamined social judgments in 13.4 can serve as practical illustrations of this principle.

4.12 As Master Cheng explains, "If you wish to obtain profit for yourself, you will inevitably harm others and thereby arouse much resentment." The gentleman is to be guided by considerations of what is right, not what is profitable (4.16, 14.12).

4.13 Here we see two themes emphasized. The first concerns the efficacy of Virtue-based government, as opposed to government by force or reward and punishment, and is related to the distaste for contention and considerations of profit expressed throughout this book.

The second theme is related to the sort of anti–Ivory Tower attitude expressed in 13.5: traditional practices are meant to be applied to the real world, not merely studied theoretically.

4.14 Again we see a distaste for self-assertion, self-aggrandizement, and contention for external goods. The gentleman focuses solely on achieving the internal goods of the Confucian Way. External recognition should and may follow, but is subject to the vagaries of fate and is not inevitable (especially in a disordered or corrupt age), and in any case is not a worthy object of concern. Cf. 14.30.

4.15 *Guan* 貫 means "thread," and Huang Kan reads it as a metaphor: everything that the Master teaches is unified theoretically by one principle, like objects strung on a single thread. The *Analects'* emphasis on practice over theory makes it likely, however, that the "single thread" is a kind of consistency in action rather than a unified theoretical principle, and this is supported by Master Zeng's elaboration.

There are quite a few passages in the *Analects* directly or indirectly concerned with *shu* (5.12, 6.30, and 15.24), and it is clear that this virtue involves some sort of considerations of others—an ability to imaginatively project oneself into another's place. There is more debate about *zhong*. One dominant line of interpretation begins with Wang Bi, who defines *zhong* as "fully exhausting one's emotions" and *shu* as "reflecting upon one's emotions in order to have sympathy with other beings." Zhu Xi and others belong to this line of thinking in defining *zhong* as "exhausting oneself" or "doing one's utmost" (*jinji* 盡己). Relying solely on relevant passages from within the *Analects* (3.19, 5.19), however, it would seem that *zhong* involves a kind of attention to one's ritual duties, particularly as a political subordinate. Understood this way, being "dutiful" (*zhong*) involves fulfilling the duties and obligations proper to one's ritually defined role. This virtue is to be tempered by the virtue of "understanding" (*shu*): the ability to, by means of imaginatively putting oneself in the place of another, know when it is appropriate or "right" (*yi*) to bend or suspend the dictates of role-specific duty. *Zhong* is often translated as "loyalty," but "dutifulness" is preferable because the ultimate focus is upon one's ritually prescribed duties rather than loyalty to any particular person, and indeed *zhong* would involve opposing a ruler who was acting improperly.

4.16 Again, the gentleman is motivated by the inner goods of Confucian practice rather than the promise of external goods. Cf. 4.2, 4.5, 4.9, and 4.12. Some commentators argue that the distinction between the gentleman and the petty person (*xiaoren* 小人) should be understood in terms of social class, because *xiaoren* is often used in Han texts to indicate simply the "common people." It is clear, though, that Confucius felt anyone from any social class could potentially become a gentleman and that social status did not necessarily correspond to actual moral worth. It is apparent that—in the *Analects* at least—the gentleman/*xiaoren* distinction refers to moral character rather than social status.

4.17 That is, one is to emulate the virtues and avoid the vices observed in others; cf. 7.22. The emphasis here is on action: not just seeing the qualities of others, but also using this insight as an opportunity for self-improvement. As Jiao Yuanxi explains, "The 'seeing' mentioned in this passage refers to that which any person can easily perceive—the difficulty lies entirely in actually beginning to do something about it. The intention of the sage [Confucius] in establishing this teaching was not merely to criticize people for not having true knowledge [of what is right], but rather to upbraid them for lacking sincerity of commitment or the courage to put their will into practice."

4.18 One owes one's parents a unique level of obedience—one that transcends legal responsibilities (13.18) and that exceeds even the demands of dutifulness in the political realm. As Zheng Xuan explains,

> The "Patterns of the Family" [chapter of the *Record of Ritual*] says, "With a regard to a son serving his parents, if he remonstrates three times and is not heeded, there is nothing left to do but, with crying and tears, go along with their wishes." However, it also says, "With regard to a minister serving his lord, if he remonstrates three times and is not heeded, he should leave his lord's service and [turn to study of the classics?]"[4] . . . Why is this? Father and son are genuinely linked to

---

[4] The quoted passages do not appear in the "Patterns of the Family" chapter of the extant *Record of Ritual*, although almost identical variants do appear in Chapters 1–2 ("Summary of Ritual"); Legge 1967, vol. 1: 114.

one another—with regard to our Heavenly nature, there is no relationship like it.
. . . Lord and minister, however, are brought together by considerations of rightness, and it is thus natural that they should have points of divergence.

4.19 Going on an extended journey would entail neglecting one's filial duties.
As for the issue of itinerary, Huang Kan comments:

> The "Summary of Ritual Propriety" [chapter of the *Record of Ritual*] says, "The
> ritual propriety proper to a son dictates that when he goes out, he must inform his
> parents, and that when he returns, he must report to them personally, and that in
> all of his travels he must keep to a fixed itinerary."[5] . . . If one travels and does not
> have a fixed itinerary, this will cause one's parents undue worry.

4.21 There are various ways to understand this, but the most plausible is that
the age of one's parents is a cause for rejoicing that they have lived so long,
while also a source of anxiety because of their advancing years.

4.22 Again we see the suspicion of glibness and an emphasis on action over
speech. Huang Zhen comments, "The distinction between the gentleman and
the petty person lies in whether or not their words and actions are consistent,
and whether or not their words and actions are consistent depends upon
whether or not their hearts are capable of knowing shame." Wang Yangming
adds sharply, "The ancients valued action, and were therefore shy with their
words and did not dare to speak lightly. People nowadays value words, and
therefore loudly flap their tongues and blabber nonsense at the slightest insti-
gation." Cf. 4.24, and 14.27.

4.24 Here again we see a concern about one's words exceeding one's actual
virtue; cf. 4.22.

4.25 A few commentators (such as Liu Baonan) believe that what it means for
Virtue not to "be solitary" (lit. "orphaned") is that Virtue is never one-sided in
a true gentleman: he is both internally respectful and outwardly righteous. A
more likely interpretation is that the reference is to the attractive power of Virtue
on others. As the *History of the Han* explains:

> When a minister learns of a king who has received the great commission from
> Heaven, he will be naturally drawn to him, in a manner beyond what human
> beings are capable of bringing about. This is the sort of good omen that manifests
> itself when one has received the Mandate. All of the people in the world will, with
> one heart, return to such a king, like children returning to their parents. Thus,

---

[5] Legge 1967, vol. 1: 68.

the auspicious signs of Heaven are brought about through sincerity.... When Confucius says, "Virtue is never alone; it always has neighbors," he is referring to the effects caused by accumulating goodness and piling up Virtue.

For this interpretation, cf. 2.1 and 15.5. Reading this passage together with 4.1, the point might also be that one requires Good neighbors and friends in order to develop Virtue; for this interpretation, cf. 12.24.

Book Five Commentary

5.1 The identity of Gongye Chang is not clear. Although he is identified by the *Record of the Historian* as a man from Qi, Kong Anguo and others describe him as a disciple of Confucius from Lu. It is not clear what his offense was, but his name later became associated with a variety of legends attributing to him the ability to understand the language of birds and other animals, including an amusing story that describes him being falsely accused of murder because he overheard a group of birds discussing the location of the body of a murder victim. He is freed only after having demonstrated his supernatural abilities to his jailer. Whatever the actual identity or supposed offence of Gongye Chang, the point of this passage is Confucius' independence from convention. The social stigma attached to former criminals in early China was enormous and inescapable, since criminals were prominently branded, tattooed, or physically mutilated. In giving his daughter in marriage to a former criminal, Confucius is flouting conventional mores and making a powerful statement concerning the independence of true morality from conventional social judgments. As Fan Ning explains, "In giving his daughter in marriage to Gongye Chang, Confucius' intention was to make quite clear the corrupt and excessive manner in which punishments were administered in his fallen age, and to provide future encouragement to those who truly held fast to rectitude."

5.4 Of course, "the gentleman is not a vessel" (2.12)—i.e., the true gentleman is more than a mere specialist. According to commentators, the *hu* and *lian* were precious jade food-offering vessels that were the most important ritual vessels in the ancestral temples of the Xia and Shang Dynasties, respectively. Commentators point out that Confucius' elaboration is double-edged: comforting, in that Zigong is no ordinary vessel, but perhaps even more critical because the *hu* and *lian* vessels were both archaic curiosities (no longer used in the Zhou rites) and extremely specialized (thus seldom used even during Xia and Shang times). Zigong was a highly accomplished statesman, skillful speaker, and successful businessman, but Confucius seems to have felt that he lacked the flexibility and sympathy toward others characteristic of Goodness. This is perhaps why Confucius uses Zigong as his audience for his teaching about understanding in 6.30 and singles out Zigong for his message that "be understanding" is the one teaching that can serve as a lifelong guide in 15.24.

5.8 Meng Wubo was the son of a minister of Lu.

The fact that Goodness functions as the ultimate telos defining the narrative arc of one's life means that no final judgment concerning whether or not a given person possesses Goodness can be delivered until that life has been completed. This is why Goodness is portrayed as a dimly perceived and ever-receding goal to a work eternally in progress in 9.11, and why Confucius is reluctant here and elsewhere (5.19, 7.33, 14.1) to pronounce anyone truly Good, including himself (7.34).

5.9 Zigong's hearing one thing and being able to grasp two is possibly a reference to 1.15 (when discussing the *Odes* and "informed as to what has gone before," Zigong is able to "know what is to come"). Zigong is realistic enough to know that even this admirable ability pales in comparison to the almost preternatural talent of Yan Hui, who apparently knows what is being taught even before he is taught it (2.9, 11.4). Some commentators believe that Confucius' last comment is intended merely to comfort Zigong, but it is possible that it is meant sincerely: Confucius was not "born knowing it" (7.20), and passages such as 2.9, 6.7, and 11.4 suggest that Yan Hui was one of those rare and superior people who are born already good (16.19).

5.10 Zai Wo obviously lacks the "native substance" (*zhi*) that serves as the background on which the "color" of Confucian self-cultivation is to be applied (3.8). As Huang Kan comments,

> Even when it comes to a famous craftsman or skilled carpenter, his carving is totally dependent upon having good wood to work with if he is to produce a perfect product. If he tries to apply his efforts to a piece of rotten wood, the result will be imperfect. Similarly, when trowelling a wall, if the earth that the wall is made out of is hard and solid, then it is easy to apply an even layer of plaster to create a smooth, clean veneer. If you try applying your trowel to a wall made out of dung, on the other hand, the plaster will crumble and fall off, resulting in an irregular surface. Confucius' purpose in invoking these two metaphors is to tell Zai Wo that if he is the kind of person who sleeps during the daytime then it is impossible to teach him anything.

The first half of the passage emphasizes the importance of native substance. The second has to do with the suspicion of language we have seen several times already: many people talk about virtue, but few actually strive to attain it in practice. As Wang Fuzhi remarks, "When it comes to learning, nothing is more crucial than actual exertion and practice. What one says is not worth paying attention to. Whether or not one gets it through exertion and practice, in turn, depends solely on whether one is diligent or lazy. A person who is able to talk well and is subsequently said to be able to understand, and who then considers himself to have already understood and thus is no longer diligent when it comes to exertion and practice—such a person is profoundly despised by the gentleman." Here again we see hints of the "paradox of wu-wei" mentioned in the commentary to 4.6: one can only attain virtue if one genuinely desires to attain it, but how does one inspire such a genuine desire in someone who does not already have it? Cf. 6.12.

5.12 Zigong's aspiration—what has been referred to as the "negative Golden Rule"—is a formulation of the virtue of understanding: the ability to temper the strict dictates of dutifulness by imaginatively placing oneself in another's place (cf. 15.24). Zigong's aspiration to the virtue of understanding is particularly amusing to Confucius because Zigong is the most unimaginative and rigid of all the disciples (cf. 5.4, 14.29). Zhu Xi says of Zigong's aspiration, "This is the sort of thing that a genuinely Good person concerns himself with, and that he does not have to be urged or forced to do. This is why the Master considers it to be something beyond the reach of Zigong" (317).

5.13 This passage has presented something of a puzzle to some interpreters, seeing that we can find one mention of human nature (*xing* 性) (17.2) in the *Analects*, and that—although the term "Way of Heaven" (*tiandao* 天道) appears nowhere else in the text—we do find quite a few mentions of the Mandate of Heaven or other topics having to do with Heaven's will. 17.2 might be dismissed as a late addition, and even if we include it with all the various mentions of Heaven, it remains true that Confucius focuses primarily on "this world"—that is, the human world of learning and self-cultivation. Thus, one way to understand this passage is that Confucius did not concern himself much with such theoretical, esoteric subjects as human nature or the Way of Heaven, but rather tried to focus his disciples' attention on the task at hand: acquiring the cultural refinement necessary to become gentlemen (cf. 6.22, 7.20, 11.12). A related interpretation is suggested by commentators who argue that "human nature" refers to the variable endowment one receives at birth (rather than to some theoretical stance about human nature as we see in the *Mencius* and *Xunzi*), and that, in classical texts, the "Way of Heaven" often refers simply to what we might call "luck" or "fate." Understood this way, "human nature" and the "Way of Heaven" collectively refer to the range of things that are beyond human control, and the point is that the Master focused on what was within human control: commitment to learning and the Confucian Way.

5.19 Ziwen was prime minister in the state of Chu who was renowned for his integrity and devotion to the state, and first took the highest office in 663 B.C.E.

Cuizi and Chen Wenzi were both ministers in the state of Qi. The former is said to have assassinated Lord Zhuang of Qi in 548 B.C.E.

We have here both substantive, edifying descriptions of two Confucian virtues and an indirect statement concerning the difficulty of attaining Goodness: even these ancient worthies, renowned for their particular virtues, had not necessarily attained complete moral perfection. Zhu Xi's comment on this passage is helpful:

> People these days become instantly hot-headed, red in the face, at the slightest loss or gain. Ziwen was given official position and had this position taken away three times, and yet showed not the slightest sign of pleasure or resentment. These days people holding even minor posts are not willing to take the time to give a quick summary of their official actions to their successors, whereas Ziwen— holding such an exalted position—nonetheless gave an exhaustive and detailed account of the official state of affairs to the incoming prime minister. These days if people develop even the slightest ties to material things they can never manage to get free of them. Wenzi, on the other hand, possessed an immense estate of ten teams of horses and yet abandoned it without a second thought, as if it were an old pair of shoes. . . . We must think about why the sage did not endorse as Goodness even the behavior of these two Masters—as elevated and exceptional as it was—and why their behavior was not seen as fully exhausting the virtue of Goodness. If we consider this carefully, and think as well upon how seldom one encounters the equals of these two Masters, it will impress upon us how rare it is to see the principle of Goodness actually realized.

5.22 Some commentators believe that this call to return home was occasioned by Lu's offer of employment for the disciple Ran Qiu (11.17). Probably the best comment on this passage is found in *Mencius* 7:B:37, which ties it together with 13.21:

> Wan Zhang asked, "When Confucius was in Chen he said, 'Oh, let us go home! Our young scholars back in Lu are wild and ambitious. They advance and seize their objectives, but cannot forget their former ways. When Confucius was in Chen, why did he think upon the wild scholars of Lu?"
>
> Mencius replied, "Confucius said, 'If you cannot get people who have achieved the Middle Way as your associates, you must turn to the wild or the fastidious. The wild plunge right in, while the fastidious are always careful not to get their hands dirty.'[1] Of course Confucius preferred those who had attained the Middle Way, but since he could not be assured of finding them, he thought about the second-best."
>
> "For what reason are some people referred to as 'wild'?"
>
> "Their ambitions are grand and their language extravagant. They are constantly saying, 'The ancients! The ancients!,' and yet if you examine their daily behavior it does not live up to their words."

Here again we have a craft metaphor for self-cultivation. Although the young followers in Lu are a bit rough around the edges, they at least have the proper "native stuff" (unlike, for instance, Zai Wo in 5.10), and merely need to have this coarse stuff shaped and properly trimmed.

---

[1] This saying constitutes *Analects* 13.21.

5.26 Yan Hui's aspiration was apparently realized before his death. Most commentators see Confucius' aspiration as the possession of all-around virtue. Huang Kan reports a family saying concerning the passage: "If the aged are comforted by you, it is necessarily because you are filial and respectful. If your friends trust you, it is necessarily because you are free of deceit. If the youth cherish you, it is necessarily because you are compassionate and benevolent." Cf. the more elaborate version of a similar conversation in 11.26.

5.27 Zhu Xi remarks, "Rare are those who, when they make a mistake, are able to realize it. Rarer still are those who, aware that they made a mistake, are able to take themselves to task inwardly. If one is able to take oneself to task inwardly, then one's sense of repentance will be profound and urgent—a necessity if one is to change oneself. The Master laments because he himself fears he will never get to see such a person, and this should be seen as a serious warning to his students."

5.28 Dutifulness and trustworthiness are relatively pedestrian virtues well within the reach of the average person, but it is the Master's love for learning that sets him apart from others (7.20) and that serves as the mark of the true gentleman. Such a love for learning—a prerequisite for attaining the supreme virtue of Goodness—was unfortunately a rare quality among his contemporaries, whose passions inclined more toward money and the pleasures of the flesh (9.18). Even among his disciples only Yan Hui was viewed by the Master as having a true love of learning (6.3). An alternate parsing proposed by Wei Guan gives the passage a more wistful than critical tone, reading the second clause as, "How is it that they do not love learning as much as I?"

Book Six Commentary

6.3 Duke Ai (r. 494–468 B.C.E.) was the nominal ruler of Lu, which was in fact controlled by the Three Families, led by the Ji Family. Commentators and Han sources disagree on the details of Yan Hui's death, but it is clear that Yan Hui was significantly younger than Confucius, and that his premature death was a source of great sorrow for the Master (11.9). We should note that Yan Hui's love of learning is manifested in terms of virtuous action, rather than theoretical knowledge. Zhu Xi comments,

> If Yan Hui was angry at Mr. X he would never shift this anger to Mr. Y, and if he made a mistake in the past he would never repeat it in the future. The fact that Master Yan's achievement in overcoming himself reached this height is why we

can say that he genuinely loved learning. . . . In saying that, "Now there are none who really love learning—at least, I have yet to hear of one," the Master is probably giving expression to his profound sorrow in losing Yan Hui, while at the same time making it clear how difficult it is to find someone who genuinely does love learning.

Beginning with Huang Kan, some commentators have also seen this passage as an indirect criticism of Duke Ai, who vented his anger randomly and constantly repeated previous mistakes.

6.5 Most commentators explain that the disciple Yuan Si was appointed to be steward of Confucius' household while Confucius was serving as minister of justice in Lu. Again, this is probably not historically accurate, and it is more likely that Yuan Si's employer is one of the Three Families. Some commentators see the point of this passage to be simply that, once one has accepted a position, it is improper to decline the salary that goes along with it, but there is probably a bit more to it than that. Reading this passage in light of the many injunctions against seeking office for the sake of material benefit found in Confucius' teachings, the disciple Yuan Si no doubt expected to be praised by the Master for declining to be paid a salary. The point of Confucius' response is that the proper course of action cannot be determined by a simple formula, but should be the result of careful reflection and consideration of the needs of others. Based on Yuan Si's one other appearance, in 14.1, as well as later legends that sprung up around him, he seems to have been one of the excessively "fastidious" (*juan* 狷) who Confucius complains about in 13.21: his obsession with remaining unsullied prevents him from effectively engaging with the world.

6.7 Again we have Yan Hui being praised for his effortless and consistent embodiment of true virtue; cf. 5.9, 6.11, and 11.4. "Three months" is probably meant in the general sense of "a long time" rather than in its literal sense.

6.10 Early commentators explain that the disciple Boniu was suffering from a disfiguring illness and did not want anyone to see him, which is why Confucius must comfort him through the "window" (possibly referring simply to an opening in a screen set up around Boniu's bed). The main point of the passage seems to be human helplessness in the face of fate. As Huan Maoyong explains,

> Whether we are successful or unsuccessful in life, and whether we live to a ripe old age or die prematurely, are things that we consign to the space between what we can know and what we cannot know. The gentleman simply cultivates that which lies within his control, and then goes along with everything else, viewing it as fate, and that is all. Fate is something that not even the sage can change or avoid . . . which is why the ancients' technique for protecting their lives consisted solely of being cautious when it came to their speech and showing restraint in their eating and drinking.

For the gentleman's attitude toward fate, see 4.14, 7.3, 7.19, 12.5, 14.36, and 20.3.

6.11 Here again we see the idea that the true gentleman, sustained by the internal goods of the Confucian Way, is indifferent to externalities (cf. 4.2, 4.5, 4.9, 7.12, 7.16). Zhou Dunyi comments, "Master Yan simply focused upon what was important and forgot what was trivial. When you focus upon what is important, your heart is at peace; when your heart is at peace, you will find satisfaction in all things." This idea of focusing on the important rather than the trivial links 6.11 with its partner passage 6.12.

6.12 Ran Qiu has already decided he cannot proceed further along the Master's Way, and so does not even really try. As we read in 4.6, there is no one who really lacks the strength to pursue the Way—what is lacking among most of Confucius' contemporaries is the kind of genuine love for the Way that sustains Yan Hui and Confucius during the long and arduous journey of self-cultivation. As Hu Anguo observes,

> The Master praised Yan Hui for his imperturbable joy [in 6.11]. Ran Qiu heard this, and this is why he says what he says here [in 6.12]. However, if Ran Qiu really did delight in the Master's Way, it would be like the palate's taking delight in the meat of grain-fed animals:[1] he would surely exhaust his strength in pursuing it, and how could he possibly worry about his strength being insufficient?

Despite his protests to the contrary, Ran Qiu actually lacks a true passion for the Way. The problem, as we have seen, is how to instill this love in someone who does not already possess it.

6.13 As discussed in the Introduction, in this context *ru* is a term that refers to a class of specialists concerned with transmitting and teaching the traditional rituals and texts of the Zhou. Most commentators see this passage as advice to Zixia before he begins to accept his own disciples. There are two general lines of interpretation of this passage. Kong Anguo (followed by the Cheng brothers and Zhu Xi) takes the "petty" *ru* to be someone like the "village worthy" of 17.13: "When a gentleman serves as a *ru*, it is in order to clarify the Way; when a petty person serves as a *ru*, it is because he is greedy for fame." In other words, the petty *ru*, according to this interpretation, is someone who is after external goods and does not really love the Way for its own sake. Another line of interpretation links this passage to 13.4 and 13.20, and sees the petty *ru* as something more akin to the narrow technician or "vessel" mentioned in 2.12. As Cheng Shude explains,

---

[1] A reference to *Mencius* 6:A:7: "Order and rightness please my heart in the same way that the meat of grain-fed animals pleases my palate."

At this time Zixia was establishing a school in Xihe to transmit the *Odes* and the *Rites*, and stood out among the Master's disciples for his cultural refinement and learning. We can sincerely describe him as a *ru*. However, if one focuses one's energies exclusively on philological studies and the explication of isolated passages one will become narrow-minded, vulgar, and shallow, and one's achievements will be trivial. In advising Zixia to be a "gentlemanly *ru*," the Master is probably encouraging him to enter the realm of broad-ranging concerns and lofty understanding.

Both interpretations are plausible.

6.17 We have here an eloquent expression of the exasperation Confucius felt with his contemporaries' perverse refusal to follow the Way of the ancients. Fan Ning understands the passage as having to do with learning: "When walking, all people know that they have to go out by means of the door, and yet none realize that it is only by means of learning that they can be truly accomplished." The *Record of Ritual* relates it to the ritualization of everyday life: "Ritual encompasses the great and the small, the manifest and the subtle. . . . Therefore the primary rites number three hundred, and the everyday rites number three thousand, but the destination to which they ultimately lead one is the same. There has never been a person who has entered a room without using the door."[2] In either case, the point is the same: the Way of the ancients is the only way to live a proper human life.

6.18 This passage is perhaps the earliest expression of an ideal that later became very important in Confucian writings: the doctrine of holding fast to the "mean" (*zhong* 中), introduced explicitly in 6.29. A perfect balance between native substance and cultural refinement is the ideal state, although if one is to err it should be on the side of substance (3.4, 3.8, 5.10, 5.22, 7.33). For the ideal of the "mean," see also 1.12, 13.21, and 17.8.

6.20 The "it" referred to is most likely the Confucian Way. There are several slightly different ways to take this passage, but under my reading what is being referred to is the increasing level of unself-consciousness and ease that characterizes the true Confucian gentleman. Bao Xian takes the "it" in the more narrow sense of learning: "One who knows about learning lacks the sincerity of one who loves learning, and one who loves learning lacks the depth of one who takes joy in it." Zhang Shi invokes an analogy to food:

> It is like the five cultivated grains. "One who knows it" knows that they are edible. "One who loves it" has eaten them and found them delicious. "One who takes joy in it" has found them delicious and has moreover eaten his fill. If you know it but are not able to love it, this means that your knowledge is not yet complete,

---

[2] Chapter 10 ("Ritual Vessels"); Legge 1967, vol. 1: 404.

and if you love it but are not able to take joy in it, this means that your love has not yet been consummated. Is not [joy in the Way] what strengthened the resolve of the ancients and allowed them to go forward without rest?

6.21 Although some commentators understand "average" to refer to overall moral character, in an alternate version of this passage in the *Guliang Commentary* it explicitly refers to level of understanding, and this is the most likely meaning here. Most commentators see this as a rationale for Confucius' practice of "skillful means": altering his teachings to accord with the level of understanding of his listeners (11.22). As Zhang Shi says, "Altering one's teachings to fit the level of understanding of one's audience is the means by which one allows them to ask and think about issues that are relevant to them, and is also the way one leads them gradually into higher levels of understanding."

6.22 Many commentators believe that Fan Chi is asking for advice in preparation for taking office, and therefore understand Confucius' answers as tailored to the duties of an official. "Social harmony among the common people" is the translation of *minzhiyi* 民之義—lit., "rightness [among] the common people." "Rightness" in this sense usually refers to observing proper social distinctions and role-specific duties, and this is the sense in which this phrase is understood in later Han texts. By himself providing an example to the common people, an official or ruler ensures that they will accord with rightness (1.2, 2.21). "Respecting the ghosts and spirits while keeping them at a distance" is understood by most as fulfilling one's sacrificial duties sincerely and in accordance with ritual (3.12), without trying to flatter the spirits or curry favor with them, and thereby also reinforcing moral behavior among the common people (1.9).

6.23 This is a famously cryptic passage. A somewhat neo-Daoist-flavored interpretation of the first two lines is provided by Bao Xian: "The wise take joy in actively exercising their talent and wisdom in governing the world, just as water flows on and on and knows no cease. The Good take joy in the sort of peace and stability displayed by mountains, which are naturally nonactive and yet give birth to all of the myriad things." The precise meaning of the last line is particularly problematic. It is unclear why only the wise (and not the Good) should be joyful, for instance. As for "the Good are long-lived" statement, some commentators attempt to reconcile it with the premature death of Yan Hui by understanding it metaphorically: it is the reputation or beneficial influence of the Good person that is long lived. Others reject this strategy, arguing that— the isolated counterexample of Yan Hui aside—the Good are long lived because they are calm and free of desire for external things. All of these interpretations are quite speculative.

6.25 A *gu* was a ritual drinking vessel. Many commentators believe that Confucius' sigh of displeasure was provoked by the fact that the sort of *gu* being made by his contemporaries was not a proper *gu* (i.e., not in accordance with ancient standards), although there is disagreement over the question of what precisely was wrong. Some claim that the offending *gu* was not of the proper size. Mao Qiling, for example, claims that the *gu* being made by Confucius' contemporaries was larger than the traditional *gu*, and sees this passage as a complaint against the excesses of Confucius' age—in this case, excessive drinking. His interpretation is supported by many of the early commentaries. Other commentators—such as He Yan or Zhu Zhongdu—see the problem as related to the shape of the *gu* or the manner in which it was manufactured, in which case the passage is similarly understood as an illustration of Confucius' strict adherence to ancient practices, his dissatisfaction with the practices of his contemporaries, and his concern for the proper use of names (cf. 13.3). Finally, Brooks and Brooks present a compelling alternate interpretation, based on the claim of William Willets that the *gu* was an exclusively Shang vessel that was no longer being manufactured or used during Confucius' lifetime, and that had been reduced to a valued, but unused, museum piece (1998: 36). This would somewhat change the meaning of the passage ("A *gu* that is not being used as a *gu*"), turning it into a lament on the part of Confucius that he—like the *gu*—was not being put to proper use.

6.27 A person who has been molded by the two main Confucian traditional forms—learning and ritual training—can be relied on to act appropriately. As Zhu Xi comments, "When it comes to learning, a gentleman desires broadness, and there is therefore no element of culture that he does not examine. When it comes to self-control, he desires restraint, and his every motion must therefore be in accordance with ritual. Having been disciplined in this way, he will not go against the Way." Some commentators believe that it is the learning or culture of the gentleman that must be restrained by the rites (rather than the gentleman himself), but 9.11 supports the first reading.

6.28 Nanzi was the consort of Lord Ling of Wei, and a woman of bad repute. Zilu is not pleased that Confucius would seek an audience with such a person. As many commentators point out, however, it is likely that ritual dictated that when arriving in a state one requests an audience with the "orphaned little lord"—i.e., the wife or consort of the local ruler. In having an audience with Nanzi on arriving in Wei, Confucius was suppressing his personal distaste for Nanzi, overcoming the disapproval of his disciples, and risking more general opprobrium in order to observe an important dictate of ritual propriety. Zilu is being presented here as similar to Chen Wenzi in 5.19: as "pure," but with a rigid fastidiousness that falls short of Goodness. Alternate interpretations of the passage see Zilu's displeasure as resulting from suspicion—either that illicit activity may have occurred during Confucius' audience with the notoriously lascivious Nanzi, or that the Master was seeking some sort of questionable political advantage in seeing her—and have Confucius defending his innocence.

6.29 An alternate reading of the final line is, "for some time now such virtue has been quite hard to find among the people." This is how He Yan and Zhu Xi take it, but alternate versions of this passage in other early texts support the reading adopted in the translation. *Yong* 庸 might also be read as "constant" rather than "application," in which case the first line would read, "acquiring Virtue through constantly holding to the mean," although the *Record of Ritual* supports the first reading when it praises the sage-king Shun: "He grasped both extremes, and applied the mean between them (*yongqizhong* 用其中) when dealing with the common people."[3] This ideal of keeping to the mean is also seen in 1.12, 6.18, 13.21, and 17.8.

6.30 We see here (as in 12.22) hints of the shift toward *ren* (Goodness) as the more specific and limited virtue of "benevolence" that is complete by the time of Mencius.[4] Many commentators see this exchange as an attempt to rein in excessive speculation on the part of Zigong and bring him back to the fundamentals of self-cultivation. As Huan Maoyong explains,

> Zigong discusses Goodness from some distant, esoteric perspective, while the Master discusses it as something intimate and close to home. Zigong talks about great and difficult to attain rewards—something on an order of magnitude that even Yao or Shun would find difficult. The Master talks about extending the self to reach other people—something that simply requires us to plumb our own minds and hearts, to start with what is near at hand in order to reach what is far away.

The final line of Confucius' advice sounds like a formulation of the virtue of understanding (*shu*)—something that we have already seen is apparently beyond Zigong's grasp (5.12).

Book Seven Commentary

7.1 There is a great deal of commentarial controversy concerning the meaning of the reference to "Old Peng"—even if one or two people are being referred to—but the least fantastic explanation is that of Bao Xian, who takes the reference to be to one person: "Old Peng was a great worthy of the Yin Dynasty who

---

[3] Chapter 32 ("Doctrine of the Mean"); Legge 1967, vol. 2: 302.

[4] Refer to Appendix 4 for more on the development of the term *ren*.

was fond of transmitting ancient tales. In comparing himself to Old Peng, Confucius indicates his reverence for those who merely transmit [and do not innovate]." Some commentators, such as Huang Kan, believe that Confucius refrained from innovating because he was not a ruler and did not have the authority to create new social institutions. It is more likely that transmission is all that Confucius countenanced for people in his age, since the sagely Zhou kings established the ideal set of institutions that perfectly accord with human needs—the "door" through which anyone wishing to become a gentleman must pass (6.17).

7.2 Repeated in a slightly different form in 7.34, these seemingly modest qualities represent the "method of Goodness" mentioned in 6.30, something far beyond the grasp of most people.

7.3 Commentators point out that the sort of "worry" (*you* 憂) mentioned here must be distinguished from the ordinary sorts of worries that other people have. In *Mencius* 4:B:28, the difference between these two types of worries is formulated in terms of a distinction between being "worried" (*you*) and "concerned" (*huan* 患):

> The gentleman has worries his entire life, but is never concerned for even a single moment. Now, the sort of worries he has are of this sort: [the sage-king] Shun was a person. I am also a person. Shun served as a model for the world worth passing down to later generations, while I still cannot manage to be more than a common villager. This is indeed something worth worrying about. What is to be done about this worry? One should merely try to become like Shun, that is all. In this way, the gentleman is never concerned. If something is not Good, he does not do it; if something is not ritually correct, he does not put it into practice. Thus, even if some sort of external problem [*huan*] arises, the gentleman is not made concerned by it.

The aspiring gentleman focuses on what is under his control (self-cultivation), and consigns the rest to fate. Cf. 4.14 and 14.36.

7.4 Huang Shisan comments, "This passage records the manner in which the sage's bearing, even when he was merely sitting at his leisure, was harmoniously adapted to the circumstances and always appeared to be in accordance with the mean." Like the accounts of Confucius' ritual behavior that constitute Book Ten, this passage describes the effortless, unself-conscious manner in which the Master embodied the Confucian Way.

7.5 The point seems to be that one's immersion in the culture of the Zhou should be so complete that it penetrates even into one's dream life. Some commentators also understand the ability to see the Duke of Zhou while dreaming as a testament to Confucius' power of concentration and his power of will (*zhi* 志).

7.6 We seem to have here, as in 2.4, an account of the stages of self-cultivation, although the various achievements mentioned are not necessarily in chronological order. The first line might also be rendered, "Set your will/intention [*zhi* 志] upon the Way," and it seems to be the crucial first step in Confucian self-cultivation: a conscious and sincere commitment to the Way of the Zhou kings. Wang Yangming emphasizes the importance of this first step in his comment on this passage:

> If you set your will upon the Way then you will become a scholar of the Way and Virtue, whereas if you set your will upon the cultural arts, you will become merely a technically skilled aesthete. Therefore, you cannot but be careful about the direction of your will. This is why, when it comes to learning, nothing is as important as focusing upon the correct goal. What the ancients referred to as the "cultural arts" were ritual, music, archery, charioteering, calligraphy, and arithmetic. These were all integral parts of their daily lives, but the ancients did not focus their will upon them—they felt that they must first establish the basics and then the rest could follow. What people nowadays refer to as the "cultural arts" are merely literature, calligraphy, and painting. What could these things possibly have to do with the needs of daily life?

The idea that the cultural arts represent the final finishing touch applied to an already substantial moral foundation is also found in 1.6 and 3.8.

7.7 There is some debate over the exact meaning of the terms *shu* 束 and *xiu* 脩, lit. "restraint/bundle" and "strip," here taken separately to mean "bundle of silk and strips [of cured meat]." The terms could also be taken as a compound, either as "bundle of cured meat" or (as in some early texts) the strip with which a man can bind his hair. Zheng Xuan explains that *shuxiu* means "over fifteen years of age," presumably because this is the age when men in ancient times began binding their hair when going out in public. In this case, the point would be that Confucius would accept anyone over age fifteen as a student. Others take the term as a metaphoric extension of the "hair tie" sense (again, relying on precedents in early texts), understanding it as a reference to the bearing of the person seeking instruction—that is, an attitude of self-restraint and self-discipline. As Mao Qiling observes, however, the verb "offering up" in the text strongly suggests that *shuxiu* refers to a literal object, and many early texts mention *shuxiu* in a context where it is clear that the term refers to small, symbolic, ritually dictated offerings made by a student seeking instruction. Most likely, then, we should follow Kong Anguo in seeing the point as being that Confucius' door was open to anyone who came willingly and in a ritually correct manner—that is, he did not discriminate on the basis of social status or wealth.

7.8 As Zhu Xi notes, this represents the flip side of Confucius' contribution as a teacher mentioned in 7.2 ("encouraging others and never growing weary"): for education to work, the student must also contribute to the process. The ideal student should come to the project possessed by an inchoate need for what study is able to provide—something like the passion for learning that causes

Confucius himself to forget to eat (7.19). While Confucius certainly saw the role of traditional knowledge as being much more essential than Socrates did, there is nonetheless a similar maieutic quality to his method. Cf. 15.16.

7.9, 7.10 These two passages fit together so neatly that some commentators argue that they should be read as one passage. One way to understand them is as examples of ritually proper behavior, and the *Record of Ritual* actually quotes both lines as models for proper mourning practice.[1] It is unlikely, however, that either of the behaviors described were explicitly dictated by the ritual standards of the time, and most commentators (from He Yan down to Zhu Xi) understand the point to be about sincerity and depth of feeling. That is, while others might observe the superficial niceties of the mourning rituals and then get on with their day, Confucius *felt* the rituals (even if they were being enacted by someone else), and remained profoundly affected by the emotions they evoked. Understood this way, the point is not that Confucius consciously refrained from eating his fill or singing, but that he was actually rendered unable to eat a full meal or engage in light-hearted activities.

7.12 Again we have the idea that the gentleman does not pursue externalities. Some commentators see this passage as a comment on fate: wealth cannot be pursued because its acquisition is subject to fate. As in 7.16, however, there seems to be more of a normative edge here: the acquisition of wealth is indeed subject to fate, but is also in itself an unworthy object of pursuit. The point here is more about rightness than fate.

7.14 The Shao is the court music of the sage-king Shun. As in 6.7, we are probably to understand "three months" in the sense of "a long time" rather than literally. According to the *History of the Han,* one of the descendents of Shun, who was enfeoffed in the state of Chen, was forced to flee to Qi, bringing Shun's court music with him. We see in this passage an association between music, joy, and forgetfulness that is also echoed by the graphic pun between the words for "joy" and "music" in ancient Chinese, which are both represented by the character 樂. The joyous rapture inspired by sublimely beautiful music is one of the internal goods of the Confucian practice that frees the gentleman from the demands of externalities.

7.16 As Huang Kan explains, the point of the last line is that "floating clouds move about on their own, up in the sky—what connection do they have with me? In the same way, what do wealth and fame improperly attained have to do with me?" We have here another expression of the gentleman's independence from externalities; cf. 4.5, 6.11, and 7.12.

---

[1] 7.9 is repeated in Chapter 3 ("Tan Gong") of the *Record of Ritual* (Legge 1967, vol. 1:147), and 7.10 is paraphrased ("on a day when one has wept [in mourning], one should not sing"), without reference to Confucius himself, in Chapter 1 ("Summary of Ritual") (Legge 1967, vol. 1:89).

7.17 The translation follows the Lu version of the *Analects* here in reading the intensifying particle *yi* 亦 in place of *yi* 易 (*[Book of] Changes*); the Gu version reads "If I were granted many more years, so that by the age of fifty I could complete my studies of the *Changes*, this might enable me to be free of major faults." Commentators who follow the Gu version generally see these words as spoken by Confucius in his mid-forties—before he had reached the stage of "understanding the Mandate of Heaven" (2.4)—and explain that understanding the Mandate of Heaven is a prerequisite for delving into such an esoteric work as the *Changes*. Most later scholars, doubting that Confucius seriously studied the *Book of Changes*, prefer to follow the Lu version.

7.18 Written Chinese characters are not directly phonetic in the manner of a Roman alphabet, and the same character can be pronounced differently by speakers of different dialects. In Confucius' age, people were apparently aware that the spoken languages of the various regions of China differed significantly from the "classical pronunciation," which Liu Baonan argues must have been the dialect spoken in the Western Zhou capital. We must assume that knowledge of these pronunciations was kept alive, at least in the state of Lu, through use in formal and ritual contexts. This passage suggests, though, that Confucius' contemporaries had begun to ignore this tradition and eschew the classical pronunciations in favor of local dialect—a Christian analogy would be the abandonment of Latin in favor of services in the vernacular. This represents a departure from the Way of the Zhou that Confucius characteristically resists. No doubt part of the motivation for abandoning the classical pronunciations was that they were no longer comprehensible, and Zheng Xuan suggests that Confucius would follow his formal recitations with explanations in local dialect. Mao Qiling argues that the "classical pronunciation" (lit. "elegant speech") also involved details of cadence, demeanor, and tone of voice.

7.19 The Duke of She was a high minister in the state of Chu; commentators explain that, since the Chu rulers had already usurped the title of "king," Chu ministers had begun calling themselves "dukes." There are two main explanations for why Zilu does not answer his query. Early commentators claim that Duke She was a power-hungry figure who was insistently trying to lure Confucius into his service, and that Zilu was leery of encouraging him in his efforts. Under this interpretation, one purpose of Confucius' response is to indicate that he is not interested in accepting a morally questionable position for the sake of a salary or other material rewards. Later commentators, beginning with Zhu Xi, portray Duke She as a more sympathetic figure who admires Confucius, and see Zilu's failure to respond as a result of the perceived ineffability of Confucius' lofty, mysterious virtue. In this case, Confucius' reaction is refreshingly straightforward: he is far from mysterious, being merely an ordinary man possessed by a great love for the Way of the ancients. The only thing that differentiates him from others is the object of his love; as Wang Yangming notes,

"The passions of ordinary people do not extend beyond being passionate about rewards, fame, wealth, and honor. . . . The nature of their passion is not different [from the Master's], it is merely the object of their passion that is different." The object, of course, makes all the difference. We see here again the idea that the unself-conscious joy derived from the internal goods of the Confucian Way renders one indifferent to externalities.

7.20 This passage serves as an elaboration of 7.19: Confucius is not especially gifted by nature; he simply knows where to look for knowledge and has the passion to sustain him in this quest. As Zheng Xuan notes, another purpose of this passage "is to encourage others to pursue learning." Cf. 7.1 and 16.9.

7.22 Alternately, Confucius may be referring to discrete qualities in his companions rather than their overall characters: in any person he can find both virtues to emulate and vices to avoid. Model emulation is the primary method of moral education for Confucius, and the implication here is that the process of education is never completed: even the Master always has something to learn. Cf. 4.17.

7.23 Huan Tui was a military minister in the state of Song who apparently wished to do Confucius harm. According to an account in the *Record of the Historian*, while in Song Confucius and his disciples were one day practicing ritual beneath a large tree when Huan Tui, in an attempt to kill Confucius, cut the tree down. The assassination attempt failed, and when the disciples urged the Master to make haste in escaping the state he delivered the remark reported here. Confucius is on a mission from Heaven (3.24), and is therefore subject only to Heaven's command (*ming*). Human beings do not have the power to alter fate, and Confucius therefore accepts whatever may befall him with equanimity, viewing it as Heaven's will. Very similar sentiments are expressed in 9.5 and 14.36.

7.24 We should probably relate this passage to 5.13: since the Master did not speak of certain topics, some of his disciples apparently felt that he was keeping some sort of esoteric knowledge from them. This is not at all the case, since all that the Master taught had to do with learning from the ancients and putting this learning into practice—a lesson that he taught every moment through his own actions and comportment. Wang Yangming's comment on this passage is quite helpful:

> When it comes to teaching disciples, there are two approaches: theoretical teaching (*yanjiao* 言教; lit. "teaching through words") and teaching by example (*shenjiao* 身教; lit. "body/personal teaching"). Theoretical teaching is certainly useful

for teaching one how to act, but it cannot match the sort of profound affect that one can achieve through teaching by example. . . . With his behavior, the Master provided the students with a model to emulate, but there were disciples who were only interested in theoretical teaching. This is why the Master had to make it clear that he was, in fact, not hiding anything from them. This was to serve as a warning to the disciples. The sense is quite similar to that expressed [17.19]: "I wish I did not have to speak (*yan* 言), what does Heaven ever say?"

Confucius' response thus also serves as a warning to the disciples not to fixate on theoretical problems, but rather to focus on the task of actual moral practice. Cf. 16.13, where Boyu, the son of Confucius, is suspected of having received esoteric training, but responds that all that he learned from his father was to study the *Odes* and to learn ritual.

7.28 The final comment is probably a reference to 7.20 (cf. 16.9): Confucius is not like those rare gifted individuals who are born with knowledge, but must instead seek it from ancient culture (cf. 7.1). On the other hand, he is better than those who recklessly innovate without first having grounded themselves in traditional learning, for such blind innovation is inevitably fruitless (2.15, 15.31). Some commentators—influenced by the traditional picture of Confucius as the author of the *Annals*—take *zuo* 作 as "creating literary works" rather than "innovation" in a general sense, but this is historically less plausible.

7.30 Bao Xian elaborates, "The Way of Goodness is not far—simply walk it and you will arrive there." Jiang Xi puts a more political spin on the passage: "If you can return to ritual for only a single day, everyone in the world will return home to Goodness—this is how extremely close Goodness is to us." The purpose of this passage is to emphasize the importance of sincere commitment to the Way, but it seems to conflict with passages such as 8.7 ("the burden is heavy and the Way is long"), and is thus symptomatic of the so-called "paradox of wu-wei" mentioned in the commentary to 4.6. For Confucius, the virtue of Goodness, as well as the power of Virtue that comes with it, can only be realized by one who truly loves them for their own sake. The point here in 7.30, however, seems to be that if one truly *does* love them, then one already has them—were a person to truly love Goodness in the same way that he loves to eat and drink, then the battle would be already won. This is no doubt the source of much of Confucius' frustration with his current age (9.18, 9.24), as well as with disciples such as Zai Wo, who presumably gives assent to the Confucian project but nonetheless lies sleeping in bed all day. The student cannot learn from the teacher unless he is passionately *committed* to learning, and this requires possessing a genuine love for the Confucian Way. The problem is that it is hard to see how the teacher can engender this sort of love in a student who lacks it. Cf. 7.34 and 9.24.

7.32 Some commentators claim that responding to another's song was a dictate of ritual, but this is more likely simply a description of Confucius' willingness and ability to learn from others (cf. 7.22). Zhu Xi comments,

> The Master would inevitably ask the other person to sing again because he wished to get the nuances and learn from the fine points. Afterward he would harmonize with them because he was happy at having gotten the nuances and grasped the fine points. Here we see the easygoing disposition of the sage: sincere in intention and cordial to the highest degree, while at the same time humble, discerning, and happy to celebrate the excellences of others.

7.33 This is perhaps merely a polite demurral (cf. 7.34), but it serves to emphasize the difficulty of obtaining in practice the proper balance between cultural refinement and native substance, and is no doubt meant as a warning against falling into "foppish pedantry"—the more insidious and common of the two failings described in 6.18.

7.34 A companion passage to 7.33 with an illuminating coda: the humble love of the Way and striving after it that Confucius is willing to grant himself as a quality is itself something beyond the ability of most people. Gong Xihua's words are very revealing and get to the heart of the paradox of Confucian self-cultivation: in order to keep oneself moving forward along on the "long journey" of self-cultivation it is necessary that one genuinely desires to reach the destination, but how does one teach such desire to a person who does not already possess it?

7.35 According to commentators, the *Eulogy* is the title of a traditional prayer text.

The point of this passage seems to be that Confucius' prayer has been his life's work. Any other sort of appeal to Heaven is unnecessary, and the Master is ready to accept whatever fate Heaven may have in store for him. We also see here the theme expressed in 3.12 and 6.22: the gentleman keeps the spirits at a distance and focuses instead on the human world and the task of self-cultivation. Brooks and Brooks' comment on this passage is quite nice:

> It is very moving, is it not? The Master patiently lets Zilu instruct him in ritual propriety, notwithstanding the fact (or what the hearer of this saying may be presumed to have regarded as fact) that he knows much more about it than Zilu. He then rejects the suggested intercession with the deities. Instead, he offers his whole life as the secular equivalent of a prayer. (1998: 44)

7.37 The gentleman is relaxed because he is sustained by the internal goods of the Confucian practice, whereas the petty person's focus on externalities exposes him to the vagaries of circumstance. As Jiang Xi notes, "The gentleman is self-possessed and at ease, relaxed and unselfish. The petty person, on the other hand, is always scrambling after glory and fighting for personal gain, constantly anxious about success or failure, and therefore perpetually full of worry." Cf. 7.38.

7.38 This companion passage to 7.37 fleshes out the description of the perfected person, who effortlessly embodies the mean of virtue. Cf. 7.4.

Book Eight Commentary

8.2 Many commentators have suggested that these two sections should be split into separate passages. The first half has to do with the ability of ritual to trim and shape native tendencies so that they fit the mean of true virtue (cf. 1.12, 12.1, and especially 17.8, where study or learning rather than ritual training is described as the force preventing virtue from falling into vice). The second half has to do with the power of charismatic Virtue as a force for bringing about political order (cf. 1.9, 12.9). One way of making the two sections cohere is to see the first as a description of how to attain the sort of individual perfection that will then enable one to bring about the political–moral suasion described in the second section. This is how Zhang Shi understands it: "If one understands what comes first and what comes last in the Way of humans, then one can be respectful without being exasperating, careful without being timid, courageous without being unruly, and upright without being inflexible, and will thereby transform the common people and cause their virtue to return to fullness [1.9]."

8.7 This passage plays on the literal and metaphoric meanings of *dao*, which means both physical path or road and the abstract moral "Way." The metaphor of self-cultivation as a lifelong journey vividly illustrates the difficulty of the Confucian Way (cf. 9.11). As Kong Anguo remarks, "Taking up Goodness as one's own personal task is a heavy burden—there is nothing heavier. Stopping only once death has overtaken you is a long journey—there is nothing longer." An alternate version of this passage found in the *Record of Ritual* is even more extreme: "The Master said, 'As a vessel, Goodness is heavy; as a way, it is long. No one is up to the task of picking it up, nor is anyone able to walk it to its end.'"[1]

---

[1] Chapter 32 ("Record of Examples"); Legge 1967, vol. 2: 334.

8.8 Here we have a more succinct version of the course of Confucian self-cultivation described in 2.4. The translation of the first phrase follows Jiang Xi's interpretation of *xing* 興 as "to inspire, stimulate": "Gazing upon the intentions of the ancients can give inspiration to one's own intention." Bao Xian takes *xing* to mean, more prosaically, "to begin": "The point is that the cultivation of the self should start with study of the *Odes*." "Taking one's place" through ritual involves, as discussed in 2.4, taking up one's role as an adult among other adults in society, something that requires a mastery of the rituals governing social interactions. Steps one and two thus represent, respectively, cognitive shaping through learning and behavioral shaping through ritual training. Finally, the joy inspired by the powerfully moving music of the ancients brings the cognitive and behavioral together into the unself-conscious, effortless perfection that is wu-wei. *Mencius* 4:A:27, which invokes the metaphor of dance, represents perhaps the best commentary on this passage:

> The substance of benevolence [*ren*] is the serving of one's parents; the substance of rightness is obeying one's elders; the substance of wisdom is to understand benevolence and rightness and to not let them go; the substance of ritual propriety is the regulation and adornment of benevolence and rightness; and the substance of music is the joy one takes in benevolence and rightness. Once such joy is born, it cannot be stopped. Once it cannot be stopped, then one begins unconsciously to dance it with one's feet and wave one's arms in time with it.

Some commentators take all three nouns in the passage as titles of classical texts—"Take inspiration from the *Book of Odes*, take your place with the *Book of Ritual*, and perfect yourself with the *Book of Music*"—but it is unlikely that such books existed in Confucius' time.

8.9 "It," of course, refers to the Way. There are several ways to understand this passage. The simplest interpretation is that the common people can be guided along the Confucian Way—most efficaciously through the influence of the gentleman's Virtue—but lack the cognitive ability to grasp the principles of the Way (cf. 16.9 and *Mencius* 7:A:5). Some early commentators alternately see it as a comment on rule by Virtue as opposed to rule by force, in which case the second clause is read more along the lines of "the common people cannot be allowed to understand it." This latter interpretation accords well with the sentiment of 2.3, where Confucius declares that ruling by a publicized legal code merely inspires the common people to devise devious ways to get around the law.

8.12 Confucius is again lamenting the fact that the majority of his contemporaries were focused on external goods, and saw learning as merely a means to an end: that is, an official position, and the prestige and salary that went with it. A great deal of commentarial ink has been spilled over the significance of the three-year period, but—as Huan Maoyong notes—"the sense is not three temporal periods; 'three years' simply means a long time."

8.13 According to Bao Xian, the fact that a state is endangered means that disorder is imminent, and Zhu Xi explains that, although one already serving as an official has a duty to remain and try to protect an endangered state, "it is permissible for an outsider to refrain from entering into such a state." Once a state has degenerated into immoral disorder—defined by Bao Xian as a situation where ministers are assassinating lords and sons killing fathers—a gentleman's duty is to leave the state rather than sully himself by remaining. The end of the passage reiterates this theme: when there is an opportunity for virtuous service, it would be shameful for the gentleman to remain in obscurity and poverty; when nothing but immorality and corruption prevails, however, it would be equally shameful for the gentleman not to withdraw.

8.19 The common people were "not able to find words to describe him" because the influence of Yao's Virtue was so subtle and pervasive that the people were transformed naturally, without being aware of what was happening. Compare this to Heaven's manner of ruling "without the need for words," as described in 17.19. As Kong Anguo observes, "Yao is being praised for modeling himself on Heaven and thereby transforming the people."

Book Nine Commentary

9.2 Daxiang is said by commentators to be the name of a small hamlet.

According to one understanding of this passage, Confucius' response is equally sarcastic as the question, expressing his contempt for limited or merely technical skills. Han and Jin Dynasty commentators, however, generally understand the villager from Daxiang as being sincere in his praise ("How great is Confucius! He is broadly learned, and yet does not achieve fame by means of any one particular art") and Confucius' answer as genuine self-deprecation— something along the lines of, "Oh, perhaps I should specialize in something and make myself useful." Charioteering was the least respectable of the gentlemanly arts, and so his choice is seen as especially humble. Under either interpretation, the sense of the passage accords with 2.12, 9.6, and 19.7, but—as Waley notes (1989: 244)—the first seems to make better sense of Confucius' response.

9.3 According to commentators, the linen cap specified by ritual was an elaborate affair—consisting of many layers and involving intricate stitching—and Confucius' contemporaries had begun replacing it with a simpler silk version. Confucius apparently feels that this does not interfere with its basic function.

When approaching a ruler or other superior sitting on a raised dais, ritual dictates bowing before ascending the stairs, but Confucius' contemporaries had taken to ascending the stairs and only bowing when directly before their ruler. This is a more substantial change—as Brooks and Brooks note, "the 'below' option implies *asking* permission to ascend; the 'above' option *presumes* it" (1998:51)—and Confucius rejects it as not ritually proper. This passage describes the sort of judgment and flexibility that can be exercised by an accomplished ritual practitioner. It is possible to exaggerate the iconoclastic character of this passage—we should note that the one change Confucius accedes to is a rather minor one, and that he does not actually *propose* changing the rite, but simply goes along with the popular practice (with possibly a hint of reluctance). Nevertheless, we can appreciate the sense of it without ignoring Confucius' profound conservatism: rites are expressive of a certain sense or feeling, and thus an alteration in the actual rite is permissible if it will not—in the opinion of one who has fully mastered the rites—alter its essential meaning.

9.5 As the *Record of the Historian* tells the story,

> Confucius was leaving Wei, and was passing through the town of Kuang on his way to Chen. There was a person named Yang Hu who had in the past done violence to the people of Kuang, and they therefore detained Confucius, because he physically resembled this Yang Hu. Confucius was imprisoned there for five days.

The account goes on to note that Yan Hui had fallen behind on this journey and was finally reunited with Confucius in Kuang. Bao Xian also claims that, to add to the confusion, one of Confucius' disciples was a known associate of Yang Hu, and happened to be driving Confucius' chariot as he passed through Kuang, further rousing the suspicions of the Kuang people. As for Confucius being the bearer of culture, the *Guliang Commentary* for Duke Ai, Year 14 (482 B.C.E) cites Confucius as saying: "The Way of Kings Wen and Wu has not fallen to the ground—it still lives on in us. King Wen having passed away, is not his Way of being cultured truly to be found in me?" For this theme of Confucius being the Heaven-appointed bearer of Zhou culture—and therefore enjoying its special protection—see also 3.24, 7.23, and 14.36.

9.10 Hastening one's step, like rising to one's feet, is a sign of respect. What is being emphasized here is probably, as Fan Ziyu says, not merely Confucius' respectfulness, but also the sincere, wu-wei fashion in which it manifested itself: "The mind of the sage is such that he grieves along with those who are in mourning, feels respect for those who hold official rank, and feels pity for those who are disabled. It is likely that the Master rose to his feet and hastened his step spontaneously, without having consciously intended it." Like 7.9, this passage resembles the descriptions of ritual behavior found in Book Ten.

9.11 The "it" referred to by Yan Hui is most likely the Confucian Way. This passage represents the most dramatic expression in the text of the difficulty of self-cultivation and the incredible strength of will needed to remain on the path—especially because it comes from the mouth of Yan Hui, the most naturally gifted of Confucius' disciples. Many esoteric and mystical interpretations of Yan Hui's words have been offered by traditional commentators, but Huang Gan is correct in rejecting them:

> The Way of the sage is certainly high and brilliant, expansive and great, so that it is indeed difficult to reach, but it still does not transcend our basic human nature. The details of one's movements and expressions; the tasks of eating and drinking, rising and resting, interacting with others and meeting one's social responsibilities; the standards that govern relations between ruler and minister, father and son, elder and junior, and husband and wife; going out in public or remaining at home, resigning or accepting office, declining or accepting reward, taking this and discarding that, along with everything else up to the implementation of government regulations—none of this lies outside the scope of the Way.

The difficulty does not lie in the Way's transcendental nature, for it is right in front of us (7.30), in the details of everyday life. The true challenge is the almost superhuman stamina and determination required to walk it to its end. Cf. 8.7 and 9.19.

9.12 Zilu means to honor his Master—and perhaps incidentally raise his own status—by having him attended as if he were a feudal lord, but this represents a serious abuse of ritual. As Li Ao explains, Confucius' concern over the ritual violations of the Ji Family—who, as we have seen, were usurping the ritual prerogatives of the Zhou kings in an attempt to impress their contemporaries and curry favor with Heaven (3.1)—no doubt accounts for some of the harshness of his rebuke, which is then softened somewhat by his final remarks. As Brooks and Brooks note, although the disciples are ashamed of their Master's lack of office and humble circumstances, Confucius himself "insists on his low rank, with devoted disciples and not sullen lackeys at his gate. Even a modern reader can hardly miss the note of intense, reproving affection" (1998: 53).

9.13 The gentleman should share his virtue with the world by taking public office, but only under a virtuous king and when approached in accordance with the Way. Confucius thus refuses to actively peddle his wares on the market, waiting instead for his virtue to be recognized by a ritually correct and morally cultivated ruler. As Fan Ziyu puts it, "The gentleman is never unwilling to serve in office, but also despises any offer that is not in accordance with the Way. The scholar waiting for the ritually proper approach is like a piece of jade waiting for the right price . . . he is certainly not going to compromise the Way in order to gain human rewards, or 'brag about his jade in pursuit of a sale.'"

9.14 The Nine Yi tribes were a group of "barbarians" who lived along the eastern coast of present-day China, possibly including the Korean peninsula. This passage is a testament to the transformative power of the gentleman's Virtue (cf. 12.19; as Ma Rong puts it, "Everywhere the gentleman dwells is transformed"), as well as the universality of the Way's power: even non-Chinese barbarians are subject to its influence.

9.17 This is a rather opaque passage, with at least two plausible interpretations. Jin Dynasty commentators generally take it as a lament on the passage of time and Confucius' sense of personal failure. Sun Chuo, for instance, comments: "The river flows on without stopping like the years ceaselessly passing away; the time is already late, and yet the Way has still not been put into practice. This is the cause of Confucius' lament." This sense ties 9.17 with 9.14. Perhaps more compelling is the interpretation of the *Luxuriant Dew of the Annals*, which claims that the river's unremitting and thorough progress toward the sea is a metaphor for the ideal student's progress along the Way toward the goal of Goodness, with all of the river's qualities mapping onto human virtues. This is how Zhu Xi takes the passage, "the Master made this pronouncement and pointed this out to people because he wanted the student to engage in constant reflection and examination without letting up for even a moment," and fits it together with the many other passages in the text that emphasize the importance of perseverance and hard work, such as 9.11.

9.18 There are two slightly different ways to take this passage. He Yan sees it as a criticism of Confucius' contemporaries: "The Master is complaining that his contemporaries viewed Virtue lightly and instead focused upon the pursuit of female beauty." This is how Sima Qian understands it as well, claiming in the *Record of the Historian* that 9.18 was inspired by an event in Confucius' life when he was publicly humiliated by Duke Ling of Wei, who honored his consort—the infamous Nanzi—over Confucius himself. Li Chong, on the other hand, sees the passage as more of a general statement about self-cultivation, a claim that "if people simply loved Virtue as much as they love female beauty, then they would discard immorality and return to rectitude." Most likely both points are intended: if only people could love the Way in the same spontaneous, wu-wei fashion that they love the pleasures of the flesh, Confucius' job would be done, but he was not optimistic about this happening anytime soon with his contemporaries. Cf. 9.24 and 15.16.

9.19 The first half of this passage echoes 1.15, 8.7, and 9.17 in emphasizing the need for constant effort and indefatigable determination if one is to completely walk the long and arduous Confucian Way. As Zhu Xi puts it, "If the student is able to steel himself and not desist, then his accumulated small efforts will result in great success. If, on the other hand, he stops halfway down the road, then he has thrown away everything he has already achieved." The second half provides some encouragement, somewhat balancing out Yan Hui's lament in 9.11: the Way is long, but with every step one is making progress. An ancillary point is that, when it comes to self-cultivation, it is the internal decisions of the individual that determine success or failure; as Zhu Xi explains, "The decision to stop or move forward lies entirely within me, and is not determined by others" (cf. 12.1).

9.22 Commentators from the Han to the Tang take this passage as specifically referring to Yan Hui's untimely death. Zhu Xi, on the other hand, takes it together with 9.17 and 9.19 as a general comment on self-cultivation: "Learning that is not completed is like this, which is why the gentleman values self-motivation." As Huan Maoyong notes, an argument in favor of this latter interpretation is that it also makes 9.22 fit well with 9.23. Both interpretations are plausible.

9.23 This forty- or fifty-year-old never-do-well is perhaps an example of the "sprout that fails to flower" or "flower that fails to fruit" mentioned in 9.22. Most early commentators take *wen* 聞 ("learning") as "reputation," but, as Wang Yangming observes, "Confucius himself said, 'This is reputation, not achievement,' so why would he consent to using reputation as a standard for evaluating a person?" Wang is referring to 12.20, where Confucius rejects public reputation as an indication of a scholar's level of achievement, and instead directs his questioner to look to a person's actual comportment and level of personal virtue. We see other passages where Confucius is suspicious of public opinion as a measure of true attainment (13.24), and that fact combined with the common theme of learning in the surrounding passages argue for *wen* as "learning."

9.24 As Sun Chuo comments, "The Master is criticizing those who consent superficially but do not transform their hearts." Nominal assent to the Confucian Way is insufficient—one must love the Way and strive to embody it in one's person. The problem is what the teacher is to do with a student who intellectually understands or superficially agrees with the Way but cannot summon up the genuine commitment required of the gentleman. Confucius' lament here is clearly related to the sarcastic 9.18: none of his contemporaries seems to have a problem finding the motivational energy required for the pursuit of sex, but their enthusiasm seems to flag when the object of pursuit is the Way. Cf. the Master's difficulties with unmotivated disciples in 5.10 and 6.12, and his comment in 15.16.

9.28 This is possibly a traditional saying, the sense of which is that it is in times of adversity that the gentleman shows his true colors. As He Yan explains, "The point of the metaphor is that even ordinary people are able to be self-possessed and orderly—and thus apparently similar to the gentleman—when living in a well-governed age, but it is only in a chaotic age that we recognize the gentleman's rectitude and air of unwavering integrity."

9.29 As Sun Chuo comments, "The wise are able to clearly distinguish between things, and therefore are not anxious. One who is at ease in Goodness is constant in his joy, and therefore is free of anxiety"; Miao Xie adds, "[The courageous person] sees what is right to do and does it, without being intimidated by physical force or threats, which is why he does not fear." Alternately, reading this passage together with 2.4, the wise are free of anxiety because they understand the Confucian Way or the Mandate of Heaven; the Good are free of worry because they examine themselves inwardly and find nothing to fault.

Book Ten Commentary

10.2 Confucius is traditionally said to have held the office of minister of justice in Lu, a relatively minor post, which means that the "officers of lower rank" were most likely his colleagues, although they may have included even more minor officials under his authority. Confucius effortlessly adapted his countenance and behavior to the demands of the social situation; he was neither overly familiar with his colleagues nor obsequious to his superiors.

10.3 Some commentators believe that receiving guests was not part of Confucius' official duties, but that he was specially summoned by the head of the Ji Family for this purpose because of his knowledge of ritual. As for his final report, it was the custom in ancient China for the guest to turn around and bow repeatedly as he left; the host (or the host's proxy, in this case Confucius) could return to his place only after this process was over. Here we see Confucius fulfilling his ritual duties with both precision and grace.

10.10 That is, he remained thoroughly focused in all of his activities. As Fan Ziyu explains, "The sage preserves his mind and is not distracted: when it is time to eat, he eats; when it is time to sleep, he sleeps. Neither of these times is appropriate for instruction or conversation."

10.11 As Zhu Xi explains,

> When the ancients took their meals, they would take a small portion of each type of food and place it on the ground, among the sacrificial vessels, as an offering to their ancestors. In thus sacrificing to those of previous generations—who were also once people, and thus ate and drank like them—they demonstrated that they did not forget their roots. Even when it came to relatively worthless things, Confucius would always make an offering, and would do so in a respectful manner. Such is the sincerity of the sage.

10.12 *Zheng* means literally "straight" as well as more abstractly "correct," and possibly both meanings are intended. Fan Ning takes *zheng* in the literal sense, observing that "a straight mat is a means of expressing reverence and respect." However, he also notes that, according to some commentators, different ranks of society had different types of seating mats they were ritually sanctioned to use, each being employed in its own proper context. Therefore, we might alternately render the passage, "He would not sit unless his mat were of the correct type."

10.17 Considering that horses were quite valuable commodities and stable hands easily replaceable, Confucius' response is both unexpected and moving—an expression, as many later commentators have put it, of Confucius' "humanism." According to the version of this passage in the *Family Sayings of Confucius*, the stables mentioned were the state stables of Lu. Most commentators, though, assume that the stables in question were those of Confucius himself, and argue that part of the point of this passage is the Master's lack of concern for his own material possessions.

10.19 Being sick, he could not rise to greet his lord or properly dress himself in court attire, but it would also be unseemly for him to receive his guest in civilian garb. He thus had himself arranged in bed so that he would be both ritually presentable and facing the door when the lord entered. Some commentators believe that the eastern orientation of the Master's head was for medical reasons—Huang Kan, for one, explains that east is the direction of *yangqi* 陽氣 ("virile/healthy-vital essence"), and thus laying in this direction when sick is advantageous for one's health. It is more likely, however, a bit of ritual decorum. The *Record of Ritual*, for instance, contains the injunction, "When sitting, the gentleman always takes a place directly facing the window, and when sleeping, his head is always towards the east."[1] Of course, this ritual injunction possibly has as its origin certain *fengshui* 風水 (Chinese geomancy; lit. "wind and water") considerations.

---

[1] Chapter 13 ("Jade-Bead Pendants of the Royal Cap"); Legge 1967, vol. 2: 5.

10.20 Setting off immediately is a sign of respect and humbleness, and we see references to the immediate response of a vassal to the summons of his lord as early as Ode 100: "He hustles, throws on his clothes upside down/By his lord he has been summoned." This ode is quoted in Chapter 27 of the *Xunzi* ("Great Compendium") after it is explained that "when a feudal lord summons a minister, the minister does not wait for the horses to be hitched to the carriage, but throws his clothes on upside down in his haste and sets out on foot. This is ritual."[2]

10.23 A gift of sacrificial meat carries with it a sort of ritual solemnity not possessed by a nonreligious gift, no matter how sumptuous it might be. As Kong Anguo comments, "Not bowing signifies that all that has transpired is an exchange of goods." There is probably no specific clause in the rites that dictate particular response; rather, Confucius, by virtue of his sensitivity to the ritual value of sacrificial meat relative to a sumptuous—but nonsacred—gift, simply *knows* how to respond properly.

10.25 The translation follows Huang Kan, who takes *xie* as referring to someone of low birth. "Respect has to do with one's position, and ancestry does not make the man," he remarks. "Therefore one must always show a respectful countenance." This accords with the passage below where Confucius shows respect to a commoner, but an alternate reading that accords better with the phrase immediately preceding is that of Mr. Zhou, who takes *xie* as "intimate, acquainted," giving us the reading: "even if they were well-known to him" (cf. 9.10).

Facing downward and grasping the crossbar of the chariot is a sign of respect. The translation follows Yu Yue's suggestion that the obscure *fuban* 負版 ("carrying tablets") should be read as *fufan* 負販 ("porter" or "peddler"), which makes this passage accord with a related comment in the *Record of Ritual*: "Ritual has to do with humbling oneself and showing respect to others—even porters and peddlers must be shown respect, how much more so the wealthy and noble!"[3]

Confucius' response to the clap of thunder is usually understood as a sign of respect for Heaven's power.

10.27 This poetic, somewhat cryptic passage has always been very problematic for interpreters and translators, and seems like a non sequitur at the end of a chapter devoted to short, prosaic descriptions of ritual behavior. Legge refers to

---

[2] Knoblock 1994: 208. See also the *Record of Ritual*, Chapter 13 ("Jade-Bead Pendants of the Royal Cap"); Legge 1967, vol. 2: 17.

[3] Chapter 1 ("Summary of Ritual"); Legge 1967, vol. 1: 65.

it as "a fragment, which seemingly has no connection with the rest of the Book" (1991a: 236), and Leys has even stronger words: "the obscurity of this entire passage has acted as a dangerous stimulant upon the imaginations of many commentators. It seems in fact that the original text has become hopelessly garbled and corrupt; there would be little point in insisting on making sense out of it" (1997: 168). Even the infinitely resourceful Zhu Xi admits to being stumped, and suggests that some explanatory text has been lost. A quite plausible way to understand it, however, is as a summary of the chapter as a whole: different in style from other passages in this book, it was probably added by the editors as a thematic capstone. While it is not entirely clear *why* the pheasant is being praised for timeliness (perhaps because it knows when to arise, when to alight, and when to fly off), the ideal of "timeliness" (*shi* 時)—according perfectly with the demands of the situation at hand—sums up fairly well the general theme of Book Ten:[4] that the Master's actions accorded perfectly with the demands of ritual propriety, no matter what the circumstances. Timeliness is Confucius' particular forte, and indeed he is known to posterity (through the efforts of Mencius, see 5:B:1) as the "timely sage"—the one whose ritual responses were always appropriate to circumstances.

Book Eleven Commentary

11.4 As Zhu Xi remarks, the comment seems to be meant ironically: the Master is in fact quite happy that Yan Hui "silently comprehends" everything that he hears (cf. 2.9). The *Discourses on the Mean* comments, "Yan Hui comprehended the essence of the sage, and therefore expressed no exhaustion or difficulties. This is why he alone achieved such an exalted reputation, and ranked at the top of the seventy disciples."

11.8 As Brooks and Brooks note, "chariots in Warring States graves . . . proclaim the power and wealth of the deceased" (1998: 71). Yan Lu is asking that Yan Hui be accorded funerary honors that were normally reserved only for high-ranking officials. Confucius' response is kind, but firm: he acknowledges Yan Lu's desire to honor his son, as well as the fact that his own son, Bo Yu, was not as talented as Yan Hui. Nonetheless, Confucius managed to refrain from according his son funerary honors to which he was not ritually entitled, and he

---

[4] If, that is, we see it as a set of descriptions of Confucius' behavior rather than impersonal ritual injunctions.

is urging Yan Lu to do the same—although gently, and couched in terms of Confucius' own need to maintain the trappings of his rank.

11.9 A touching comment on the importance of Yan Hui for the Master and the affection with which he was viewed. As He Yan notes, "[The Master laments] 'Heaven has bereft me!' because losing Yan Hui was like losing himself, and the repetition emphasizes the depth of the Master's pain and sorrow." Beginning with Han Dynasty commentators, we also find the theory that Heaven provided Yan Hui as a helper and companion to the sage Confucius, which makes his loss particularly poignant and disturbing.

11.12 In this passage—often cited by Western commentators as an expression of Confucius' profound "humanism"—we clearly see Confucius' practical orientation: the aspiring gentleman is to focus his energy on virtuous conduct and concrete learning rather than empty speculation. As Huang Kan remarks, "the teachings of the Zhou Dynasty and of Confucius have to do solely with the here and now." More metaphysically oriented commentators such as Zhu Xi contend that the Master did have esoteric teachings about death and spirits, but that Zilu is simply not yet ready to hear about them, and must complete more basic levels of education before he can receive the esoteric teachings. This, however, is unlikely.

11.17 Ran Qiu was serving as the household steward for the Ji Family under Ji Kangzi. An alternate version of this story appears in the *Zuo Commentary*:

> The head of the Ji Family wanted to institute a land tax, and dispatched Ran Qiu to ask for Confucius' counsel. Confucius replied, "I know nothing about such matters." Several attempts were made, and finally the head of the Ji Family sent Ran Qiu with a message for Confucius, "You are a respected elder in this state, and I await your help in carrying out this action. How is it that you do not answer me?" Confucius did not send an official reply, but privately he remarked to Ran Qiu, "The conduct of the gentlemanly ruler is measured by ritual. In giving he is generous, in his affairs he upholds the mean, and in levying taxes he follows moderation. For a ruler like this, taxation according to the Qiu [丘] model[1] is already sufficient. However, if a ruler does not measure himself with ritual and lets his greed grow to insatiable proportions, then in the end even a land tax will not prove to be enough for him. If the Ji-sun Family head wishes to act in accordance with proper models, he has the standards passed down by the Duke of Zhou. If, on the other hand, he wants to proceed according to his own personal whims, what good will my counsel be to him?" Confucius' words were not heeded.[2]

---

[1] An ancient taxation system, the details of which are the subject of long and rather tedious commentarial debate.

[2] Duke Ai, Year 11 (485 B.C.E.); Legge 1991d: 826.

Drums were sounded not only when going into battle, but also to summon people to witness public executions and other punishments, and some commentators try to soften Confucius' final words by suggesting that he meant only that the disciples should publicly chastise Ran Qiu—that is, they should metaphorically rather than literally attack him. A more elaborate version of this story is also found in *Mencius* 4:A:15.

11.22 For Ran Qiu's excessive caution or timidity, see 6.12. This is a paradigmatic example of how the Master's teachings were variously formulated depending on the individual needs of his students. As Zheng Xuan puts it, "Each piece of advice was aimed at correcting the fault particular to each person." Han commentators and early texts take this passage as having to do specifically with household financial decisions. Bao Xian's commentary reads, "[This passage is about] matters having to do with saving people from penury or succoring them in need," and Huang Kan elaborates by explaining that the issue is when it is necessary to consult with one's elders before providing gifts to friends in need. In contrast, later commentators and Western translators generally take the unspecified thing that is heard of or learned (*wen* 聞) to be a bit of moral teaching or knowledge. Understood this way, the questions asked by the disciples would be rendered: "learning this teaching/moral principle, should one immediately put it into practice?" This interpretation fits better with 6.12, where Ran Qiu's timidity has to do with self-cultivation, rather than practical decision making.

11.26 The Master's initial smile is one of disapproval, probably of Zilu's abrupt manner as well as the content of his answer. The disciples that follow are noticeably more cautious in their responses.

According to commentators, the Yi River was near Confucius' home, and the Rain Altar was located just above the river. The "Rain Altar" was so named because traditionally it was a site where ceremonies were performed to pray for rain during times of summer drought, although here it seems to be featuring merely as a pleasant destination for an excursion.

The point of Confucius' final remark is that Zihua's aspiration also involves high-level diplomacy and statecraft, despite the surface humility of his response. According to one plausible interpretation of this passage, the Master is equally disapproving of Zilu's, Ran Qiu's, and Zihua's aspirations—all of which are overly focused on statecraft techniques—although only Zilu's response is audacious enough to provoke a smile. The point is that true government is effected through the superior virtue gained by ritual practice, and the task of the gentleman is to focus on self-cultivation and attaining a state of joyful harmony with the Way. Such wu-wei harmony with the Way is exemplified by Zengxi's musical bent, his reluctance to speak about his aspirations, and the sense of spontaneous joy in the cultivated life conveyed by his answer. As Li Chong puts it, "Only Zengxi has transcendent aspirations, only he is able to stir up the sounds of Virtue and give expression to the Master's style and sensibility. His words are pure and remote, his meaning lofty and fitting, and his diligence is certainly something with which one with sagely Virtue would feel an affinity. By comparison, the answers of the other three disciples seem vulgar."

Book Twelve Commentary

12.1 There is a long-running debate in the commentarial tradition concerning how to understand the phrase *keji*. The translation follows early commentators such as Ma Rong and Huang Kan in taking *ke* 克 (often "defeat," "overcome") in the sense of "cutting" or "trimming," and thus as "imposing restraint" (*yue* 約). This accords with the common metaphor of ritual as a tool for restraining, regulating, or reshaping one's native substance (see 1.2, 6.27, 8.2, and especially 9.11, where Yan Hui notes that the Master "restrains me with the rites"). For the contrast between looking within oneself and looking to others, cf. 4.14, 14.24, and 15.21.

Liu Baonan's commentary on the second half of 12.1 is very helpful:

> Looking, listening, speaking, and moving are all things that come from oneself, not from others, which is why the key to achieving Goodness lies within oneself and does not come from others. . . . If only I am able to restrain myself and return to ritual, whenever I am confronted with something that is not in accordance with ritual, I will have within myself the means to restrain my eyes and not look at it, restrain my ears and not listen to it, restrain my mouth and not speak of it, and restrain my heart and not put it into action. This is all that is meant by "restraining oneself and returning to ritual."

12.5 Sima Niu came from a prominent military family in Song, and in fact left behind several brothers when he went abroad. Huan Tui,[1] one of these brothers, planned and carried out an unsuccessful revolt against the rightful lord of Song in 483 B.C.E., and was forced to flee the state. Another of Sima Niu's older brothers, Xiang Chao, was also a military official in Song; he was apparently a somewhat arrogant and self-aggrandizing man, and was also forced to flee the state after Huan Tui's attempted revolt, along with the remaining elder Xiang brothers. Sima Niu—apparently uninvolved in the revolt or its aftermath—resigned his official post in disgust and emigrated, ending up eventually in Lu, where he presumably had the conversation with Zixia recorded here. His comment that "he

---

[1] The family's ordinary surname was Xiang 向, but as descendents of Duke Huan 桓, they were also allowed to use this surname, and the military title of *sima* 司馬 (Master of the Horse) had been in the family so long that it was also used by them at times as a surname.

alone has no brothers" is thus not meant literally: the point is either that he has no brothers truly worthy of being considered brothers, or that all of his brothers are in exile or in constant danger of losing their lives, and therefore as good as dead. Sima Niu is bemoaning the fate that has left him effectively without family, an exile from his home state.

Presumably Zixia heard the phrase cited in his response from the Master. The *Garden of Persuasions* quotes Confucius as saying, "Be diligent with regard to your conduct, cultivate your ritual propriety, and then even a thousand miles away people will treat you intimately, as if they were your brothers. If you are not diligent in your conduct, or are not in accordance with ritual, then even right outside your front door you will make no progress." We see two themes at work here. The first concerns fate: if the gentleman focuses on what is in his control (self-cultivation), he has no need to be anxious or worry about things out of his control, which will take care of themselves (cf. 4.14, 7.3, 7.37, 9.29). The second theme is the universality of ethical culture: a ritually correct person will find acceptance wherever he goes—even in foreign lands—because human beings throughout the world respond to the efficacy of the Zhou rituals (cf. 9.14). As Bao Xian remarks, "The gentleman distances himself from those who are bad and befriends those who are worthy, because every person in the entire world can be made an intimate by means of ritual."

12.7 Wang Yangming's comment on this passage is helpful:

> Once you have lost the hearts of the people, how can the rest be relied upon? Even if you have grain, would you even get to eat it? Even if your soldiers are numerous, this may merely set the stage for a rebellion. During the Sui Dynasty, Emperor Yang [r. 604–618] caused the fortress of Luokoucang to be built, and during the Tang Dynasty, Emperor Dezong [r. 780–805] built the Qionglin Treasury. They had an overflowing abundance of riches, and piles of grain as high as mountains; when their armies took the field, it was if a forest of trees had sprung up, and their assembled armor and horsemen covered the earth like clouds. Even then, they could not avoid losing their states and ruining their families, because they did not possess the hearts of the people. One who wishes to govern skillfully should think carefully upon this!

This passage is primarily advice to the aspiring ruler. Li Chong additionally sees it as reflecting Confucius' valuing of morality and the Way over physical life itself: "Confucius valued being able to 'hear in the morning that the Way was being put into practice, and thus dying that evening without regret' [4.8], while Mencius celebrated the ability to 'abandon life in order to hold fast to rightness' [6:A:10]. From ancient times we have had the imperishable Way, and yet there have never been imperishable people. Therefore, to allow one's body to die is not to necessarily to sacrifice the [true] self, while to keep oneself alive at any cost in fact involves losing oneself."

12.8 The "team of horses" comment is a traditional saying, meaning that foolish words, once uttered, cannot be taken back.

Ji Zicheng is described by commentators as a minister of Wei, but nothing else is known about him. Zigong served as an official in Wei for some time, and this is probably when this exchange took place. Zhu Xi believes Ji Zicheng's comment to be a criticism of his contemporaries, who have carried cultural refinement to an excessive extreme, but Chen Tianxiang is probably correct in seeing it as a jab specifically directed as Zigong, known for his sedulous—if limiting—specialization, perhaps a compensation for some lack of native talent (cf. 5.4, 5.9, 5.12, 14.29). Zigong's response invokes an interesting metaphor for the relationship of native substance and cultural refinement: although native substance is required (as an animal requires a hide), a gentleman possessing substance but unadorned by cultural refinement would be like a tiger or leopard shaved of its beautiful pelt—indistinguishable from any ordinary creature. Cf. 6.18.

12.9 According to the *Annals*, the traditional ten percent tithe on agricultural production was doubled by Duke Xuan of Lu in 593 B.C.E., and then continued as standard practice. It is possible that this exchange between Duke Ai and Master You took place during the Lu famine of 484 B.C.E. (Year 14 of Duke Ai's reign), which occurred after back-to-back plagues of locusts in 484 and 483 B.C.E. Master You is thus suggesting a return to a taxation rate over one hundred years old—quite a radical cutback. Probably the best commentary on this passage is a story from the *Garden of Persuasions*:

> Duke Ai of Lu asked Confucius about governing. Confucius replied, "The purpose of the government is to make the common people rich." Duke Ai asked, "What do you mean by that?" Confucius said, "Lighten the burden of levies and taxes, and this will make the common people rich." The Duke replied, "If I did that, then I myself would become poor." Confucius responded, "An ode says, 'All happiness to our gentleman-ruler/Father and mother of his people' [Ode 251]. I have never seen a situation where the children were rich and the parents poor." (844)

The point, of course, is that if the Duke comported himself as the parent of his people, as he properly should, his sole concern would be for their welfare, not his own financial needs.

12.11 In Duke Zhao, Year 25 (516 B.C.E.), Confucius arrived in Qi to find that Duke Jing, near the end of his reign, was in dire straights. His nominal minister, Chen Qi, had usurped control of the state, and the Duke's plan to pass over his eldest son for the succession had set off contention among his sons. Confucius' advice is thus very topical. His point is that if everyone would simply concentrate on conscientiously fulfilling their role-specific duties, order would result naturally—there is no need for some special technique or theory of "governing" (cf. 2.21, 13.3). Many commentators have seen this passage as concerned with the theme of "rectifying names" (*zhengming* 正名) mentioned in 13.3, whereby the actualities of one's behavior should follow the standard set by one's social role ("name"). This is the import of similar passages in the *Annals of Lü Buwei*:

> Those who govern must make establishing clear distinctions (*dingfen* 定分) their first priority. When lords and ministers, fathers and sons, and husbands and wives all occupy their proper positions, then the lower member of each pair will refrain from overstepping their place, and the higher member will refrain from behaving arbitrarily. Juniors will not be audacious or unrestrained, and seniors will not be careless or arrogant. . . . The difference between what is similar and what is dissimilar, the differentiation between noble and base, and the proper distinction between elder and junior are things about which the Ancient Kings were very careful, and constitute the guiding principle for controlling disorder.[2]

As Zhu Xi observes, Confucius' attempt to advise the duke was ultimately for naught: "Duke Jing praised Confucius' words, but did not subsequently put them into practice. In the end, he failed to clearly establish a successor, and thereby set the stage for the disaster of the Chen clan assassinating their lord and usurping control of the state."

12.13 A classic expression of the Confucian suspicion of rule by law; cf. 2.3, 13.12, and 13.18. A good ruler morally transforms the people and renders them obedient through the suasive power of his Virtue, and therefore litigation never arises. As Wang Su notes, "One can bring it about that there is no litigation at all by transforming the people beforehand." This is similar to the manner in which a good moral example on the part of the ruler obviates the need for punishments (12.17–12.19), and is the basis of noncoercive, wu-wei government (2.1, 15.5). 12.13 is repeated in the "Great Learning" chapter of the *Record of Ritual*, followed by the comment: "Those with frivolous complaints do not get the chance to fully air them, because the minds of the common people have a proper sense of respectful awe."[3]

This valuing of social harmony over the adversarial assertion of individual interests has become an enduring feature of societies in the Confucian cultural sphere.

12.17 As Zhai Hao notes, a passage in the *Book of Documents* reads: "If you are able to make yourself correct, how can others dare not to be themselves correct?"[4] This is also probably a proverbial saying and is found in various permutations in several early texts.

---

[2] Chapter 25.5 ("Keeping to One's Lot in Life"); Knoblock and Riegel 2000: 637.

[3] Legge 1967, vol. 2: 416.

[4] Chapter 25 ("Jun Ya"); Legge 1991a: 580.

12.18 Kong Anguo comments, "The point is that the common people are transformed from above, and they do not act in accordance with what their superiors explicitly command, but rather with what their superiors themselves personally desire." A similar and more elaborate exchange is found in the *Zuo Commentary*. There we read that Lu was plagued by robbers, and that the head of the Ji Family said to Zang Wuzhong, minister of crime at the time, "You are the Minister of Crime, why are you not able to deal with these robbers?" Wuzhong's reply is similar to that of Confucius:

> You, Sir, invite foreign robbers to come to our state and then treat them with great ritual honor—how am I supposed to put a stop to the robbery in our state? . . . Shu Qi stole cities from Zhu and arrived here, and yet you gave him wives from the Ducal line, as well as other cities, and gave gifts to all of his followers. . . . I have heard it said that those above can rule others only after they have purified their own hearts, learned to treat others consistently, and regulated their trustworthiness by means of models and regulations, so that their trustworthiness is clear for all to see. For the model set by the actions of their superiors is what the common people will turn to."[5]

Again, the key to political order is personal self-cultivation on the part of the ruler.

12.19 An alternate version of this story is found in the *Exoteric Commentary*:

> The state of Lu had a case of a father and son filing civil complaints against each other, and Ji Kangzi wanted to have them executed. Confucius said, "You cannot execute them. . . . When the common people do something that is not right, it is only because their superiors have lost the Way. . . . If the superiors make manifest their teachings and then take the lead in obeying these teachings, the common people will then follow as if being impelled by a wind."[6]

In this passage, we see again a suspicion of recourse to legal means and reliance on punishment—widespread disorder among the common people is a sign of immorality among the ruling class, and in such a situation it is actually cruel and unfair to punish the people for their transgressions. Throughout traditional Chinese texts on rulership the common people are portrayed as childlike and easily influenced by their superiors, and therefore not totally accountable for their behavior. Some modern scholars of Confucianism present passages such as *Analects* 12.17–12.19 as examples of how traditional China had something like the modern Western liberal–democratic ideal of governmental accountability, but it is important not to lose sight of how distinct from modern liberal ideals the early Confucian conception actually was.

---

[5] Duke Xiang, Year 21 (551 B.C.E.); Legge 1991d: 490.
[6] Chapter 3.22; Hightower 1952: 100–101; see also 3.24: 105–106.

12.22 In this passage we have the first and only hint in the *Analects* of *ren* 仁 as specifically "benevolence"—the sense it will have in later Warring States texts—rather than general moral excellence.

The Master also explains that wisdom—here, specifically in the context of rulership—involves being a good judge of character, a theme that will be appear several times in Book Fourteen. Tang was the legendary founder of the Shang Dynasty, and Gao Yao and Yi Yin were famously virtuous ministers. Regarding this "press-frame" metaphor for virtuous influence, cf. 2.19.

12.24 Friends in virtue are drawn to each other by their common interest in learning and culture—their common love of the Way—and then support each other in these endeavors. A related passage in the *Record of Ritual* reads:

> When it comes to instruction in the great learning, every season has its appropriate subject, and when the students withdraw to rest, they are required to continue their studies at home. . . . Therefore, when it comes to learning, the gentleman holds it dear, he cultivates it, he breathes it, he rambles in it. Because of this, he is at ease while learning and feels affection for his teacher, takes joy in his friends and trusts in the Way. This is why, even when separated from the support of his teacher, he does not go against what he has been taught.[7]

A passage in the *Garden of Persuasions* puts it more succinctly: "Having worthy teachers and excellent friends at his side, and the *Book of Odes*, *Documents*, *Ritual*, and *Music* spread out in front of him—few indeed ever abandon the Way and go bad in such an environment."

Book Thirteen Commentary

13.3 Lit. the gentleman should "leave a blank space" (*que* 闕).

Reading this passage in light of 12.11 ("let the fathers be true fathers, the sons true sons"), it can be seen as a barb against the ruling family of Wei, whose disordered family relations eventually threw the state into chaos. The "Duke of Wei" referred to in Zilu's initial question is thus probably Duke Chu, grandson of Duke Ling and son of Kuai Kui. As Zhu Xi observes, "At this time, Duke Chu was not treating his father as a father, and instead was performing the paternal ancestral sacrifices to his grandfather. In this way, name and actuality were confused, and this is why Confucius saw the rectification of names as the first priority." Huang Kan quotes a passage from the *Exoteric Commentary* that shows Confucius putting the rectification of names into practice in the state of Lu:

---

[7] Chapter 16 ("Record of Learning"); Legge 1967, vol. 2: 85.

Confucius was seated in attendance at the side of the head of the Ji-sun Family. The Ji-sun's steward, Tong, said, "If you, lord, send someone to borrow a horse [from one of your ministers], would it in fact be given to you?" [Before the head of the Ji-sun could reply] Confucius remarked, "When a lord takes something from a minister, it is called 'taking,' not 'borrowing.'" The Ji-sun head understood Confucius' point, and reproved his steward, saying, "From now on, when speaking of your lord taking something, call it 'taking,' do not call it 'borrowing.'" In this way, Confucius rectified the names involved in the expression, "borrowing a horse," and thereby established clearly a relationship of rightness between lord and minister.[1]

The passage then quotes *Analects* 13.3, as well as Ode 339: "The lord should not lightly utter his words." For other examples of the "rectification of names," see 12.11 and 12.17.

13.4 Part of the theme here is clearly the proper distinction between the vocations of the "great person," or gentleman, and the "little person," or commoner. The *Book of Documents* says that "Knowing the painful toil of sowing and reaping . . . one knows the livelihood of the commoner";[2] similarly, we read in *Mencius* 3:A:4 that plowing the fields is the "work of the commoner." There are at least two ways to understand how this relates exactly to Confucius' response. Commentators such as Li Chong read this passage together with 15.32 ("the gentleman focuses his concern on the Way, not on obtaining food"), as well as the hints of Fan Chi's acquisitiveness in 6.22 and 12.21, understanding Confucius' point to be that the gentleman does not give up the pursuit of moral excellence in order to pursue externalities such as food or money. Others, such as Cheng Shude and Jin Lüxiang, read it together with *Mencius* 3:A:4 as an attack on the so-called "Divine Farmer" (*shennong* 神農) or "primitivist" movement. This movement—which produced a host of writings recorded in the *History of the Han*, and which was probably also the incubator of the famous Daoist text *Laozi*—advocated a kind of agricultural communism: educated people should withdraw from public life into isolated agricultural communities, where social distinctions would be abolished and the educated would plow the fields alongside the commoners, everyone sharing in the tasks required to sustain life. In 3:A:4, Mencius defends Confucian social distinctions and division of labor against this "leveling" doctrine, arguing that, just as the heart-mind is the ruler of the body, those who work with their minds should rule over those who work with their bodies. We can see Confucius' response here as a similar counterargument to primitivist doctrines, by which Fan Chi has apparently been at least partially seduced. This understanding of the passage is supported by 14.39 and 18.6, which present encounters between Confucius and his disciples with disillusioned former officials who have apparently turned to the

---

[1] Chapter 5.33; Hightower 1952: 190.

[2] Chapter 15 ("Against Luxurious Ease"); Legge 1991a: 464–465.

practices of primitivism. The appeal of primitivism to educated elite troubled by the chaos of the late Spring and Autumn and Warring States periods in China should not be unfamiliar to those acquainted with the various "back to nature" movements popular in the West in the 1960s and 1970s, which arose among elite, educated people disillusioned with the ills brought about by modern industrial capitalist societies—and among whom the *Laozi* was quite popular in English translation.

13.5 The words of the *Odes* formed part of the repertoire of an accomplished statesman of the time, who would often quote an apt phrase to make a point or invoke a relevant historical allusion (cf. 16.13, 17.9–17.10). The point here, though, is that merely memorizing the *Odes* is not enough to make one a good messenger or envoy—one must also learn to think on one's feet. As the *Book of Etiquette and Ritual* observes of serving as an envoy, "The words one are to speak cannot be determined ahead of time; one must speak in accordance with the situation."[3] A story from the *Exoteric Commentary* refers obliquely to 13.5 in its portrait of a skillful envoy in action:

> Duke Jing of Qi dispatched an envoy to Chu. The King of Chu accompanied him in ascending his nine-level throne-dais. Fixing his gaze upon the envoy, the King of Chu asked, "Does the state of Qi have a dais the equal of this?" The envoy replied, "My lord has a place to sit when dealing with governmental affairs. It has three levels of earthen stairs, a roughly made thatched hut at the top, and unadorned wooden rafters. Even still, my lord feels that he has overworked those who made it, and worries also that he who sits in it will be overly proud. How could my lord have a dais the equal of this one?" Thereupon the King of Chu was ill at ease. Because of his ability to engage in repartee, this envoy can be said to have not disgraced his lord's commission.[4]

Here we see again the theme that learning involves not merely the acquisition of scholastic knowledge, but also the ability to flexibly apply this knowledge in a situation-specific manner (cf. 2.11).

13.6 A passage in the *New Arrangement* elaborates on 13.6:

> If you sing and others do not harmonize with you, or you move and others do not follow, it is invariably because there is something lacking within yourself. There-fore, do not descend from your place in order to set the world straight; simply look within yourself [13.6]. This is the reason the Former Kings were able to simply assume a reverent posture and beckon, and have everyone within the Four Seas respond. This is a case of the regulation of sincere Virtue manifesting itself on the outside. Thus, the ode [263] says, "Because the King's plans are sincere and reli-able, the people of the Xu region come immediately [and submit to his rule]."

---

[3] Chapter 15 ("Rites Concerning Official Missions"); Steele 1917, vol. 1: 233.
[4] Chapter 8.12; Hightower 1952: 266–267.

Again, we have the theme of wu-wei rulership through personal moral perfection and the power of Virtue; cf. especially 2.1, 2.3, 2.21, 12.17, and 15.5.

13.16 The duke, personal name Zigao, was lord of the walled city of She within the powerful state of Chu. Alternate versions of this encounter appear in many Warring States texts; the only significantly different one, found in the *Mozi*, gives Confucius' answer as: "Those who are good at governing draw close to them those who are far away, and renew that which is old."[5] The point seems to concern rule by Virtue, whereby common people are naturally drawn to the kind and Good ruler. The message may be especially intended for the Duke of She because of the harsh Legalist practices apparently practiced in the state of Chu, as well as Chu's policy of aggressive military expansion (cf. 13.18).

13.18 This represents the classic statement of the Confucian valuing of familial relations over considerations of public justice that so infuriated the Mohists and statecraft thinkers such as Hanfeizi. Some commentators see this passage as a specific response to Hanfeizi (and thus of quite late provenance), but legalist tendencies probably had their beginning in China long before they were systematized by the late Warring States statecraft theorists. In the Confucian view, proper relations between father and son are the root of Goodness (1.2), and Goodness—rather than rule of law—is the only way to properly order a state (cf. 2.3, 12.13, 12.17–12.19, 13.6). Comparing 13.18 to *Mencius* 7:A:35 is also helpful:

> Tao Ying asked, "When Shun was serving as the Son of Heaven, and Gao Yao was his minister, if the Old Blind Man [Shun's father] had committed murder, what would have been done?" Mencius replied, "The Old Blind Man would simply have been apprehended." "Would Shun not have prevented it?" "How could Shun have prevented it? Gao Yao had his rightful duty to perform." "So what would Shun have done?" "Shun would have regarded giving up his rulership of the world no differently than throwing away an old pair of sandals: he would have secretly taken his father on his back and fled into exile, taking up residence somewhere along the coast. There he would have spent the rest of his days, cheerful and happy, with no thoughts of his former kingdom."

The emphasis is slightly different here, in that the rightfulness of legal punishment is not denied, but the basic theme is the same: it is the duty of the filial son to sacrifice himself in order to prevent the law from being applied to his father.

---

[5] Chapter 46 ("Geng Zhu"); Mei 1929: 216.

13.20 Here again the flexibility and true grace of the gentleman is contrasted with those who are simply "renown" (cf. 17.13, 17.18) and those who are too narrowly focused on trustworthiness (cf. 13.18). As *Mencius* 4:B:11 observes, "The great person is not always necessarily true to his word [*xin*], because he is concerned only with rightness." Apparently even such narrow, rigid officials are to be preferred to the "vessels" (2.12) or "petty functionaries"—*doushaozhiren* 斗筲之人, lit. "peck and basket men," which we might have rendered more colloquially as "bean counters"—who dominated public life in Confucius' age.

13.21 In the commentary to 5.22 we have already cited portions of *Mencius* 7:B:37, which discusses both 5.22 and 13.21. The "wild" (*kuang* 狂) have a preponderance of native substance insufficiently shaped by refinement (5.22), while the "fastidious" (*juan* 狷) lack the passion, flexibility, and courage possessed by a true gentleman. Zilu might serve as an example of the former, while examples of the latter include the excessively "pure" Chen Wenzi in 5.19, the excessively scrupulous disciple Yuan Si in 6.5 and 14.1, or the various principled recluses presented in Books Fourteen and Eighteen. These two types represent extremes of the ethical spectrum, and each has its strengths, but it is the mean between these two extremes that is truly desirable.

13.24 We see again the suspicion of public opinion voiced in 15.28, 17.13, and 17.18. This is related to the deeper problem of separating appearance from substance that motivates both Confucius' suspicion of glibness and flattery and his tendency to favor native substance over refinement.

Book Fourteen Commentary

14.1 Yuan Si is the disciple who, serving as a steward for one of the Three Families in 6.5, makes a show of declining his salary, and is then reproved for it by the Master. According to the later legends that sprang up around Yuan Si, he became a recluse and led a strict, ascetic lifestyle. An account in the *Record of the Historian* reads:

> Yuan Si lived in an obscure, humble abode, reading books and embracing the solitary enactment of gentlemanly Virtue. He was righteous and would not compromise with his contemporaries, and in return his contemporaries mocked him. Therefore, he lived out his days without complaint in an empty room with a thornwood gate, clad in hemp and subsisting on vegetables and millet. It has now been over four hundred years since his death, and still the memory of him has not died out among his disciples.

The Master's answer to Yuan Si's initial question (cf. 8.13) seems to be an endorsement of his reclusive tendencies, which is perhaps why he is embold-ened to offer his other achievements for the Master's approval. This approval is, of course, denied (as in modern Japanese, we have the polite locution, "I do not know," to soften the impact of the real message, "No"). As mentioned in the commentary to 6.5, Yuan Si's extreme and rigid adherence to principle seems to mark him as one of the overly "fastidious" criticized by the Master in 13.21. Yuan Si's achievements, though impressive, are all purely negative—the truly Good person displays a degree of flexibility, creativity, and positive concern for others lacking in the fastidious or "pure" (*qing* 清).

14.4 An observation concerning both the problem of glibness (1.3, 16.4) and the unity of the virtues: a virtue such as courage becomes a vice when not bal-anced by other virtues (cf. 17.23). As Zhu Xi remarks, "One who possesses Virtue harmoniously and effortlessly accumulates it inside, so that eventually it flowers forth on the outside [in the form of words]. On the other hand, those who are able to speak well are sometimes merely glib and loquacious. In his heart, the Good person is not concerned with himself, which means that, when he sees what is right to do, he simply must do it. On the other hand, those who display courage are sometimes merely driven by an overly belligerent physio-logical disposition."

14.5 Kong Anguo identifies Nangong Kuo as a minister in the state of Lu, an unusually virtuous member of the Three Families, and son of Meng Yizi. Zhu Xi believes him to be the Nan Rong mentioned in 5.2. Both Yi and Ao were legendary martial heroes of the Xia Dynasty with questionable morals: Yi usurped the throne of one of the kings of the Xia Dynasty, and Ao was the son of one of Yi's ministers. Ao subsequently murdered and dethroned Yi, and was in turn slain and overthrown by one of his own ministers.[1] Yu and Hou Ji, on the other hand, were moral worthies and heroes of civilized arts: Yu tamed the Yellow River and introduced irrigation, receiving the rulership of the world from Shun in return, while Hou Ji ("Lord Millet") is the mythical founder of agri-culture and progenitor of the Zhou royal line.[2] The point is that the world is won through moral cultivation and civilization rather than martial prowess; cf. 14.4 and 17.23, where mere martial courage is dismissed as inferior to the balanced moral courage of the gentleman. Zhu Xi suggests that Nangong Kuo meant to compare Confucius to Yu and Ji, and that Confucius remains silent out of modesty: "Probably Kuo brought up Yi and Ao as analogies to the

---

[1] For the legend concerning these two figures, see the *Zuo Commentary*, Duke Xiang, Year 4 (568 B.C.E.); Legge 1991d: 424.

[2] See the *Book of Documents* 55 ("Punishments of Lu"; Legge 1991b: 595) for legends of these two figures.

wielders of power in Confucius' time, and Yu and Ji as analogies to Confucius himself, and this is why Confucius did not answer."

14.12 Zang Wuzhong (grandson of Zang Wenzhong) and Meng Gongchuo were both respected officials in Lu, and Zhuangzi was an official in the walled city of Bian, on the eastern border of Lu, who was legendary for his courage. The point here is that only the possession of all of these virtues allows one to merit the description "complete" or "perfect" person (*chengren* 成人), just as the gentleman, who possesses the overarching virtue of Goodness, is often presented as having a number of the lesser virtues in their proper proportions (14.4, 15.18). Confucius' qualification in the second paragraph seems analogous to his characterization of "second-rate" (*ci* 次) scholar-officials in 13.20: in Confucius' corrupted age, it is perhaps too much to ask for true perfection. Some commentators also see this concession to the lowered standards of his age as an encouragement to Zilu, who may have felt intimidated by the likes of former worthies such as Zang Wuzhong and Zhuangzi of Bian.

14.13 Gongshu Wenzi is the posthumous title of Gongsun Ba (alternately Gongsun Zhi), a worthy minister in Wei who apparently passed away before Confucius' first visit to that state. Little is known about Gongming Jia, but he was presumably Gongshu Wenzi's disciple or retainer. Gongshu Wenzi clearly had a reputation for virtuous restraint, but what his disciple or retainer is claiming for him is in fact even more impressive. As Huan Maoyong notes, "Not speaking, not laughing, and not taking are all negative restrictions that someone wishing to affect virtue or make a name for themselves could force themselves to adhere to, whereas speaking only when the time is right, laughing only when genuinely full of joy, and taking only what it rightful to take are qualities of the timely sage." Confucius' disbelief probably stems from the fact that Gongming Jia is claiming that his master was a true gentleman, embodying the Way in a wu-wei fashion, rather than merely one of the lesser, fastidious men whom Confucius is accustomed to encountering.

14.24 Kong Anguo and Huang Kan understand this in terms of the words versus actions dichotomy we have already seen several times. Kong explains, "Those who study for their own sake actually personally put it into practice, whereas those who do it for the sake of others are only able to talk about it." Huang elaborates:

> The ancients learned about those things in which they themselves did not yet excel. Thus, they would study the Way of the Former Kings, desiring thereby to personally put it into practice and perfect themselves, nothing more. People in Confucius' age, on the other hand, did not learn in order to remedy flaws in their own behavior, but rather with the sole purpose of lording it over others and having others praise them as excellent.

Reading this passage along with 4.2, 4.5, 4.9, 4.12, 4.16, and 14.23, a related interpretation is to see the issue as one of motivation: the gentleman learns for the sake of his own improvement and out of love of the Way, whereas the petty person learns in order to acquire an official position and salary. This is how Xunzi understands it; after quoting 14.24, he adds: "The gentleman learns in order to improve himself, whereas the petty person uses learning like a ceremonial offering of birds and calves [i.e., to attract their superior's attention]."[3]

14.25 Qu Boyu was a virtuous minister in the state of Wei. He is also mentioned in the *Zuo Commentary* for 558 B.C.E. as a principled minister who leaves a state rather than participate in an uprising against his lord,[4] and must have been significantly older than Confucius. He also appears in the *Zhuangzi* and *Huainanzi*. The former text says that "Qu Boyu has been going along for sixty years and has changed sixty times, and there has never been a case where he did not start out saying something was right and end up rejecting it as wrong,"[5] and the latter that "Qu Boyu, at age fifty, realized that he had been wrong for forty-nine years." Commentators cite this as evidence that Qu Boyu was, indeed, someone who earnestly wished to reduce his faults, but never felt that he was done. Zhu Xi claims that Confucius stayed with Qu Boyu during his time in the state of Wei, and that this is why they remained in touch, but there is no independent evidence to support this. There are probably at least two points to this passage. First of all, Confucius approves of Qu Boyu's noble intentions and realistic evaluation of himself, indications of both an unflagging commitment to further self-improvement (especially impressive at Qu Boyu's age; cf. 8.7) and a commendable degree of modesty (cf. especially 14.27–14.29). The second point relates to the theme of knowing the character of others and properly employing people. Qu Boyu clearly knows how to find a messenger who can "engage in repartee" (13.5) and accurately represent the intentions of his master, while the messenger himself displays an admirable degree of perspicuity. As Huang Kan observes, "In saying, 'But he has not yet been able to do so,' the messenger shows that he has understood the mind of Boyu and is not deceived about his character."

14.27 As Huang Kan explains, "The gentleman is the type of person who pays attention to his words and is careful about his behavior." Cf. 1.14, 2.13, 4.22, and 4.24.

---

[3] Chapter 1 ("Encouraging Learning"); Knoblock 1988: 140. Also cf. the comparison of the "learning of the gentleman" and the "learning of the petty person" earlier in the same chapter (Knoblock 1988: 140).

[4] Duke Xiang, Year 14 (558 B.C.E.); Legge 1991d: 465.

[5] Chapter 25 ("Ze Yang"); Watson 1968: 288.

14.29 Despite the importance of being able to evaluate the character of others that has been stressed throughout this book, one must not be too eager to pass judgment on others. Even the Master did not presume to declare himself a true gentleman or sage (cf. 7.34), and in that light Zigong's pretension to be an arbiter of virtue becomes even more absurd. This passage might also be compared to other passages where Zigong is criticized by Confucius for being too strict and judgmental with others—i.e., for not moderating his duty-defined demands on others with understanding.

14.30 As Wang Kentang comments, "This is because having ability or not is something that lies within one's own control, whereas whether or not one is recognized is under the control of others." Cf. 4.14 and 15.19.

14.34 The initial quoted phrase appears in the *Laozi* (Chapter 63)—and Confucius' response to it is certainly anti-Laozian in flavor—but it was likely a traditional saying not necessarily identified with the *Laozi* itself. As He Yan notes, *de* here is used in the more archaic sense of "kindness." The point of 14.34 seems to be that order is brought about through proper discrimination. Each type of behavior has a response that is proper to it: injury should be met with sternness, whereas kindness is to be rewarded with kindness. Failure to discriminate in this way is an invitation to chaos; as Huang Kan notes, "The reason that one does not repay injury with kindness is that, were one to do so, then everyone in the world would begin behaving in an injurious fashion, expecting to be rewarded with kindness. This is the Way of inviting injury." For Confucius, being impartial or just (*gong* 公) means to discriminate properly, giving to each his due.

14.35 Another comment on the Master's failure to find employment or official recognition (cf. 9.13), but the hint of bitterness is then tempered, perhaps in response to the injunction in 14.30 to "not worry that you are not recognized by others, but rather worry that you yourself lack ability." Confucius pursues that which lies within his own control—the study of the Way—and does so for his own self-improvement (14.24), consigning the vagaries of official recognition or attainment of office to fate. Kong Anguo understands that which is "below" as "human affairs," and that which is "above" as "knowing the Heavenly Mandate." Probably what is being described is similar to the progression found in 2.4, where learning and ritual lead to an understanding of Heaven and a wu-wei harmony with the Way of the Ancients. In the end, Confucius thus finds comfort in the thought that, though he is neglected by the rulers of his time, at least Heaven understands him.

14.36 Zilu was at this time presumably working as steward for the Ji Family. Zifu Jingbo, a minister in the state of Lu—Liu Baonan claims that he was a kinsman of the Meng Family—is claiming that he has enough influence with Ji Kangzi that he can both convince him of Zilu's innocence and see to it that his fellow minister, Gongbo Liao, is punished for his slander. The punishment in such a case of ministerial malfeasance would be public execution, after which, according to Zhou custom, the corpse would be displayed in public for three days. Confucius, sure of his correctness and the correctness of his disciple, sees no need for such machinations. The attitude expressed here is not so much passive fatalism as a surety in one's own rectitude and a confidence that Heaven's will shall be done (cf. 9.5). As Zhang Erqi comments,

> That which is certain and cannot be evaded when it comes to the Way of human beings is rightness; that which is original and cannot be disputed when it comes to the Way of Heaven is fate. The fact that poverty, wealth, nobility, baseness, attainment, loss, life, death are all regulated and cannot be forced is the same, whether you are a gentleman or a petty person. . . . The gentleman, by means of rightness, makes his peace with fate, and therefore his heart is always calm. The petty person, on the other hand, used cleverness and force in order to struggle against fate, and therefore his heart is always filled with resentment.

Some commentators identify both Gongbo Liao and Zifu Jingbo as disciples of Confucius, but this is unlikely.

14.38 Most commentators believe the Stone Gate to be one of the outer gates of the capital of Lu, and explain that Zilu is returning from having traveled about with the Master in search of employment. The Lu gatekeeper may be a principled recluse,[6] or simply an ordinary functionary, but in any case he shares the view of Weisheng Mou and the recluse that, confronted wherever he goes by indifferent or actively immoral rulers, Confucius should simply give up.

Book Fifteen Commentary

15.1 Confucius is playing on the word *chen*, which is both a noun referring to military formations and a verb meaning "to arrange" or "set out," often with

---

[6] As was mentioned with regard to the border guard at Yi in the commentary to 3.24, disillusioned officials sometimes retired by withdrawing from active life and taking some minor post, such as gatekeeper, that would at least serve to feed their families.

reference to ritual vessels. The point, of course, is that the true ruler causes his state to prosper by means of Virtue rather than military force. Some commentators read 15.1 and 15.2 as one passage, arguing that the troubles in Chen described in 15.2 occurred after Confucius left Wei because of his conversation with Duke Ling, but there is no compelling reason to read the passages together.

15.2 As Huang Shisan observes, the point of this passage is that "it is only in adversity that the gentleman reveals himself. 'A fierce blaze or intense fire only adds to the luster of gold'—how true is this proverb!" Besides an oblique reference in a passage not include in this selection, this is the only appearance of this incident in the *Analects*, but it was a very popular story in later Warring States texts.

15.5 Although the concept of wu-wei, or "effortless action," can be found throughout the *Analects*, this is the only place in the text where the term "wu-wei" appears. There are two distinct lines of interpretation concerning what it would mean to rule by means of wu-wei. One, beginning with He Yan, understands this passage to be referring to what might be called "institutional wu-wei." Under this interpretation, "wu-wei" is to be understood more in its literal sense of "doing nothing," the point being that, if the ruler can fill his ministerial posts with able people and effectively set the machinery of government in motion, the state will more or less run itself, without any need for action on the part of the ruler himself. As He Yan puts it, "The point is that if you fill your posts with the right people, you can 'do nothing' and yet the state will be governed." This interpretation of 15.5 accords with some of the passages in Book Fourteen that emphasize the importance of employing the right people. Considering the general drift of the *Analects*, however, it is far more likely that ruling by wu-wei refers to ruling by means of Virtue: the ruler morally perfects himself and thereby effortlessly transforms everyone around him. "Wu-wei" in this sense is thus not meant literally ("doing nothing"), the point rather being that one does not force anything or attempt consciously to achieve results—one simply "follows the desires of the heart" (2.4) and everything else falls into place. As Wang Fuzhi explains in his commentary on 15.5,

> Shun's wu-wei is similar to Confucius' not innovating [7.1]: in both cases, the point is that one follows along with the times and thus utilizes them effectively, thereby gradually accumulating one's achievements. "Making oneself reverent" refers to cultivating Virtue within oneself; "taking one's position facing South" refers to allowing one's regulating force to be applied to the common people. All of this refers to the constant Way of the ruler, and cannot really be spoken of as "doing" anything in particular.

This idea of "ruling by not ruling"—concentrating on self-cultivation and inner Virtue and allowing external things to come naturally and noncoercively—has been a constant theme throughout the *Analects*, but cf. especially 1.12, 2.19, 2.21, 12.17–12.19, and 13.6. Zhu Xi somewhat bridges the two different interpretations with his observation that "ruling by means of wu-wei refers to the sage accumulating Virtue and thereby transforming the common people, so that there is no need to wait for him to actually do anything in particular. . . . Moreover, in this way he also attracts the right people to fill the various offices, which makes it even less likely that one will see traces of the ruler's actions."

15.9 As Kong Anguo remarks, the point is that "the scholar-official of noble intention and the Good person do not overly cherish their own lives." An alternate version of Confucius' statements is found in *Mencius* 3:B:1 and 5:B:7, which recount a story from the *Zuo Commentary* where a gamekeeper risks death by refusing to answer a ritually improper summons from his lord, and then quote Confucius as remarking, "The scholar-official of noble intention never forgets that he may end up in a roadside ditch, and the courageous scholar-official never forgets that he may lose his head." The idea is that the true devotee of the Confucian Way values it over life itself. This is not to say that such a person is foolhardy or suicidal, merely that, for him, issues of rightness take precedence over self-preservation. As we read in *Mencius* 6:A:10,

> Fish is something that I desire; bear's paw [a rare delicacy] is also something that I desire. If it is not possible to obtain both at the same time, I would give up the fish and take the bear's paw. Life is something that I desire; rightness is also something that I desire. If it is not possible to obtain both at the same time, I would give up life and take rightness. This is because, although life is something that I desire, there are things that I desire more than life. Therefore, life is not something that I seek to preserve at any cost. Death is something that I hate, and yet there are things that I hate even more than death. This is why there are troubles that I do not choose to avoid.

The *Mencius* passage is targeted at the self-preservationist school exemplified by Yang Zhu, and it is possible that 15.9 has a similar target.

15.11 The calendar of the Xia—which was in fact something like a combination calendar and almanac, providing instructions for what to do at various points in the year—began the year in the spring, and was apparently well adapted to the cycles of the seasons and the needs of farmers. The state carriage of the Shang, according to commentators, was stately but relatively unadorned, while the ceremonial cap of the Zhou was elegant and practical; according to Bao Xian, it shielded both the eyes and ears, making it easier to resist distractions and concentrate on ritual. Both the Shang carriage and Zhou cap thus realized the perfect harmony of form and function without being overly ostentatious.

The Shao and Wu, as we saw in 7.14, represent the best of classical, properly formed music, in contrast to the licentious, seductive popular music of Zheng that was the rage among Confucius' contemporaries. The lyrics of the Zheng music were somewhat racy,[1] and although little is known about the exact nature of the music, commentators assert that it had a simple but catchy beat, was sung by mixed groups of men and women, and gave rise to sexual improprieties—all of which should sound very familiar to concerned parents of any nation or age. As Waley notes,

> Toward classical music, the "music of the former kings" (*Mencius* 1:B:1), ordinary as opposed to serious-minded people had the same feelings as they have towards our own classical music today. "How is it," the Prince of Wei asked Zixia, "that when I sit listening to old music, dressed in my full ceremonial gear, I am all the time in terror of dropping off asleep; whereas when I listen to the tunes of Zheng and Wei, I never feel the least tired?"[2]

Like moralists of our own age, early Confucians were very concerned about the effect of music on people's dispositions, and properly regulating music was seen as a crucial part of ordering the state. For more on Confucian education and music, cf. 8.8. The tunes of Zheng were seen as counterfeits of true music, just as glib speakers were viewed as counterfeits of genuinely virtuous people. The two are mentioned together because the danger they represent is similar: because of their surface appeal, both can easily lead people astray, and this is why someone wishing to order a state must carefully prevent either one from taking hold. As Kong Anguo remarks, "Both the tunes of Zheng and glib people have the power to move people's hearts, the same sort of power possessed by classical music and worthy men. In the former case, however, this power causes people to fall into licentious disorder and imperils the state, which is why the two things must be gotten rid of and kept at a distance." A very similar point in made in 17.18, where Zheng music and glib people are condemned along with flashy new colors for corrupting traditional standards and leading to disorder.

15.16 The translation follows Zhu Xi, but the Han commentators read it rather differently, along the lines of, "One might say, 'What can be done? What can be done?', but there is now nothing that I can do." Li Chong, for instance, comments that "one must make plans to deal with problems before they have man-

---

[1] Refer to the *Book of Odes*, "Airs of Zheng" (numbers 75–95).

[2] Waley 1989: 250; the citation is from the *Record of Ritual*, Chapter 19 ("Record of Music"); Legge 1967, vol. 2: 116–177. In his response to the prince, Zixia defends the salutary effects of ancient music, condemns the bizarre excesses of the new music, and concludes by reproving the prince for his taste with words that should sound familiar to any curmudgeon fed up with the latest musical fad: "what you just asked about, Sir, was music, but what you happen to like is mere sound."

ifested themselves, and regulate situations before they have become disordered. Therefore, what use is it to wait until one is faced with difficulties and only then say, 'What can be done?'" There is some textual support elsewhere in the *Analects* for this interpretation, but it requires reading the text in a somewhat awkward fashion, and Zhu Xi's interpretation is confirmed by an alternate transmission of this passage found in the *Luxuriant Dew*. The point is one that we have seen before: the Master cannot teach someone who is not driven by a need to learn, and he cannot impart the Way to someone who does not, at some level, already love it. This accounts for the frustration expressed above: there is nothing the Master can do with someone who loves female beauty more than Virtue. Cf. 7.8.

15.18 As in 6.18, the gentleman is portrayed as the balanced product of native substance refined by cultural refinement, with both elements portrayed as crucial. As Xia Xichou observes, "The first level [rightness, substance] is the marrow—without it, one would become one of those types who associates with and participates in the corruption of the village worthy. Without the second level [cultural refinement], however, one would possess the fault of excessive bluntness, or would fall into the trap of becoming like the excessively fastidious. This emphasis on both is why the teaching of the sage is comprehensive, balanced, and free of flaws." The focus on rightness also sets up an implicit contrast between the gentleman, who focuses on goods internal to Confucian practice such as rightness, and the petty person, who focuses on externalities. As Wang Yangming remarks, "It is only the gentleman who takes rightness as his substance, in the same way that the petty person takes profit as his substance [4.16]. When one takes profit as one's substance, one loses entirely the fundamentals of character. Then selfish desires take over the heart and become the ruler of the self; the eyes and ears, hands and feet all become the slave of these desires; and all of one's movements, words, and actions are subject only to their command."

15.24 This is an alternate version of 4.15, which identifies the "single thread" that unifies the Master's teaching as dutifulness coupled with understanding. It is probable that dutifulness is dropped in 15.24 not only because Zigong asked for "one word," but also because Zigong already possesses dutifulness to a fault, and in fact needs to learn how to moderate it with understanding (cf. 5.4, 5.12).

> The fact that you yourself hate hunger and cold allows you to understand that everyone in the world desires food and clothing. The fact that you yourself hate labor and bitter exertion allows you to understand that everyone in the world desires rest and ease. The fact that you yourself hate poverty and deprivation allows you to understand that everyone in the world desires prosperity and sufficiency.

Knowing these three things, the sagely king can order the world without ever having to descend from his seat. Thus, "the Way of the gentleman is none other than dutifulness and understanding, that is all" [4.15].[3]

For more on understanding and the "negative Golden Rule," cf. 6.30.

15.28 Again we have the suspicion of public opinion; cf. especially 13.24. As Wang Su comments, "Sometimes one can play to the crowd and please others in a partisan fashion, and sometimes one takes an unpopular stand in opposition to the crowd. This is why both love and hatred must be carefully examined." Yang Shi connects this passage to 4.3: "Only the Good person is able to properly love or despise another. If you accept the love or hate of the masses without examining it, you will sometimes fall victim to selfish distortions." A similar passage in the *Guanzi* is more narrowly focused on the issue of a ruler knowing his underlings:

> If a confused ruler does not examine the achievements of his ministers, he will simply reward those who are praised by the masses. If he does not look carefully into their transgressions, he will simply punish those who are condemned by the masses. In this way, wicked ministers with no achievements will end up being rewarded, and innocent, dutiful ministers will end up being punished.[4]

15.29 As Cai Mo explains, "The Way is silent and without action, and requires human beings in order to be put into practice. Human beings are able to harmonize with the Way—this is why the texts reads: 'Human beings are able to broaden the Way.' The Way does not harmonize with humans—this is why the text reads, 'It is not the Way that broadens human beings.'" Liu Baonan similarly argues that the point of this remark is that it is human ability that allows the Way to manifest itself in the world, quoting a line from the *Record of Ritual* that says, "If you are not able to fully realize virtue, the complete Way will not have nowhere to make itself concrete,"[5] as well as a passage from the *History of the Han*:

> When the Way of the Zhou declined with the accession of [the wicked kings] You and Li, it was not that the Way was lost, only that You and Li failed to follow it. With the accession of King Xuan, who focused upon and treasured the Virtue of the Former Kings, that which was stagnant was reinvigorated, and that which was flawed was made complete; the achievements of Kings Wen and Wu were brought back to light, and the Way of the Zhou made its splendid resurgence.

The Way thus is transcendent, in the sense that it continues to exist even when it is not being actively manifested in the world, but it requires human beings to be fully realized.

---

[3] Chapter 3.38; Hightower 1952: 123.

[4] Chapter 67 ("Explanation of 'Making the Law Clear'"); Rickett 1998, vol. 2: 162.

[5] Chapter 32 ("Doctrine of the Mean"); Legge 1967, vol. 2: 323.

15.30 Cf. 1.8. An alternate version of this saying attributed to Confucius in the *Exoteric Commentary* reads, "If you make a mistake but then change your ways, it is like never having made a mistake at all."[6]

15.31 Cf. 2.15, which presents thinking and learning as equally important. 15.31, in contrast, stresses the danger of thinking in isolation. Rather than attempt to pointlessly reflect on one's own, the accumulated wisdom of the classics should form the very basis of one's thinking. Thinking outside the context of learning might be compared to randomly banging on a piano in ignorance of the conventions of music: a million monkeys given a million years might produce something, but it is better to start with the classics (cf. 17.10). We find a very similar theme in the *Xunzi*, which provides a more succinct version of 15.31, "I once spent the entire day doing nothing but thinking, but this is not as good as even a single moment devoted to learning," and adds:

> I once stood on my tiptoes to look into the distance, but this is not as good as the broad view obtained from climbing a hill. Climbing a hill and waving your arms does not make your arms any longer, but they can be seen from farther away; shouting downwind does not make your voice any louder, but it can be heard more clearly; someone who borrows a carriage and horses does not improve the power of his feet, but he can travel a thousand *li*; someone who borrows a boat and paddle does not thereby become able to swim, but he can cross great rivers. The gentleman by birth is not different from other people—he is simply good at making use of external things.[7]

15.36 Deference to elders and teachers is a virtue, but, when it comes to being moral, any hesitation or deference is both unnecessary and harmful. As Zhang Ping comments, "Putting others before oneself, showing no concern for one's physical well-being but caring for things, treading the way of modesty and dwelling in humbleness—these are the means by which one practices Goodness. Acting in this way does not mean that one is not fond of showing deference, it just means that the Way is something with regard to which one does not defer."

15.37 Again we have the concern about petty or rigid trustworthiness (*liang* 諒); for the dangers of excessive or inflexible trustworthiness, cf. 13.18, 13.20, and 17.8, and for the importance of flexibility in general, cf. 19.11. As Huang Kan comments, "The gentleman uses discretion to respond to changing circumstances and does not have any single, constant way of doing things. In his handling of affairs he must sometimes bend the rules in order to harmonize with

---

[6]Chapter 3.17; Hightower 1954: 94.

[7]Chapter 1 ("Encouraging Learning"); Knoblock 1988: 136.

the Way and properly realize principle. Therefore, when the gentleman does something, he is not bound by petty fidelity (*xin*) like those who 'strangle themselves in some gully or ditch.'"

15.39 It is probably best to read this passage together with 17.2 ("By nature people are similar; they diverge through practice") and such passages as *Mencius* 3:A:1 and 4:B:32, or the *Xunzi* passage quoted in the commentary to 15.31, which all emphasize that the sages are no different in innate endowment than ordinary people. As Kong Anguo comments, "The point is that there are no differences in kind when it comes to what people bring to the process of education." What distinguishes a sage from an ordinary person is that they are well educated, learn to love the Way, and then work hard at perfecting it. Cf. 7.20 and 7.34, where Confucius denies having any special talents, other than a love for and dedication to the Way. The basic educability of all human beings—even non-Chinese barbarians—has remained a central tenet of Confucianism down to the present day. Notice, however, the contrast with passages such as 16.9. Another grammatically plausible way to render the passage is, "In education there are no distinctions concerning whom is taught," which may be understood as meaning that instruction is open to all, regardless of social class. This would accord with 7.7, as well as a passage from the *Annals of Lü Buwei*: "In offering instruction, a teacher does not challenge a student on the issue of whether he is socially inconsequential or important, noble or humble of birth, rich or poor. Rather, he challenges him as to whether or not he truly seeks the Way. If the person in himself is acceptable, instructing him cannot but be acceptable."[8] Finally, "no distinctions" may refer to the subject matter that is taught, the sense being that instruction is comprehensive in scope rather than specialized, which would accord with passages such as 2.12, 6.13, 9.2, 9.6, 13.4, and 19.7.

15.41 As a general statement, this is probably meant as a warning against glibness or cleverness of speech—i.e., allowing the embellishments of cultural refinements to overwhelm the basics of native substance. This is the point of the grammatically very similar 19.14, which concerns ritual behavior rather than speech: "Mourning should fully express grief and then stop at that." As Kong Anguo remarks, "In all things, never allow the substance of the matter to be exceeded. When words convey their point, leave it at that—do not needlessly complicate matters with refined and voluptuous [*wenyan* 文豔] words." Gui Fu notes a parallel passage in the *Book of Etiquette and Ritual* where the context more narrowly concerns the speech of an official envoy: "If one's words are excessive, one comes off as pedantic; if one's words are too few, however, the point [of the mission] is not conveyed. The

---

[8] Chapter 4.2 ("Encouraging Learning"); Knoblock and Riegel 2000: 119.

perfection of meaning is realized when words are just adequate to convey the point."[9]

15.42 The post of Music Master was traditionally filled by blind persons in ancient China, both in order to give them a trade in which they could excel and because their sense of hearing was considered more acute than that of the sighted. Music Master Mian has presumably been brought to Confucius' residence by an assistant, who then leaves him in Confucius' care.

As Brooks and Brooks note, Zizhang's question is probably inspired by Confucius' "extra solicitude, which seems to sacrifice Confucius' dignity as a host, but which is explained as situationally appropriate" (1998: 135). Reading this as a pair with 15.41, part of the point is no doubt the economy of expression of the Master, who puts aside the normal ritual behavior of a host in order to deftly and respectfully serve as a guide for the blind Music Master, without being overly fussy or condescending. As Xue Xuan comments,

> Observing the Master speaking with the Music Master, we see that his words are casual and relaxed, yet also thoroughly sincere and cordial—truly inspiring in us a rare sort of admiration. Ordinary people know to be respectful when they encounter an important person, but this respectfulness diminishes somewhat when they run into a rival, and often degenerates into nothing more than arrogant casualness when they are dealing with inferiors. The sage, on the other hand, met everyone—superior or inferior, stranger or friend—with the same spirit of sincerity and respect.

Some of the Master's actions here are presented as ritual injunctions in later ritual texts,[10] so an additional point is possibly the Master's effortless accordance with ritual in this particularly complex situation, which is worthy to serve as a model for others. As Zhu Xi remarks, "This passage demonstrates the manner in which the students in the sage's school remarked and carefully reflected upon his every word and gesture."

Book Sixteen Commentary

16.4 We see here again the importance of choosing one's friends properly; cf. 12.24 and 16.5. As Wang Yangming comments,

---

[9] Chapter 18 ("Ritual for Official Visits"); Steele 1917, vol. 1: 233–234.

[10] Cf. the *Record of Ritual*, Chapter 17 ("Smaller Rules of Demeanor"); Legge 1967, vol. 2: 80: "When someone who does not have a candle arrives late, they should be informed as to who is present. One should also do the same with blind people."

In life, it is impossible to go without friends, and when making friends it is unacceptable not to be selective. Befriending those who are upright, true to their word, and broadly learned, you will always get to hear of your own transgressions, learn things that were previously unknown to you, develop your excellences and remedy your faults, open and expand your heart, and every day make further progress in rendering both your Virtue and learning bright and noble. On the other hand, associating with clever flatterers, dissemblers, and the glib will make you dependent upon flattery and constant affirmation; no one will demand excellence of you, and you will grow self-satisfied and complacent; arrogance will develop and you will pursue wrongness, to the point that every day your Virtue and learning will descend further into the depths of immoral crudeness. The benefit and harm provided by friendship are not to be underestimated, and therefore you cannot but be careful in choosing your friends!

16.5 In this companion passage to 16.4, we see how one's affective responses have significance for moral cultivation: one must learn to take joy in the right sorts of things, because only one who actively takes joy in the Way can genuinely master it (6.20). Both Confucius and Yan Hui seem to have naturally possessed this joy in the Way, but of course the trick is how one can instill this joy in a person who lacks it or, conversely, how one who lacks this joy can go about acquiring it. Cf. 4.6, 5.10, 6.12, and 7.30.

16.7 A similar passage in the *Huainanzi* reads, "It is the general nature of human beings that, when young, they are prone to be wild and undisciplined; when in their prime, they are prone to be violent and aggressive; and when old, they are prone to be greedy." Confucius' comment therefore probably reflects common wisdom of the time. This passage is interesting because it is the only place in the *Analects* where human vices are explicitly linked to psychophysiological factors, and it represents the first evidence we see in the text of the influence of medical theories concerning the blood and vital essence (*xueqi* 血氣) that later had such a large impact on the thought of Mencius, Zhuangzi, and Xunzi. This may be an indication of a relatively late date for this passage. Cf. 9.18.

16.8 This parallel to 16.7 can perhaps be compared to 2.4, where recognizing or understanding (*zhi* 知) the Mandate of Heaven is presented as an essential step in comprehending the Way and achieving wu-wei perfection. Two views on how to understand "great men" can be traced back to He Yan and Zheng Xuan, with He Yan arguing that it refers simply to morally great people, such as the sages, and Zheng Xuan arguing that it refers specifically to sociopolitical superiors. Either interpretation is plausible, but the metaphorical structure of the concept of the "Mandate of Heaven" supports the

latter, suggesting a parallel between submitting to fate and showing due deference to a political superior. Things that are beyond the immediate control
of the individual (wealth, fame, health, life span) are metaphorically
"commanded" or "mandated" by the Heavenly ruler, and thus the true gentleman—understood in the metaphor as a loyal minister—submits to these "decisions" without anxiety or complaint. The petty person, on the other hand, has
no respect for rank, does not know his place, and is always scrambling to get
ahead.

16.9 Yan Hui seems to have belonged to the first category (2.9, 5.9, 6.7, 11.4),
and Confucius to the second (7.20). In contrast to 15.39, we have here a hierarchy of native ability presented, but the point seems ultimately to be the same:
although perhaps more difficult for the less gifted, learning the Way is within
the reach of all who are willing to dedicate their life to its pursuit and never
give up (cf. 8.7 and 9.11). As Yang Shi observes, "All three of the first categories,
although different in terms of native substance, are the same in eventually
attaining knowledge. This is why the gentleman values learning, and nothing
else. It is only someone who does not learn because he finds it difficult who is
ultimately dismissed as inferior."

16.13 Boyu is Confucius' son, and the disciple Ziqin is curious to see if,
because of his special relationship to the Master, he has obtained any sort of
esoteric learning not shared with the other disciples.

Along with 8.8, this passage serves as one of the clearer expressions of the
constitutive function of the Confucian tradition: learning the *Odes* provides one
with the resources to speak (cf. 13.5, 17.9–17.10), and learning ritual provides
a model for everyday behavior, allowing one to "take one's place" among other
adults in society (cf. 2.4, 12.1, 20.3). As Huang Kan notes, "The rites are the
root of establishing one's self by means of reverence, frugality, gravity, and
respectfulness. With the rites, one can be at ease; without the rites, one will be
imperiled." Regarding the principle of "keeping one's son at a distance," Sima
Guang remarks, "To 'keep at a distance' refers not to being cold or alienating,
but rather to being timely in the way one allows one's son to approach, and
always receiving him with ritual propriety. The point is simply that father and
son do not consort with one another day and night in an indecently familiar
manner." A passage from the *Summary of Discussions* suggests that such formality does not extend to the third generation: "The gentleman keeps his sons
at a distance, but is familiar with his grandsons." Boyu's denial that he has
received any esoteric instruction accords with the Master's statement in 7.24
that he "hides nothing" from his disciples, as well as the *Analects*'s general
eschewal of abstruse concerns in favor of the everyday practicalities of self-
cultivation (5.13).

Book Seventeen Commentary

17.2 Although not a primary concern for Confucius, the topic of human nature (*xing* 性) became a central focus of debate in later Confucianism. Mencius famously declared that "human nature is good [*shan* 善]," and repeatedly defended this claim against his opponents. Xunzi chose human nature as the center of his confrontation with Mencius, famously entitling one of his chapters, "Human Nature Is Bad." The character of human nature was a topic of lively debate throughout pre-Tang Confucian thought, with various positions—it is good; it is bad; it is neutral; it is mixed (some people are born good, others bad)—all being defended as expressions of Confucius' original view. The lack of theoretical consistency in the *Analects* makes it possible to argue for any of these positions. Passages that emphasize the importance of native substance (*zhi* 質) (3.4, 3.8) sometimes seem to imply that at least some people are born with the "stuff" of virtue that merely needs to be refined into full Goodness; passages such as 2.9, 5.9, 11.4, and 16.9 imply that some exceptional sages (such as Yan Hui) are born fully good, while 5.10 and 17.3 similarly imply that some are born hopelessly flawed. The general tenor of the *Analects*, however, seems to be summed up fairly well here in 17.2: all people, even non-Chinese barbarians, are born with more or less similar basic stuff, and it is the quality of the tradition into which they are socialized—the consequences of "practice" (*xi* 習)—that really makes the difference.

17.3 Some commentators read 17.2–17.3 as a single passage, but the "Master said" locution marks 17.3 as a separate passage. In any case, it is clearly related to 17.2, clarifying that, although people are generally similar by nature, there are exceptions. Commentators are probably correct in reading this passage along with 16.9: the "wisest" are those who are "born understanding it," and the "stupidest" are those "who find it difficult but do not even try to learn." The former do not really need education, whereas the latter either refuse to benefit from it, or are constitutionally unable to do so.

17.8 As Kong Anguo explains, "Zilu had stood up to answer the Master [as required by ritual], and therefore the Master tells him to take his seat again."

The "six words" are the six virtues named, each paired with an attendant vice (*bi* 蔽; lit. "obscuration"). Learning is presented as a force able to restrain or regulate the inherent emotional "stuff" of human beings, which would tend toward excess if left to develop on its own; cf. 8.2, where the restraining force is ritual. The discipline provided by training in traditional cultural forms allows one to reshape one's native substance and hit on the mean of virtue (cf. 1.12). This description of the "six virtuous words" and their attendant vices is reminiscent of Aristotle's discussion of the virtues and their excesses and deficiencies. Aristotle describes his virtues as the mean (*mesotes*) point between two extremes: truthfulness or straightforwardness, for instance, is the mean between the vice of excess (boastfulness) and the vice of deficiency (self-deprecation).[1] Although Confucius discusses his virtues in pairs (the virtue and its excess when not restrained by the rites or learning) rather than triads (the virtue and its excess and deficiency), the basic conceptual structure of the "mean"—in Chinese, *zhong* 中, or "the center of an archery target"—is very similar, based as it is on the metaphor of a physical continuum with extreme ends or edges and a desirable midpoint. For more on the mean in the *Analects*, cf. 6.29 and 13.21.

17.9 For the *Odes* as a source of inspiration, cf. 8.8, and as a resource for interpersonal communication, cf. 13.5. This passage fleshes out Confucius' comment in 16.13 to his son, Boyu, that "unless you learn the *Odes*, you will be unable to speak." As Zhu Xi comments,

> The *Odes* stimulate the mind and inspire the ambition, and examining them allows one to understand success and failure. They express harmony without getting carried away, and express complaint without falling into anger. With regard to the Way of human relationships, there are none which are not contained in the *Odes*; these two [i.e., serving one's father and one's lord] are cited because they are the most important. Moreover, the remainder of the *Odes* is able to serve as a broad resource for a knowledge of things in the world.

The *Odes* play a broad role in fostering in the individual the ability to speak and interact socially, providing the student with everything from quotations and turns of phrase useful in social situations to exemplary models of the most important role-specific duties. Seen in this light, the Master's rebuke of Boyu in 17.10 is quite understandable.

17.10 The "South of Zhou" and "South of Shao" are the first two sections of the "Airs of the States" portion of the *Book of Odes*, and here probably stand in for the *Odes* as a whole. The sense of this passage is thus similar to 16.13 and 17.9: without the knowledge provided by the *Odes*, one will lack the means to think clearly or associate with others. Some commentators believe that it is merely these two sections of the *Odes* that Confucius has in mind, but the sense is in any case much the same. As Liu Baonan remarks,

> It seems to me that these two sections of the *Odes* are entirely concerned with the Way of husbands and wives, which in turn is the first step in kingly moral transformation. Thus, the gentleman, in reflecting upon himself, must first cultivate it

---

[1] *Nicomachean Ethics* 1127a–b.

inside. Only then can he use it to discipline his wife, extend it to his brothers, and finally rely upon it to manage the state. The *History of the Han* says, "Once the Way of the household is cultivated, the principle of the world is obtained." This is exactly what I mean. Is it not also possible that, at the time this dialogue occurred, Boyu was establishing his household, and the Master therefore particularly singled out the "South of Zhou" and "South of Shao" in order to instruct him?

17.11 Reading this passage together with 3.3 and 3.12, one point could be that, just as true music requires not merely instruments, but also sensitive musicians to play them, so true ritual requires not merely traditional paraphernalia, but also emotionally committed, sensitive practitioners. Most commentators, however, understand the message as concerning the confusion of means and ends among Confucius' contemporaries. As Wang Bi comments,

> The governing principle of ritual is respect; jade and silk are merely the means for expressing and adorning respect. The governing principle of music is harmony; bells and drums are merely the tools with which music is made. In Confucius' age, that which went by the name of "ritual" emphasized gifts and offerings at the expense of respect, and that which went by the name of "music" failed to harmonize with the Ya and Song, despite its profusion of bells and drums. Therefore Confucius is here attempting to rectify the meanings of these words.

Understood this way, this passage may serve as another example of the "rectification of names" that Confucius held to be so important (cf. 6.25, 12.11, 13.3).

17.13 Probably the best commentary on this passage is *Mencius* 7:B:37, where Mencius quotes 17.13, and then is asked for further explanation by the disciple Wan Zhang:

> "What sort of person is this, who is referred to as a 'village worthy'?"
>
> "He is the type of person who says, 'Why be so grandly ambitious?' His words have nothing to do with his actions, and his actions have nothing to do with his words. Such a person then goes on to declare, 'The ancients, the ancients, why were they so standoffish and cold? When you are born in an age, you should accommodate yourself to it. As long as you do so skillfully, this is acceptable.' Someone who, in this way, tries to surreptitiously curry favor with his contemporaries—this is the 'village worthy.'"
>
> "If everyone in a village praises a man as being worthy, and nowhere can you find someone who does not consider him worthy, what did Confucius mean by calling such a person a 'thief of Virtue'?"
>
> "Those who try to censure him can find no basis; those who try to criticize him can find no faults. He follows along with all the vulgar trends and harmonizes with the sordid age. Dwelling in this way he seems dutiful and trustworthy; acting

in this way, he seems honest and pure. The multitude are all pleased with him— he is pleased with himself as well—and yet you cannot enter with him into the Way of Yao and Shun. This is why he is called the 'thief of Virtue.' Confucius said, 'I despise that which seems to be but in fact is not. I despise weeds, for fear they will be mistaken for domesticated sprouts. I despise glibness, for fear it will be mistaken for rightness. I despise cleverness of speech, for fear it will be mistaken for trustworthiness. I despise the tunes of Zheng, for fear they will be mistaken for true music. I despise the color purple, for fear it will be mistaken for vermillion [17.18]. I despise the village worthy, for fear that he will be mistaken for one who truly possesses Virtue.' "

The village worthy is one who carefully observes all of the outward practices dictated by convention and so attains a measure of social respect, but who lacks the inward commitment to the Way that characterizes the true Confucian gentleman. Confucius refers to him as the "thief of Virtue" because from the outside he *seems* to be a gentleman laying a false claim to Virtue. By serving as counterfeit models of virtue for the common people, the village worthy is in effect a false prophet, not only blocking the development of true virtue in himself but also leading others astray. This is why Confucius despises him. Cf. 13.24, 15.28, and especially 17.18.

17.18 Vermillion—the color of the Zhou—was the traditional and proper color for ceremonial clothing, and purple a mixed, more "modern," and increasingly popular variant; cf. 10.6 and *Mencius* 7:B:37, quoted in the commentary to 17.13. A passage in the *Hanfeizi* tells how purple was popularized by Duke Huan of Qi (685–643 B.C.E.), who started a craze for purple garments among his people by wearing purple himself, apparently because he possessed a stock of purple garments he had to unload and wished to create a profitable market for them. "Duke Huan of Qi was fond of wearing purple," the *Hanfeizi* says. "The people of Qi esteemed it as well, and were willing to exchange five plain garments for a single purple one."[2] The target of Confucius' scorn is thus perhaps the first recorded marketing fad in history. For the political trouble caused by both the Zheng music and the clever of tongue, see 15.11. The danger represented by all of these phenomena—purple, the tunes of Zheng, clever speakers—derives from the fact that, as Liu Baonan concludes, "they seem to be the real thing, but in fact are not."

17.19 Reading this passage together with the ones that precede it, the theme is related to the suspicion of glibness and hypocrisy: whenever there is speech, there is the danger of a discrepancy between speech and action, which is

---

[2] Chapter 32 ("Outer Congeries of Sayings, The Upper Left Series"); Liao 1959, vol. 2: 53–54.

why Confucius elsewhere has been led to declare that "the Good person is sparing of speech" and "reticence is close to Goodness." We see here again the metaphor of Heaven as ruler: Heaven governs the natural world in an effortless fashion, without having to issue orders, and the counterpart to Heaven in the social world is the sage-king of old, someone like Shun, "who ruled by means of wu-wei" (15.5). We have already seen the analogy between the wu-wei manner of ordering the human world and the spontaneous harmony effected by Heaven in the natural realm in 2.1, where one who rules by means of virtue is compared to the Pole Star. Like the natural world, then, a properly ordered human society functions silently, inevitably, and unself-consciously. Confucius' somewhat exasperated remark here is therefore inspired by the contrast between the natural, silent, and true order that prevailed in ancient times and the garrulous, self-righteous, hypocritical disorder that characterizes his own age.

17.21 There is some evidence from early texts, such as the *Book of Odes*, that a three-year mourning period (usually understood as *into* the third year—i.e., twenty-five months) for one's parents had at least some currency. As we have already seen in 14.40, however, this three-year period was viewed as impractical by many of Confucius' contemporaries, and we mentioned the claim of an official in Teng, recorded in *Mencius* 3:A:2, that such was not even the practice of the ancients. Both of these arguments against the three-year period were later raised and pursued in detail by Mozi.[3] Here Zai Wo appears as a critic of the practice from within Confucius' own school, repeating Zizhang's implicit criticism that three years is impractical and counterproductive, and then adding a novel cosmological twist: if people want to model their behavior on Heaven, the one-year Heavenly cycle should be their standard. Ma Rong explains that the "rekindling of the fire" mentioned by Zai Wo refers to a ritual of renewal whereby, at the beginning of each season, a new ceremonial fire was lit from the wood of a tree appropriate to that season. After the passage of four seasons, the cycle was complete, and thus—Zai Wo claims—should one's mourning for one's parents' death also come to an end. This concern with cosmology marks this passage as rather late.

While mourning his parents, a son is restricted to ordinary millet to eat—rice being an unusual luxury in northern China of this time—and rough hemp for clothing, and is to refrain from such pleasures as music or sex. He is also to dwell in a specially built mourning hut rather than his ordinary chambers. Refer to the commentary for 14.40.

Kong Anguo understands the final judgment of "not Good" to signify that Zai Wo "lacks a feeling of benevolence [*ren'en* 仁恩] toward his parents"; such an understanding of *ren* as a kind of feeling (compassion, empathy) would also mark this passage as rather late (cf. 12.22). Miao Bo, however, argues

---

[3] See especially Chapter 25 ("Simplicity in Funerals"); Mei 1929: 123–134.

for a more standard *Analects* understanding of *ren* as general moral excellence cultivated by means of ritual: Zai Wo's failure is not one of feeling, but rather of ritual propriety. What is certainly new here, in any case, is defense of a ritual standard in terms of an essential characteristic of human biology: the fact that an infant is helpless at birth and is completely dependent on his or her parents for the first three years of life. The implication is that the length of the mourning period is not an arbitrary cultural artifact, but is rather grounded in the very nature of human experience. This sort of direct link between Confucian practice and human nature is rarely postulated in the *Analects*, but later becomes one of the major elements in the thought of Mencius.

17.23 "Gentleman" and "common person" are here meant in terms of social rank. The general point is that virtues must be balanced by one another: an individual virtue like courage, possessed in isolation, is potentially dangerous. More particularly, some commentators suggest that Zilu has been singled out for this teaching because courage uninformed by other virtues, such as wisdom, was his particular fault (cf. 11.22). For the more general idea of virtues unbalanced by traditional restraints turning into vices, see 17.9.

17.25 This is an infamously misogynous passage that some later commentators have sought to soften. The use of the word *yang* 養 ("manage," "care for," "raise") suggests the context of aristocratic household management, which is why *xiaoren* 小人 is best translated in its more concrete social sense of "servants" or lower-class people. Some claim that, considering this household management context, "women" (*nuzi* 女子) is meant only to refer to slave women or female servants. Such women were certainly still being kept in aristocratic households in Confucius' age, but so were male slaves and servants, which means that even under this interpretation we have the problem of why women in particular are being singled out. In the *Zuo Commentary* we read, "Female attractive power (*nude* 女德) is infinite, and there is no end to the resentment of women."[4] Du Yu's commentary on this passage paraphrases 17.25: "The disposition of women is such that if one is familiar with them they do not know when to stop or when is enough, whereas if one is distant with them their resentment knows no bounds." The danger of "female power" is a constant theme in traditional texts from the earliest times, usually manifesting itself in two ways: more generally, as a force analogous to alcohol that intoxicates men and leads them into immorality, and more specifically in the form of the deleterious influence of concubines or dissolute wives who hold the ear of the ruler and thereby lead the state into moral and political ruin.[5] We have already seen examples of

---

[4] Duke Xi, Year 24 (635 B.C.E.); Legge 1991d: 192.

[5] This is the context of the *Zuo Commentary* passage previously quoted.

the former sense in 9.18, and the latter in the person of the infamous Nanzi of Wei in 6.28. With this in mind, the sense of 17.25 is probably one that would not seem particularly strange to a man in Victorian Europe: considering their potentially dangerous sexual power and inability to control themselves, household women (i.e., wives and concubines), like servants, need to be managed firmly, but with respect, if they are to remain obedient and not overstep their proper roles.

Book Eighteen Commentary

18.6 Confucius and his entourage were apparently attempting to cross a nearby river, but this passage is probably also to be read allegorically: the "ford" is the way out of the "great flood" of chaos mentioned below. The use of self-consciously primitive technology by these two figures (most plows were ox drawn by this time), as well as their knowledge of Confucius' identity revealed below, makes it clear that they are no ordinary commoners, but rather educated, primitivist recluses who have deliberately rejected society and culture. Like many of the figures in the *Zhuangzi*, their names appear to be allegorical (*changju* 長沮 means "Standing Tall in the Marsh" and *jieni* 桀溺 "Prominent in the Mud"); the appearance of this literary technique and the complex narrative quality of this passage mark it as quite late.

This characterization of these recluses as "living like the birds and beasts" sums up the Confucian criticism of the primitivist–Laozian project: rightful social duties and the elaborations of culture are part of any properly human life, and to abandon these to lead a solitary, primitive lifestyle is to abandon one's humanity. Confucius' compassion for the suffering of the world is such that he cannot take what he views as the easy way out—simply withdrawing from society and living the life of a noble, unsullied recluse—although his mission as the "bell-clapper of Heaven" (3.24) is grueling and fraught with difficulties and frustrations. At least two stories in the *Zhuangzi* are apparently inspired by this passage. In Chapter 6, Confucius is portrayed somewhat sympathetically as one "punished by Heaven," who admires the wild and free Daoist masters but is fated to act in the conventional world, whereas in Chapter 20 the Daoists get the last say, and Confucius is portrayed as finally abandoning the social world and going to dwell as a recluse among the birds and beasts.[1]

18.7 The old man's initial comment is a rhyming verse in the Chinese—an indication that again we are not dealing with an ordinary, illiterate farmer. Its

---

[1] For the former, see Watson 1968: 87, and the latter Watson 1968: 214.

target is both Zilu and Confucius: in his scholar-official dress and with his unsoiled hands, Zilu is clearly not suited to manual labor in the fields. The farmer is gently mocking both Zilu's uselessness and the sort of education that produced it. Zilu does not respond to this rather rude remark, probably out of respect for the old farmer's age, and his quiet, dignified demeanor apparently wins the old man over.

Commentators believe that Zilu's final remarks are delivered to the old farmer's two sons, presumably to be passed on when he returns. The point is that the old recluse clearly recognizes the first set of relationships (between elders and juniors) in requiting Zilu's formal hand clasping—an expression of respect by a younger man for an elder—by providing Zilu with proper hospitality and formally presenting his sons, but he ignores the second (between ruler and minister) by living in reclusion and avoiding any sort of official contact. Cf. the account of a similar encounter between Confucius, Zilu, and a recluse in the *Zhuangzi*.[2]

Book Nineteen Commentary

19.6 Here the combination of learning and personal reflection is presented as one of the keys to attaining Goodness; cf. 2.15.

19.7 Jiang Xi is probably correct in thinking that part of the point here is that learning is something that one needs to acquire through hard work: "A craftsman is certainly not born skillful. He must spend time in his workshop in order to broaden his knowledge, and as his knowledge broadens, his skill is perfected. Similarly, the gentleman is not able to intuitively comprehend everything he needs to know—he must learn in order to broaden his thinking, and as his thinking is broadened, his Way will become perfected." Zixia is likening the practice of the gentleman to more mundane craft practices (cf. other craft metaphors for self-cultivation in 1.15, 3.8, 5.10), but with the clear implication (especially after 19.4) that the way of the gentleman is the higher and more inclusive path.

19.11 An illustration of this principle is found in a story from the *Exoteric Commentary*, where it is put into the mouth of Confucius:

> When Confucius encountered Cheng Muzi in the region of Yan, he lowered the canopy of his carriage and talked with him for the rest of the day. After some time, he turned to Zilu and said, "Make up fourteen bundles of silk and present them

---

[2] Chapter 12 ("Ze Yang"); Watson 1968, 285–286.

to the gentleman." Zilu replied, "I have heard from the Master that scholar-officials do not receive one another when on the road."[1] Confucius said., "As long as one does not transgress the bounds when it comes to important Virtues, it is permissible to cross the line here and there when it comes to minor Virtues."[2]

For similar themes in the *Analects*, cf. 9.3 and 15.37. An alternate interpretation is offered by Kong Anguo and Huang Kan, who take the passage to be referring to two levels of people, along the lines of "Those with great Virtue do not transgress the bounds; when it comes to people of small Virtue, crossing the line here and there is acceptable." This reading is supported by a comment attributed to Confucius in the *Xunzi*: "Correct when it comes to important regulations, but occasionally crossing the line here and there when it comes to minor regulations—such is the middling gentleman [*zhongjun* 中君]."[3] The interpretation adopted in the translation seems preferable, however, having more support in the *Analects* itself.

19.12 Ziyou is criticizing Zixia for making his younger disciples practice minor ritual tasks instead of teaching them about the "important" issues, but what he fails to understand is that only someone who starts at the beginning of the Way of the gentleman can truly walk it to its end. This means that the teacher must distinguish between the "grass" (the younger students at the beginning of the path) and the "trees" (the more mature students capable of advanced work), and target his instruction accordingly—forcing students to learn things of which they are not yet capable leads only to exhaustion. As Bao Xian notes, "Zixia's point is that those who are taught the Way too early will inevitably be the first to grow tired, and therefore he starts his disciples off with minor tasks, and only later instructs them in great matters." A further import of the metaphor is that the manner with which one comports oneself with regard to small matters is connected organically to how one will develop in the end; therefore, one cannot neglect the "roots," nor can one rush the process. As Huang Kan remarks, "Because the great Way of the gentleman is so profound, the only way to study it broadly is in stages." For the "root" metaphor, cf. 1.2 and 3.4, and for the importance of the details of daily behavior in judging and cultivating one's character, cf. 2.10. An alternate reading of the final line is, "Possessing both the beginning and the end [at the same time]—surely only the sage is like this!" Under this interpretation, the point is that, while most people have to proceed in a stepwise fashion, there are rare sages who possess it all at birth.

19.14 Reading this passage together with 3.4 and 15.41, this is a warning against allowing cultural refinement to overwhelm native substance. Kong Anguo and

---

[1] I.e., without observing the formalities of presenting an introduction and being ritually received.

[2] Chapter 2.16; Hightower 1952: 54–55.

[3] Chapter 9 ("On the Regulations of the King"); Knoblock 1990: 97.

Huang Kan read it rather differently, however, seeing it as a warning against allowing oneself to be overwhelmed by grief to the point of personal harm. As Huang Kan puts it, "Although mourning rituals are based upon the emotion of grief, the filial son cannot allow excessive grief to harm his health."

19.21 Huang Kan's interpretation of this metaphor seems apt:

> An eclipse of the sun or the moon is not the result of deliberate action on the part of the sun or moon; in the same way, a gentleman's transgression is not intentional. . . . Everyone sees an eclipse of the sun or moon, in the same way that everyone sees the transgression of the gentleman, because he does not attempt to conceal it. . . . When an eclipse of the sun or moon passes, darkness is transformed into light, and everyone in the world together cranes their neck to gaze upon it. In the same way, the Virtue of the gentleman is not permanently sullied by prior transgressions.

Cf. the importance of "making emends" (*gai* 改) when one has erred (7.22), as well as the repetition of 19.21 in *Mencius* 2:B:9.

Book Twenty Commentary

20.3 *Ming* 命 here probably refers to "fate" rather than the "Mandate of Heaven" (cf. 2.4), although of course the two concepts are related. Kong Anguo remarks, "Fate refers to the allotment of success and failure." Huang Kan elaborates,

> When it comes to those things in life that are subject to fate, whether or not one receives them is up to Heaven, therefore one must understand fate. If one does not understand fate and tries to forcibly pursue those things that are subject to it, one will not be able to perfect the Virtue that will allow one to become a gentleman.

Similar observations about fate are found in the *Mencius*. 7:A:1 reads, "Preserving one's heart-mind and nourishing one's nature are the mean by which to serve Heaven. Considering with equanimity an untimely death or long life, and cultivating oneself in order to simply await what comes—these are the means by which to establish fate." In 7:A:3, the issue of fate is linked to the distinction between internal and external concerns:

> "Pursue them, and you will get them; let go and you will lose them."[1] This refers to a situation where pursuing it helps one to get it, because the search lies within

---

[1] A quotation from *Mencius* 6:A:6, where the reference is to the Confucian virtues— the proper object of pursuit for a Confucian gentleman.

oneself. "Pursuing it requires a technique; whether or not you actually get it is a matter of fate." This refers to a situation where pursuing it does not help one to get it, because the search lies outside oneself.

The point is that the aspiring gentleman needs to focus his energy on the internal goods of the Confucian practice, the attainment of which is within his control, instead of wasting his time pursuing such externalities as wealth or fame; cf. 4.14 and 12.5. With regard to ritual, the aspiring gentleman must understand it because it is the means by which he becomes socialized, and therefore a true human being (16.13). As Huang Kan observes, "Ritual governs reverence, dignity, temperance, and respectfulness, and thus is the root of establishing oneself. A person who does not understand ritual lacks the means to establish himself in the world." Zhu Xi adds, putting it more vividly, "A person who does not understand ritual has no idea where to focus his eyes and ears, and has no place to put his hands and feet." Finally, with regard to understanding words, most commentators take this to refer to an ability to judge others' characters from their utterances. As Liu Baonan remarks, "Words are the voice of the heart. Words can be either right or wrong, and therefore if one is able to listen and distinguish between the two types of words, one will also be able to know the rightness or wrongness of the speaker."

APPENDIX 2

Traditional Chinese Commentators Cited

Short biographical notes for each of the commentators cited are included below. Only brief information is provided for minor commentators mentioned only once or twice, most space being reserved for major, frequently cited commentators. Western-style dates are provided when available; otherwise simply the dynastic period is indicated. For more extensive notes, as well as an explanation of sources, visit www.hackettpublishing.com.

Bao Xian 包咸 (c. 6 b.c.e.–65). Han Dynasty. A high official and scholar who moved in imperial circles, Bao was trained in the Lu version of the *Analects*, and taught this version of the text to the Han prince.

Cai Mo 蔡謨 (281–356). Jin Dynasty. Cai was a successful general and high civil official, known for both his strategic acumen and broad scholarly knowledge. His commentary to the *Analects* is quoted in Huang Kan's subcommentary.

Chen Tianxiang 陳天祥 (1230–1316). Yuan Dynasty. Scholar, official, and general.

[Master] Cheng 程子. Refer to the entry for Cheng Yi.

Cheng Yi 程頤 (1033–1107). Song Dynasty. The younger brother of Cheng Hao, both of whom studied for a year with Zhou Dunyi and had intellectual ties to Zhang Zai. Cheng is credited with setting the intellectual tone for what would become the Cheng-Zhu school, transmitting his teachings through his disciple Yang Shi to Yang's disciple Li Tong, who in turn was the teacher of Zhu Xi. Cheng Yi and his older brother were instrumental in making "principle" the central focus of neo-Confucian thought, with Cheng Yi coining the famous saying, "Principle is one, but its manifestations are many." His emphasis on correcting the mind through study and rectification of one's dress and demeanor can be seen as giving the Cheng-Zhu school its characteristic externalist bent. It is presumed that most of the commentary to the *Analects* attributed to "Master Cheng" in Zhu Xi's *Collected Line-by-Line Commentary to the Four Books* refers to Cheng Yi, although which brother is being quoted is difficult to establish for certain.

Fan Ning 范甯 (339–401).   Jin Dynasty. Blocked from public service early in his life because of a powerful enemy of his family, he eventually rose to high office after this person's death, only to be eventually relieved of his duties as the result of a financial scandal. Fan disapproved of what he saw as his contemporaries' tendency to disregard both rituals and laws, and since he attributed this decline of morals to the flourishing of the "Mysterious Learning" school associated with Wang Bi and He Yan, he was a frequent critic of these two scholars.

Fan Ziyu 范祖禹 (1041–1098).   Song Dynasty. Official, philosopher, and historian, Fan was a member of the Hanlin Academy,[1] prominent participant in the compilation of official histories, and lecturer to the emperor. He studied with the Cheng brothers, and his thought and writings—especially his commentary to the *Analects*, cited in Zhu Xi's *Collected Line-by-Line Commentary to the Four Books*—was very much derived from them. He was politically conservative and particularly known philosophically for his emphasis on the importance of sincerity (*cheng* 誠) for both personal self-cultivation and political order. Although he believed sincerity was part of inborn human nature, he thought that most people had to struggle to regain it, and advocated as the primary method for doing so the Confucian practice of "dutifulness and understanding." In this respect, Fan was a vociferous opponent of Daoism, arguing that, by deemphasizing the importance of the Confucian virtues and moral self-cultivation, it led human beings into chaos and confusion.

Gui Fu 桂馥 (1736–1805).   Qing Dynasty. Philologist and classicist, Gui is particularly known for his work on early dictionaries such as *Explaining Words* and his work on reconstructing archaic pronunciations.

Guo Xiang 郭象 (c. 252–c. 312).   Jin Dynasty. Renowned official and "Mysterious Learning" thinker, Guo is famous for his annotated edition of the *Zhuangzi*, but passages from his otherwise lost *Commentary to the Analects* (*lunyu zhu* 論語注) are quoted in Huang Kan.

Han Yu 韓愈 (768–824).   Tang Dynasty. Often identified as the forerunner of neo-Confucianism, Han Yu is best known for his attacks on Daoism and Buddhism (personally quite costly for him at the time), which he believed to be disruptive of natural human relations; his focus on human nature as a topic of inquiry, and his theory of the "three grades" of human nature; his insistence of the importance of "correct transmission" of Confucian doctrines, and his placement of Mencius in this orthodox lineage; and his citations from the *Book of Changes* and "Great Learning" and "Doctrine of the Mean" chapters of the *Record of Ritual*, which helped to put these works at the center of later neo-Confucian metaphysics.

---

[1] The Hanlin Academy was an elite imperial academic institution founded by the Emperor Xuan Zong (r. 712–756) in the Tang.

He Yan 何晏 (c. 190–249).   Three Kingdoms Period. Together with Wang Bi, He Yan is traditionally cited as the founder of the so-called "Mysterious Learning" school. He was a rather prominent figure, grandson of a great general of the Eastern Han Dynasty, and adopted son of the famous Cao Cao 曹操, who attempted—but failed—to unify China after the collapse of the Han. He Yan was renown both for his intellect and physical beauty, married a princess, and eventually entered the ranks of the nobility as Marquis-consort. He was killed in 249, after the failure of the Cao Shuang 曹爽 revolt in which he participated. He was a student of Daoism and the *Book of Changes*, and is often described as interpreting the *Analects* through the lens of such "Daoist" concepts as "nothingness" (*wu* 無) and "emptiness" (*xu* 虛). He is traditionally credited with editing *Collected Explications of the Analects* (*lunyu jijie* 論語集解)—one of our main sources for otherwise lost Han Dynasty commentaries—although this attribution has been disputed by some modern scholars.

Hu Anguo 胡安國 (1074–1138).   Song Dynasty. Classicist and philosopher, he was a close associate of Xie Liangzuo, Yang Shi, and You Zuo, and considered Cheng Yi to be his intellectual inspiration. Hu emphasized the importance of hard work in self-cultivation, which he saw as being based on dutifulness and trustworthiness, the extension of knowledge, and personal respectfulness. His commentary to the *Analects* is cited in Zhu Xi's *Collected Line-by-Line Commentary to the Four Books*.

Huan Maoyong 宦懋庸.   Qing Dynasty.

Huang Gan 黃榦 (1152–1221).   Song Dynasty. Student and son-in-law of Zhu Xi, Huang was dedicated to the transmission of the "orthodox" Cheng-Zhu school of interpretation.

Huang Kan 皇侃 (488–545).   Northern and Southern Dynasties Period. Huang Kan had scholarly inclinations from a very early age, and studied the classics under a famous Confucian scholar as a young man, specializing in the early ritual texts, the *Classic of Filial Piety*, and the *Analects*. He was also a practicing Buddhist and created a variety of intellectual and practical links between Buddhism, Daoism, and Confucianism. He was the author of the *Subcommentary to the Meaning of the Analects* (*lunyu yishu* 論語義疏), based on He Yan's commentary, which was lost in China, but then rediscovered in Japan in the eighteenth century. This eclectic subcommentary (*shu* 疏) contains Huang's own comments, as well as the comments of more traditional Confucian scholars, Daoist thinkers, and Buddhist monks.

Huang Shisan 黃式三 (1789–1862).   Qing Dynasty. A scholar broadly versed in the classics, particularly early ritual texts and the thought of Zheng Xuan, Huang shared the general Qing distaste for metaphysical speculation. He believed that the world consisted of material force alone, in which principle was embedded, and felt that any attempt to discuss principle or the Way outside of the context of the physical world would lead to nonsense. He also opposed Zhu Xi's distinction between human "moral nature" and "material nature," arguing that there is no human nature apart from the physical body and its needs. He similarly dismissed the common neo-Confucian conception—shared by both the Cheng-Zhu and Lu-Wang schools, and ultimately derived from Buddhism—that human desires are inherently evil, believing that it is only desires that have not been corrected and regulated by ritual and other cultural standards that are problematic. In this respect, he differed from the idealism of the Lu-Wang school in arguing that ritual and other standards are tools that are both external to human nature and essential for properly shaping it.

Jiang Xi 江熙.　Jin Dynasty. Generally characterized as a Daoist-inclined scholar, Jiang compiled *Collected Commentaries on the Analects* (*lunyu jijie* 論語集解), no longer extant, portions of which are quoted in Huang Kan.

Jiao Hong 焦竑 (1540–1620).　Ming Dynasty. Jiao was a prominent scholar of the classics who was placed first in the Palace Examination of 1589, and who was subsequently appointed to high academic posts at the imperial court. He believed that Buddhism and Confucianism were fundamentally reconcilable, devoting much of his scholarly effort to demonstrating parallels between the Buddhist canon and Confucian classics. He argued that the Buddhist sutras served as the best commentaries on the *Analects* and the *Mencius*. His syncretism also embraced the Daoist classics, for which he authored several commentaries.

Jiao Xun 焦循 (1763–1820).　Qing Dynasty. Classicist, mathematician, and drama critic. Unsuccessful in his official examinations, Jiao retired to his studio and devoted his life to writing and study, acquiring broad expertise in the entire classical canon. He was particularly devoted to the *Mencius* and *Book of Changes*, analyzing the latter in terms of mathematical theory, and believing that the *Changes* could in turn be used to explicate the other classics. Philosophically, he believed that the Way or principle was inseparable from material force, representing the pattern of the movement of material force. He was also a fatalist, believing that fate, in the form of the cyclic movement of material force, could not be altered. He also opposed the Cheng-Zhu rejection of desire as inherently bad, believing that true benevolence consisted of regulating and harmonizing human desires so that they could be properly satisfied.

Jiao Yuanxi 焦袁熹 (1661–1736).　Qing Dynasty. A classicist who held the post of lecturer on the *Analects* at a regional academy, Jiao was a specialist in the study of the *Annals* and a close associate of Lu Longqi.

Jin Lüxiang 金履祥 (1232–1303).　Song-Yuan Dynasty. Jin was a classicist and neo-Confucian thinker in the Cheng-Zhu school. He held some minor academic posts early in his life, but then went into retirement after the fall of the Song and dedicated himself to textual studies and writing. An accomplished scholar of the *Book of Odes* and *Book of Documents*, he interpreted these and other early texts in such a way that their message would be consistent with that of the Cheng-Zhu branch of neo-Confucianism.

Kong Anguo 孔安國 (156–74 B.C.E.).　Han Dynasty. An eleventh-generation descendent of Confucius, Kong held a variety of important posts, including governor of Linhuai, although he died at a young age. Little is known about his thought. Kong's commentary to the *Analects* is cited from the *Collected Explications of the Analects*, although many scholars believe that the commentary attributed to him is, in fact, a forgery.

Li Ao 李翱 (fl. 798).   Tang Dynasty. Student or friend of Han Yu, and along with him one of the forerunners of the neo-Confucian movement. See the entry on Han Yu.

Li Chong 李充.   Jin Dynasty. Scholar, official, and "Mysterious Learning" thinker, reputedly fond of Legalist thought in his youth. Passages from his otherwise lost collected commentary to the *Analects* are cited in Huang Kan.

Liu Baonan 劉寶楠 (1791–1855).   Qing Dynasty. Both a successful administrator and classical scholar, Liu dedicated the scholarly activities of the latter part of his life to putting together a state-of-the-art critical edition of the *Analects*. Because he considered both Huang Kan's and Xing Bing's commentarial editions to be full of errors, he used He Yan's *Collected Explication of the Analects* as his basis, adding other Han commentaries, selected Song commentaries and subcommentaries, and the best products of Qing philology and textual history. Because of the demands of his administrative duties, Liu passed away before the fruit of these labors, the *Correct Meaning of the* Analects (*lunyu zhengyi* 論語正義), could be finished, but this work was completed by his son. The governing hermeneutical strategy of this work was to "let the classics explain the classics"—in other words, to use other classical Confucian texts in order to elucidate the meaning of the *Analects*, in order to avoid importing anachronistic philosophical baggage.

Lu Longqi 陸隴其 (1630–1692).   Qing Dynasty. Important scholar and official, known for his incorruptibility and concern for the well-being of the common people. Lu was also an impassioned defender of the Cheng-Zhu orthodoxy, declaring that "the teaching of Zhu Xi is the door to Confucius and Mencius; trying to study Confucius and Mencius without going through Zhu Xi would be like trying to enter a room without going through the door." The belief behind this sentiment was that the message of Confucius and Mencius had been lost in the intervening centuries, and only recovered again by the Song neo-Confucians. Lu was also highly critical of the Lu-Wang school, because in his view their radical internalism—essentially a form of Chan-Zen Buddhism in Confucian garb—was fundamentally opposed to the proper Confucian concern with "things and affairs" in the outside world.

Ma Rong 馬融 (77–166).   Han Dynasty. A classicist and thinker in his own right, Ma adhered to the "Yin-Yang" cosmology of his time, which held that certain patterns in the Heavenly realm were mirrored in the human realm, with the two realms influencing one another through a kind of analogical resonance. For instance, if the emperor manifested obedience in his own person, this would help the seasons to follow their proper course; similarly, disruptions in the natural order of things would manifest themselves in social and political disorder. Ma was a famous commentator and teacher of the classics in his own age, and produced a number of outstanding students, including Zheng Xuan. Although an adherent to the so-called "Ancient text" school,[2] he often employed New Text readings when appropriate, and thereby helped to blur the line between the two school's approaches to the classics. He was also somewhat eclectic philosophically; although a Confucian, he had an interest in Daoist texts such as the *Laozi* and *Zhuangzi*. This interest in Daoism, as well as his somewhat free and easy personal manner, is thought to have had an influence on the later "pure talk" movement that eschewed ritual standards and conventional morality. His commentary to the *Analects* is cited in He Yan's *Collected Explications of the Analects*.

Mao Qiling 毛奇齡 **(1623–1716).**   Ming-Qing Dynasty. Well-known classicist, philosopher, and writer. Mao briefly went into reclusion after the fall of the Ming, but then reentered public life, enticed by the special national examination held in 1679 by the Qing to lure reclusive Ming-loyalists back into public service. He was one of only fifty people to pass the exam and was subsequently assigned to the Hanlin Academy, where one of his duties was to help compile the official *History of the Ming*. Mao was a man of wide talents, famous for his poetry as well as his extensive mastery of the classics. He was also fond of controversy and debate, and took a special interest in refuting the views of previous scholars when it came to textual analysis of the classics. A follower of the Lu-Wang school, he believed that this school represented the true legacy of Confucius, and expended much intellectual effort in demonstrating how the entire Confucian canon could be reconciled with the teachings of the "learning of the mind." In his view, self-cultivation consisted of nothing more than recovering one's original mind. He reaffirmed Wang Yangming's doctrine of the unity of knowledge and action, and emphasized the pernicious influence of human desires—the primary barrier to one seeking to recover the original mind. Mao also acknowledged the parallels between Lu-Wang neo-Confucianism and Chinese Buddhism, but believed that neo-Confucianism differed from Buddhism in its emphasis on putting the original mind to work in the social world.

Miao Xie 繆協.   Jin Dynasty. Little is known about this figure, other than that he authored a short text called *Explaining the Analects* (*lunyu shuo* 論語説) that is no longer extant, but that is partially preserved in Huang Kan's subcommentary.

Sima Guang 司馬光 **(1019–1086).**   Song Dynasty. Famous historian, politician, political theorist, philosopher, and member of the Hanlin Academy. In his writings, he emphasized the importance of ritual, believing it to be the key to both realizing one's own nature and ordering the state.

---

[2]The "Ancient text" school was devoted to the set of texts written with archaic versions of Chinese characters that began to be discovered in the Han Dynasty, especially in the first c. B.C.E., whereas the "New text" school believed these texts to be spurious and preferred to use the received versions of the classics, written with contemporary-style Chinese characters.

Sun Chuo 孫綽 (320–377). Jin Dynasty. A scholar and writer, he held a variety of posts in the imperial court. As a young man, he was fascinated with Daoism, and eventually became a devotee of the "Mysterious Learning" school. Sun was of the opinion that Confucianism, Daoism, and Buddhism were all ultimately the same teaching, with Buddhism and Daoism teaching the "inner" aspects of the Way and Confucianism focusing on its "outer" application in the world. Sun also believed that human nature is originally pure, but then is "agitated" by contact with the world and the arousal of human desires. His commentary to the *Analects* was lost sometime after the Tang Dynasty, but is partially preserved in Huang Kan's subcommentary.

Wang Bi 王弼 (226–249). Three Kingdoms Period. Famous "Mysterious Learning" thinker, scholar, and official, Wang is best known for his annotated edition of the *Laozi*, the basis of the received version of the text and oldest extant commentary on it. Philosophically, he is best known for his emphasis on "nonbeing" (*wu* 無) and principle, both referents to a kind of transcendent, fundamental reality that Wang believed was the basis of the phenomenal world. His commentary to the *Analects* is cited in Huang Kan.

Wang Fuzhi 王夫之 (1619–1692). Ming-Qing Dynasty. A scholar and Ming Dynasty loyalist, the thirty-three-year-old Wang led a small force in ill-fated resistance against Qing forces when they invaded his native Hunan Province. After his defeat, he went into retirement rather than serve the new Qing Dynasty, and devoted the rest of his life to scholarship. He is sometimes described as a "materialist" for opposing the Cheng-Zhu school dichotomy of principle and material force, as well as the monism of principle advocated by the Lu-Wang school, with the claim that only material force exists in the world, and that principle is nothing more than patterns of this material force. Wang is also famous for his view of history, which was fairly radical at the time: he saw history as a progressive rather than cyclic, and felt that patterns from the past cannot necessarily be used to govern the present. Wang was also extremely critical of the influence of Daoist and Buddhist metaphysics on Confucianism, and in his exegesis of the Confucian classics attempted to recover what he saw as their essentially practical, this-worldly emphasis. In this desire to purge *Analects* interpretation of Song and Ming neo-Confucian metaphysics, in many ways, Wang anticipated the more historically sophisticated approach of later Qing Dynasty scholars.

Wang Kentang 王肯堂. Ming Dynasty. Scholar, official, and physician.

Wang Yangming 王陽明 (1472–1529). Ming Dynasty. Famous neo-Confucian thinker, follower of the teachings of Lu Deming 陸德明 (1139–1193), and founding figure in the Lu-Wang 陸王 "learning of the mind" (*xinxue* 心學), or "idealist" school of neo-Confucianism. Like Lu Deming, Wang was a vocal critic of Zhu Xi and the Cheng-Zhu brand of neo-Confucianism, arguing that their concern with "study and inquiry" and the gradual accumulation of knowledge led to a pedantic, disjointed, overly theoretical grasp of Confucianism. Unlike Zhu Xi, Wang was a man of action in addition to being a scholar, serving as a high official as well as a general responsible for putting down uprisings in the south of China, and was a popular and charismatic teacher. He is most famous for his claim that there is nothing in the world but principle, which is identical to the human mind—that is, observable phenomena are not the result of the interactions of material objects composed of material force, but are rather emanations of the mind. This means that Zhu Xi's dualism of principle and material force is incorrect, and Zhu's program of acquiring knowledge through the "investigation of things" is therefore doomed to failure, since there are no things in the world to investigate. All necessary moral knowledge is already in the mind in the form of principle, which means that the task of self-cultivation consists of nothing more than activating this "innate knowledge" through the elimination of selfish desires, achieving a sincere "unity of knowledge and action" where innate knowledge is instantly and spontaneously translated into action in the world. Although Wang's extreme internalism seems rather foreign to the *Analects*, his claim that Confucius was more concerned with action than theoretical study is basically sound, and served as an important corrective to the teachings of the Cheng-Zhu school.

Wei Guan 衛瓘 (220–291). Jin Dynasty. A high official and author of *Collected Commentaries on the Analects* (*lunyu jizhu* 論語集注), portions of which are preserved in Huang Kan.

Xia Xichou 夏錫疇 (1732–1798). Qing Dynasty. A scholar in the Cheng-Zhu tradition, he believed that this school of neo-Confucianism represented the orthodox transmission of the spirit of Confucius.

Xue Xuan 薛瑄 (1389–1464). Ming Dynasty. A prominent neo-Confucian scholar and member of the Cheng-Zhu school. He continued the Cheng-Zhu emphasis on the importance of learning, although he slightly modified the orthodox metaphysics by suggesting that since principle resides in material force, it is impossible to know which should be given priority.

Yang Shi 楊時 (1053–1135). Song Dynasty. Philosopher, scholar, and official, one of the four renowned disciples of the Cheng brothers. He particularly followed Cheng Hao in his thought, emphasizing that all of principle is contained within the self, and often in his writings seeking to blur the distinction between the inner-self and outside things. He followed the Chengs in seeing the "investigation of things" as the key to recovering principle, but tended to emphasize the importance of internal recognition over external acquisition of knowledge. In this respect, his views anticipate certain themes in the Lu-Wang school. He was also somewhat influenced by Daoist ideals. His commentary to the *Analects* is cited in Zhu Xi's *Collected Line-by-Line Commentary to the Four Books*.

Yu Yue 俞樾 (1821–1906). Qing Dynasty. One of the most prominent figures in Qing philology and textual studies, Yu was a member of the Hanlin Academy and served in a variety of academic posts before retiring from official life and devoting himself full time to classical studies. He believed that the most important techniques in rendering the classics readable for contemporary readers were restoring original word and sentence orders (sometimes altered in transmission), establishing the proper senses of individual words, and—most importantly—being more aware of the use of "phonetic loan words." Phonetic loan words are Chinese characters that are used with the intended sense of another word with a different graphic form but similar pronunciation; especially in pre-Qin texts, before the Chinese written language was standardized, this phenomenon was quite common. Yu believed that many of the difficulties encountered in reading the classics were due to a failure to recognize the use of loan characters—an often quite challenging task, requiring an intimate knowledge of ancient Chinese phonology—and in his commentaries, he often raises the possibility of this phenomenon to suggest alternate readings. Yu's analyses of the classics are widely admired for their philological acumen, and he has had a large influence on both Chinese and foreign students of the Chinese classics, particularly in Japan.

Zhai Hao 翟灝 (1736–1788). Qing Dynasty. A scholar and professor, Zhai was widely versed in the classical canon, particularly specializing in the Four Books. His commentaries are carefully considered and nonpartisan, drawing on both Han and Song commentaries in formulating his opinions.

Zhang Erqi 張爾岐 (1612–1699). Qing Dynasty.

Zhang Ping 張憑. Jin Dynasty. Official and scholar, whose commentary to the *Analects* is cited in Huang Kan's subcommentary.

Zhang Shi 張栻 (1133–1180). Song Dynasty. Famous scholar and thinker. Although Zhang followed Cheng Yi's thought in most ways, he also emphasized the importance of the mind and is seen by some as a transitional figure between the Cheng-Zhu and Lu-Wang schools of neo-Confucianism. Ethically, he believed that, because of the deleterious influence of human desires, making a proper distinction between rightness and profit-benefit was crucial to the individual's moral development. His commentary to the *Analects* is cited in Zhu Xi's *Collected Line-by-Line Commentary to the Four Books*.

Zheng Xuan 鄭玄 (127–200). Later Han Dynasty. Famous classicist and commentator. As a commentator to the *Analects*, Zheng focused on glossing archaic characters and explaining the text in terms of other classics. His *Mr. Zheng's Commentary to the Analects* (*lunyu zhengshi zhu* 論語鄭氏注) was extremely important and influential up through the Tang Dynasty, officially recognized by the imperial court and the subject of national university chairs, but was suddenly lost sometime between the late Tang and early Song Dynasties. Parts of it were preserved in other works, and this is the source of the Zheng Xuan comments cited in Cheng Shude and reproduced in our work.

Mr. Zhou 周氏. Han Dynasty. Author of a commentary to the *Analects* quoted in He Yan's *Collected Explications of the Analects*, and about whom nothing else is known.

Zhou Dunyi 周敦頤 (1017–1073). Song Dynasty. Traditionally considered to be the founder of neo-Confucianism, Zhou was a syncretic Confucian thinker who set the tone for later neo-Confucianism by giving Confucianism a cosmological grounding, deriving the idea of a transcendent unity to the cosmos from Chinese Buddhism and the *Book of Changes*. The Cheng brothers visited and studied with him for a year, and in later genealogies, he is identified as the founder of the Cheng Yi–derived line of transmission.

Zhu Xi 朱熹 (1130–1200).   Song Dynasty. It is probably not an exaggeration to say that Zhu Xi is the most influential thinker in Chinese history after Confucius. A third-generation student of Cheng Yi (through Yang Shi and Li Tong), Zhu Xi avoided public office for most of his adult life, preferring to devote himself to scholarship. He established a school of neo-Confucian thought— later known as the Cheng-Zhu 程朱, "learning of principle" (*lixue* 理學), or "rationalist" school—that remained the dominant orthodoxy throughout the Chinese cultural sphere into the twentieth century, and which continues to inform the beliefs of many contemporary neo-Confucians. One salient feature of the Cheng-Zhu school is a dualism with regard to principle and material force. Principle is identical to the Way, perfectly good, and prior to material force. It requires material force to manifest itself in the world, however, at which point it immediately becomes contaminated by this contact, in the same way that clean water is fouled when flowing in a dirty channel. The clean water is not changed in its essence, however—being merely mixed with something alien to it—and thus can be returned to its originally pure state if this contaminant is somehow removed or settled out. This dualism with regard to principle and material force corresponds to a dualism with regard to human nature: although all human beings possess a "moral nature" that is identical to principle, as soon as they take on physical form, this original nature becomes contaminated with material force, resulting in the mixed "material nature" with which we are burdened at birth. Desires, which are essentially bad, spring from this corrupt material nature. The task of self-cultivation, then, is to attempt to gradually purify the material nature and recover the original moral nature. Meditation is helpful in this respect, since it helps to calm the material force, but since our own nature is already hopelessly corrupted, outside help is essential. This help comes in the form of one's teacher, who is able to guide one in the process of the "investigation of things" (*gewu* 格物). A term from the "Great Learning" chapter of the *Record of Ritual*, the "investigation of things" for Zhu consisted of the cumulative and extensive study of physical things in the world and—more importantly—the texts of the Confucian tradition, which collectively contain within them all of the elements of original principle. By means of a lifetime of intensive study, the student could gradually piece together again the elements of original principle that are obscured in him, and thereby come to clear away the obscurations of material force and eventually manifest the original moral nature in his own person. Like all neo-Confucians, then, Zhu Xi accepted the Mencian theory that human nature is good, but not in the radically subjective sense of Wang Yangming: although originally good, we lose this goodness immediately on birth, and therefore need to rely on external training and study to recover it. With this essentially externalist bent, Zhu's views seem to correspond more closely with that of the original Confucius than those of Wang Yangming. One of Zhu's most enduring contributions to Chinese intellectual life was his editing of the *Analects*, the *Mencius*, and the "Great Learning" and "Doctrine of the Mean" chapters of the *Record of Ritual* to form the so-called "Four Books," which eventually became the basis of the civil service examination from 1313 to 1905, and which were therefore studied and memorized—along with Zhu's commentary to them—by all educated Chinese during this period and beyond. Zhu's commentary to the *Analects* still dominates the way the text is understood in both Asia and the West, and although in many places he understands Confucius through the lens of anachronistic, neo-Confucian concepts, the enduring influence of his commentary stems in no small part from its eloquence, brilliance, and frequently profound insight.

Zhu Zhongdu 褚仲都.   Northern and Southern Dynasties. In a biography of Zhu's son in the *History of the Liang*, Zhu is described as a specialist in the *Book of Changes*, a historian-official, and an expert in the Five Classics. His *Analects* commentary exists only in isolated quotations in Huang Kan's work.

APPENDIX 3
DISCIPLES OF CONFUCIUS

The following list of disciples is confined to those cited in this edition, and the accounts omit most of the later traditions about the disciples of Confucius that were developed in such Han texts as the *Family Sayings* and the "Biographies of Disciples of Confucius" chapter of the *Record of the Historian*, the historical accuracy of which is not certain. Since many of Confucius' sayings seem to be tailored to the needs of the disciple receiving the teaching, it is helpful to have some sense of each disciple's character. For this purpose, a finding list of passages in which each disciple appears is provided. Italics in the finding list refer to commentary rather than main text.

Boniu 伯牛. Style-name of Ran Geng 冉耕. He was a native of Lu, known for virtuous conduct, and died young of a terrible disease, possibly leprosy. 6.10.

Bo Yu 伯魚. Style-name of Kong Li 孔鯉, son of Confucius, who died relatively young. 11.8, 16.13, 17.10.

Fan Chi 樊遲. Common name for Fan Xu 樊須, style-name Zichi 子遲, native of Qi 齊. The fact that he is repeatedly warned against acquisitiveness (6.22) is understood by some commentators to imply that greed was his particular flaw. 6.22, 12.22, 13.4.

Master You 有子. Respectful form of address for You Ruo 有弱, style-name You 有, a native of Lu. His honorific title indicates that he was the head of his own school of disciples after Confucius' death. 1.2, 1.12, 2.21, 12.9.

Master Zeng 曾子. Respectful form of address for Zeng Shen 曾參, style-name Ziyu 子輿, native of Lu, and son of Zeng Dian 曾點 (style-name Zengxi 曾皙), who in turn was probably one of Confucius' earliest disciples. Master Zeng was known particularly for his filial piety, and authorship of both the "Great Learning" chapter of the *Record of Ritual* and the *Classic of Filial Piety* were later attributed to him. As his honorific title indicates, he became the head of his own school after Confucius' death, and the *History of the Han* records the existence of a book—no longer extant—recording his teachings. His grandson Zisi 子思 was supposedly the teacher of Mencius, thus—in the eyes of Song neo-Confucians, at least—assuring the direct orthodox transmission of Confucius' teachings to Mencius. 1.4, 1.9, 2.12, 4.15, 8.7, 11.8, 11.26, *12.5*, 12.24, *17.11*.

Ran Qiu 冉求. Style-name Ziyou 子有, also known as Ran You 冉有, a native of Lu. Ran Qiu was skilled in statecraft, administration, and the cultural arts, but is harshly criticized by the Master for his behavior as steward for the Ji Family of Lu, and for not being sufficiently eager when it came to self-cultivation. *2.12*, 5.8, *5.22*, 6.12, 11.17, 11.22, 11.26, 14.12.

Sima Niu 司馬牛. Style-name Ziniu 子牛, proper name Sima Geng 司馬耕. He has traditionally been identified with a figure of the same name who appears in the *Zuo Commentary*, Duke Ai 14 (483 B.C.E.),[1] the youngest brother of a prominent military family in the state of Song. His older brothers included the Song military minister, Huan Tui 桓魋,[2] who threatened Confucius' life in 7.23, and who planned and executed an unsuccessful revolt against the rightful lord of Song in 483 B.C.E. Another of Niu's older brothers, Xiang Chao 向巢, was also a military official (minister of the left) in Song. Xiang Chao was apparently a somewhat arrogant and self-aggrandizing man, who was forced to flee the state after Huan Tui's attempted revolt. The Sima Niu of the *Zuo Commentary* resigned his official post in disgust after the flight of his two older brothers and emigrated in 483 B.C.E., apparently ending up in Lu, where he presumably had the conversation with Zixia recorded in 12.5. Some later commentators reject this identification of the disciple Ziniu with the figure Sima Niu in the *Zuo Commentary*, but this identification goes back to the Han dynasty and seems to make sense of the passages in which this disciple appears. 12.5.

Yan Hui 顏回. Style-name Ziyuan 子淵, also known as Yan Yuan 顏淵. Native of Lu, born into poverty, and the Master's most gifted disciple. Tragically, he died at a young age (there is some debate about how young), a loss that affected Confucius profoundly. *1.1*, 2.9, *4.2*, 5.9, *5.26*, 6.3, 6.7, 6.11, 9.11, 11.4, 11.8, 11.9, 12.1, 15.11, *16.5*, *16.9*.

Yuan Si 原思. Common name of Yuan Xian 原憲, style-name Zisi 子思. Little is said about this disciple in the *Analects* other than the report in 6.5 that he was appointed steward and wished to decline his official salary, and the account of his question about shame in 14.1, but it is apparent that he was one of the excessively "pure" or "fastidious" men of whom Confucius disapproved. Later legends arose documenting his austerities and harsh reclusive lifestyle, and he apparently had his own quite substantial line of disciples, despite the dismissive treatment in the *Analects*. 6.5, *13.21*, 14.1.

Zai Wo 宰我. Common name of Zai Yu 宰予, style-name Ziwo 子我. Employed by Duke Ai of Lu as a ritual specialist, but criticized by Confucius for his laziness and lack of Goodness. 5.10, 17.21.

---

[1] Legge 1991d: 839–840.

[2] The family's ordinary surname was Xiang 向, but as descendents of Duke Huan 桓 they were also allowed to use this surname, and the military title of *sima* 司馬 (Master of the Horse) had been in the family so long that it was also used by them at times as a surname.

Zengxi 曾皙.   Style-name of Zeng Dian 曾點, father of Master Zeng and one of the senior disciples of Confucius, presented in a very favorable light in his sole appearance in the text. 11.26.

Zigong 子貢.   Style-name of Duanmu Ci 端木賜. Important disciple of the Master, featured prominently in Book Nineteen, but criticized in other parts of the text for his inflexibility and overspecialization. 1.10, *1.15*, 2.12, 3.17, 5.4, 5.9, 5.12, 6.30, 9.13, 12.7, 12.8, 13.20, 13.24, 14.29, 14.35, 15.24, *17.11*, 17.19, 19.21.

Zihua 子華.   Style-name of Gongxi Chi 公西赤, also known as Gongxi Hua 公西華, a native of Lu. Apparently skilled at ritual tasks, and employed at some point by the Three Families of Lu. 5.8, 11.22, 11.26.

Zijian 子賤.   Style-name of Fu Buqi 宓不齊 of Lu, who became governor of Shanfu 單父.

Zilu 子路.   Style-name of Zhong You 仲由, native of Lu and one of Confucius' earliest disciples. Zilu was a former warrior and was admired by Confucius for his courage, but seems to lack other virtues (such as good judgment) that would balance out his courage. Zilu died a violent death during a civil war in Lu. 2.12, 5.8, 5.26, 6.28, 7.19, 7.35, 9.12, 10.27, 11.12, 11.22, 11.26, 13.3, *13.21*, 14.12, 14.35, 14.38, 15.2, 17.8, 17.23, 18.6, 18.7, *19.11*.

Ziqin 子禽.   Style-name of Chen Kang 陳亢, native of Chen. 1.10, 16.13.

Zixia 子夏.   Style-name of Bu Shang 卜商, a native of Wei particularly known for his learning, cultural refinement, and quick grasp of the Master's teachings, credited in later traditions with the transmission of many classical texts. He is sometimes criticized by Confucius for being too cautious. He apparently became the head of his own school after Confucius' death since Book Nineteen of the *Analects* is dominated by his sayings. 2.8, 3.8, 6.13, 12.5, 12.22, *15.11*.

Ziyou 子游.   Style-name of Yan You 言游, also known as Yan Yan 言偃. Little is known about this disciple, other than that he served as steward of a city in Lu, and was praised by the Master for his mastery of the arts. 2.7, 19.12.

Zizhang 子張.   Style-name of Zhuangsun Shi 顓孫師, a native of Chen, skilled at ritual, but apparently prone to excess and overly concerned with externalities. 2.18, 5.19, 15.42.

APPENDIX 4
Glossary of Terms

Below is a list of terms appearing in the text of the *Analects*, the commentary, or the appendices that may be unfamiliar to readers, at least with regard to their significance in the Confucian context. Certain terms from the *Analects* itself (e.g., Goodness, the gentleman) appear so often in the text that providing passage references would not be helpful; for other terms, reference is made to passages that shed light on their meanings.

benevolence (*hui* 惠). A virtue particularly important when it comes to superiors' actions toward those in their charge, or the behavior of parents toward their children. Also the translation of *ren* 仁 ("Goodness") in post-*Analects* texts. 4.11, 5.16, 14.9, 17.5, 20.2.

Cheng-Zhu 程朱 School. A school of neo-Confucianism named after Cheng Yi 程頤 (1033–1107) and Zhu Xi 朱熹 (1130–1200), sometimes alternately referred to as the "learning of principle" (*lixue* 理學) or "rationalist" school. See the entry on Zhu Xi in Appendix 2 for more details.

courage, courageous (*yong* 勇). A virtue inherited from the Zhou martial ideal of the gentleman, but subordinated in the Confucian context to more important virtues such as wisdom or rightness. The disciple Zilu, a former warrior, often serves as an example of the danger of impetuous courage uninformed by other virtues (5.7, 11.13; cf. 7.11, 8.10, 17.23), and we might contrast him with figures who are presented as displaying modest, genuine courage (6.15). In its proper place, however, courage is an important quality of the gentleman, allowing him to pursue the moral Way without fear (9.29, 14.28).

culture, cultural refinement (*wen* 文). Lit. referring to writing, *wen* often serves in the *Analects* as a general term pertaining to the sort of acculturation—training in ritual, the classics, music, etc.—acquired by someone following the Confucian Way (6.27, 9.5). In this respect, it is often portrayed metaphorically as a kind of adornment or refinement of the "native substance" (*zhi* 質) an uneducated person brings to the process of acculturation. It is often emphasized that cultural refinement requires a suitable substrate of native substance, as in 3.8, where *wen* is compared to cosmetics applied to a beautiful face, but ultimately a proper balance between the two must be struck (6.18, 12.8). Sometimes *wen* is also used in the more narrow sense of a set of specific practices like those later formalized as the so-called "six arts" of ritual, music, archery, charioteering, calligraphy, and mathematics, in which any gentleman was trained (see 1.6; similar to the sense of *yi* 藝, "arts," in 7.6).

153

Daoism, Daoist (*daojia* 道家).   Lit. the "School of the Way," this is a term retrospectively applied to thinkers such as the author(s) of the *Laozi*, the *Zhuangzi*, and the *Liezi*, who were viewed as emphasizing common themes, including an opposition to the Confucian project of acculturation and an emphasis on naturalness. See Graham 1989: 170–172 for more on the term "Daoism" and its referents.

Duke (*gong* 公).   Title held by those families given fiefs by the Zhou kings, and who, in the traditional feudal system, were answerable only to the king himself.

dutifulness, dutiful (*zhong* 忠).   Dutifulness is the virtue of fulfilling one's role-specific obligations, and is often linked to political duties (especially of a subordinate toward his superior) and to ritual obligations. Although *zhong* is often translated as "loyalty," "dutifulness" is preferable because the ultimate focus is on one's ritually prescribed duties rather than loyalty to any particular person. Indeed *zhong* involves opposing a ruler who is acting improperly (13.15, 13.23, 14.7). Examples of dutiful behavior are found in 5.19 and 14.21, descriptions of the restrictions placed on one's behavior by the demands of duty are found in 8.14 and 14.26. For its relationship to the virtue of "understanding," see 4.15.

fate (*ming* 命).   Also see "Mandate." In the sense of "fate," *ming* refers to the whole range of circumstances that are both external to the Confucian practice itself and beyond the control of human beings. Even when used in the sense of "fate," *ming* continues to preserve its connection to Heaven and the metaphor of "mandating" or "commanding": fate is what is mandated by Heaven, the normative standard of the universe. It is therefore not only pointless, but also morally wrong, to struggle against it. The proper attitude of the gentleman is to accept what fate brings and focus his attention on things actually within his control, such as self-cultivation. See 6.10, 7.3, 7.19, 11.18, 12.4–12.5, 14.36, 19.1, and 20.3.

filial piety, filial (*xiao* 孝).   The virtue of being a dutiful and respectful son or daughter, considered by Confucius to be the key to other virtues developed later in life. See especially 1.2, 2.5, 2.7–2.8, and 19.18. For an observation on the debt owed to parents, see 17.21.

gentleman (*junzi* 君子).   Meaning lit. "son of a lord," *junzi* referred in Western Zhou times to a member of the warrior aristocracy. In Confucius' hands, it comes to refer to anyone capable of becoming a kind of moral aristocrat: an exemplar of ritually correct behavior, ethical courage, and noble sentiment—in short, a possessor of Goodness.

glibness, glib (*ning* 佞).   Glibness is a negative quality that is attacked throughout the text. The original Zhou meaning of *ning* was something like "attractive or noble in speech," but in giving it the negative sense of "glibness," Confucius portrays *ning* as the false, external counterfeit of true, inner "Goodness" (see especially 1.3). This is no doubt the sentiment behind such passages as 12.3

("The Good person is sparing of speech") and 13.27 ("reticence is close to Goodness"), as well as Confucius' general suspicion of language and outward show.

Goodness, Good (*ren* 仁). In the *Analects*, Goodness refers to the highest of Confucian virtues. In pre-Confucian texts such as the *Book of Odes*, *ren* was an adjective referring to the appearance of a handsome, strong, aristocratic man, and the term is cognate with the word meaning "human being" (*ren* 人). In this context, *ren* would thus perhaps be best rendered as "manly." One of Confucius' innovations was to transform this aristocratic, martial ideal into an ethical one: *ren* in the *Analects* refers to a *moral*, rather than physical or martial ideal. In post-*Analects* texts, it has the more specific sense of empathy or kindness between human beings—especially for a ruler toward his subjects—and in such contexts is therefore usually translated as "benevolence." Although we see hints of this later usage in the *Analects* (12.22, 17.21), it is much more commonly used there in the more general sense of "Goodness," the overarching virtue of being a perfected human being, which includes such qualities as empathetic understanding (*shu* 恕) or benevolence (*hui* 惠).

Heaven (*tian* 天). The tribal god of the Zhou, who is deliberately conflated in Zhou writings with the Shang's god, the Lord on High. Early graphic forms of *tian* seem to picture a massive, striding, anthropomorphic figure, who is from the earliest times associated with the sky. Hence "Heaven" is a fairly good rendering of *tian*, as long as the reader keeps in mind that "Heaven" refers to an anthropomorphic figure—someone who can be communicated with, angered, or pleased—rather than a physical place. From Zhou times on, Heaven is viewed as the source of normativity in the universe, the all-powerful Being who, when pleased with proper ritual conduct, charges its representative on earth with the Mandate to rule, as well as the power of virtue that made realizing the Mandate possible. Heaven is also viewed as responsible for everything beyond the control of human beings (things relegated to "fate") and—in Confucius' view—for revealing to human beings the set of cultural practices and texts collectively known as "the Way."

hermeneutics, hermeneutical. Referring to interpretation or the theory of interpretation, from the name Hermes, Greek messenger of the gods.

Hegemon (*ba* 霸). Alternately translated as "Lord Protector," this was a position officially recognized by the Zhou kings in 681 B.C.E., when Duke Huan of Qi was appointed first hegemon to unite the Chinese states in defense against barbarian invasion. Although theoretically merely regents of the Zhou king, the hegemons in fact ruled independently, and the post itself represented an important erosion in the authority of the Zhou kings.

learning (*xue* 學). The common alternate translation of this term is "study," which gives it too much theoretical flavor. Although "learning" generally does focus on classical texts, its point is the actual practice of emulating and internalizing ideal models of behavior and speech exemplified in these works. In addition, the scope of learning extends beyond textual study, and includes observing and benefiting from the behavior of others (7.22, 19.22). The role of classical texts, such as the *Book of Odes*, is not only to give one the language to express oneself (16.13, 17.9), but the accumulated wisdom of the ancients that they represent is to form the very basis of one's thinking (*si* 思). See especially 1.1, 1.7, 5.28, 6.3, 16.13, 17.8, and 19.5–19.7.

Legalism, Legalist (*fajia* 法家). More accurately, though awkwardly, referred to as the "School of Statecraft," this is a retrospective term for a group of thinkers, such as Hanfeizi or Shen Buhai, who emphasized the importance of impartial, amoral techniques for state management, including a strong emphasis on punishment and reward.

li 里. Unit of measurement, equal to approximately one-third of an English mile.

Lord on High (*shangdi* 上帝). The Lord on High seems originally to have been a non-human god who gradually came to be viewed as the first human ancestor of the Shang people, and—by virtue of seniority—the most powerful of the ancestor spirits. The Lord on High and the other ancestor spirits of the Shang were viewed as dwelling in a kind of netherworld somewhere above the human realm (hence the Lord "on High"). From this vantage point they continued to monitor the behavior of their descendents, receive sacrificial offerings from them, hear questions and requests, and control all of the phenomena seen as lying beyond human control, such as weather, health and sickness, and success or failure in battle.

Lu-Wang 陸王 School. A school of neo-Confucianism named after Lu Deming 陸德明 (1139–1193) and Wang Yangming 王陽明 (1472–1529), sometimes alternately referred to as the "study of the mind" (*xinxue* 心學) or "idealist" school. See the entry on Wang Yangming in Appendix 2 for more details.

Mandate (*ming* 命). Also see "fate." *Ming* refers literally to a command issued by a political superior to an inferior or a decree issued by a ruler. In a metaphorical and religious sense, it refers to Heaven's command to his proxy on earth, the king, to rule the human world. In Shang and Zhou times, the Lord on High or Heaven was believed to grant the Mandate to rule the world to the ruler who maintained ritual correctness. Zhou texts claim that the Shang lost the Mandate because of gross ritual improprieties and general immorality, which motivated the Lord on High/Heaven to withdraw the Mandate from the Shang and give it to the Zhou. Since the holder of the Mandate was believed to also receive virtue from Heaven as a sign of its favor, he would be able to rule by means of wu-wei. 2.4, 16.8.

material force (*qi* 氣). Refer to the entry "Neo-Confucianism."

Mysterious Learning (*xuanxue* 玄學). Refers loosely to a syncretic movement that flourished in the Wei-Jin Period (220–420), related to the so-called "Pure Talk" (*qingtan* 清談) movement (the two movements are sometimes subsumed under the rubric "neo-Daoism"). It focused metaphysically on the concept of "nonbeing" (*wu* 無), seen as the mysterious progenitor of the entire phenomenal world; politically on the concept of effortless action or wu-wei as a means of ruler-ship; and personally on the importance of attaining "emptiness" (*xu* 虛) and living in a free and easy manner, unconstrained by social norms. Although much of the metaphysics was drawn from Daoism, this movement also drew heavily on Confucian social and political thought, and many of its advocates—the most prominent being Wang Bi, He Yan, and Guo Xiang—wrote commentaries on the Confucian classics.

native substance (*zhi* 質). Native substance refers to the moral "stuff" that a person brings to the process of acculturation, probably consisting of both inborn qualities and characteristics developed in early childhood. Although Confucius felt that a balance between native substance and cultural refinement was ideal (6.18, 12.8), his dislike for hypocrisy at times caused him to place more emphasis on the importance of native substance (3.3, 3.4, 5.10, 5.22).

neo-Confucianism (*lixue* 理學). Collective term for the various schools of Confucianism that arose during the Song and Ming Dynasties as a conscious reaction against the dominance of Buddhism in the Tang. They saw their task to be eliminating the "alien" influence of Buddhism and the antisocial influence of Daoism, and thereby bringing China back to the original teachings of Confucius. Despite this professed mission, modern scholars have noted that the various schools of neo-Confucianism—despite their differences—generally share a set of characteristics that distinguish them from "classical" Confucianism. To begin with, neo-Confucians believe that Mencius was the true follower of Confucius and that Mencius' view that "human nature is good" was shared by Confucius, and that this is a view that must be embraced by any orthodox Confucian. This is by no means an accurate portrayal of pre-Qin Confucian thought and probably stems from a desire (though probably unconscious) to accord with the Chinese Buddhist teaching that all human beings possess a pure Buddha-nature. In addition, neo-Confucians understand the nature of Mencius' claim in what might be characterized as a Buddhist sense; whereas Mencius believes that human beings are born *potentially* good, neo-Confucians understand his claim to mean that human beings are born with goodness already complete somewhere within them, which means that it only needs to be uncovered in some fashion. They also pick up from Han syncretic Confucianism and Chinese Buddhism a strongly metaphysical slant, evinced most obviously in their use of a dichotomy between "principle" (*li* 理) and "material force" (*qi* 氣). Principle, identical to the Way, is perfectly good and contains all of the ordering structure of the universe. The second term, *qi*, means something like "vital essence"—the animating force in all living things—in pre-Qin writings, but by the Han came to refer, in philosophical writings, to the dynamic and yet tangible material "stuff" that makes up the visible universe (hence "material force"). Generally, this material force is understood to be structured by principle, although there is a great deal of controversy among neo-Confucians about the precise relationship between the two (or even if they are ultimately distinct or identical). These "neo-Confucian" philosophical assumptions are shared by virtually all of the commentators from the Song to the Ming

Dynasties quoted in our translation, as well as many of the Qing scholars, although in the Qing some effort was made to approach *Analects* interpretation in a more historically responsible manner.

primitivism, primitivist.   A retrospective term referring in particular to the followers of Shen Nong 神農 ("The Divine Farmer"), a group of "levelers" who believed that stratified societies, vocational specialization, and advanced technology should be abandoned as unnatural, and that everyone—from ruler down to common person—should work together in the fields. The primitivists are often associated with the Daoists, and indeed one of the primary Daoist texts, the *Laozi*, features many primitivist themes. For an encounter between some followers of Shen Nong and Mencius, see *Mencius* 3:A:4, and for more on primitivism and its influence on early Chinese thought, see Graham 1989: 64–74.

principle (*li* 理).   Refer to the entry "Neo-Confucianism."

purity, pure (*qing* 清).   A minor virtue having to do with refraining from unworthy behavior or avoiding disgrace, generally discussed in the text with regard to its being taken to an inflexible extreme, as in 5.19, 14.1, and 18.8.

rightness, right, righteous (*yi* 義).   This term generally refers to a kind of cultivated sense of what is right and morally proper (4.10, 4.16, 5.16, 15.18, 17.23, 19.1), although at times it has the more specific sense of "rightful duty" in a political context, as in 18.7.

ritual, ritual propriety (*li* 禮).   A set of traditional religious and moral practices, which in the Confucian context were believed to have been revealed to the Zhou kings by Heaven. The scope of ritual is quite broad, encompassing not only sacrificial offerings to the spirits, but also aspects of one's daily life that we might be tempted to label as "etiquette," such as the manner in which one dresses, takes one's meal, approaches one's ministers, etc. (see especially Book Ten). By submitting to and internalizing ritual forms, an aspiring gentleman is able to restrain improper inborn tendencies (8.2, 12.1), acquire the means to "take his place" (*li* 立) among other adults in society (2.4, 8.8, 16.13, 20.3), and thereby win the favor of Heaven. Ritually acquired virtue is also portrayed as the only proper way to rule the world (3.11, 12.11, 14.41).

***ru* 儒.**   This term, which later came to mean "Confucian," appears only once in the *Analects* (6.13), and referred in Confucius' time to a class of specialists concerned with transmitting and preserving the traditional rituals and texts of the Zhou Dynasty. Confucius was probably a *ru*, although he sought to distance himself from *ru* who pursued cultural training solely in order to obtain official positions, social prestige, and salary.

scholar-official (*shi* 士).   The lowest of the three classes of public office holders, this term originally referred to an aristocratic warrior, but had, by the time of Confucius, come to refer to a class of people who filled the middle and lower ranks of state governments, primarily in civil posts. Like Confucius, it seems that a subset of these scholar-officials were also *ru* 儒.

thinking (*si* 思). This term might also be rendered as "concentration" and refers to focusing one's attention on a subject or the attempt to process or reflect on information that one has learned. While learning takes place within a certain structured context, it involves more than simply the passive absorption of knowledge; learning (what one hears from teachers and reads in the classics) and thinking (how one processes and integrates this knowledge) must be properly balanced (2.15, 15.31). Indeed, the ideal student must come to the project possessed by an inchoate need for what learning is able to provide and a passion for acquiring it (7.8, 9.31).

trustworthiness, trustworthy (*xin* 信). In certain contexts, this term is also rendered as "true to one's word." A minor, but nonetheless useful, virtue that unfortunately—like purity or uprightness—can easily be taken too far by those who are not virtuous in other ways. For trustworthiness in the positive sense, see especially 2.22 and 16.4. For the problems of excessive trustworthiness (sometimes rendered "petty fidelity"), see 13.18, 13.20, 14.17, 15.37, and 17.8. Also refer to the contrast of trustworthiness and rightness in 1.13.

understanding (*shu* 恕). The character itself is made up of components meaning "comparing" (*ru* 如) and "heart-mind" (*xin* 心), and is defined in the *Analects* in terms of what might be called a "negative" version of the Golden Rule: "Do not impose on others what you yourself do not desire" (15.24; cf. 5.12). It might thus be rendered as "understanding," in the sense of an ability to show sympathy, through putting oneself imaginatively in another's place or "being able to take what is near at hand as an analogy" (6.30). In 4.15, coupled with dutifulness (*zhong* 忠), it is described as the "single thread" tying together all that Confucius taught, and in 15.24 it is described as the "single teaching which can be a guide to conduct throughout one's life." "Understanding" seems to refer to an intuitive ability to amend or suspend the dictates of dutifulness—or to apply them flexibly—when holding to them rigidly would involve "imposing on others what you yourself do not desire," and the ability to combine role-specific properness with some sort of context sensitivity is an essential aspect of the overall virtue of Goodness.

uprightness, straightness (*zhi* 直). Refers to a kind of moral rectitude (6.19, 18.2), and also has the sense of "forthright"—i.e., not being shy about informing others of their faults—and in this sense represents the opposite of obsequiousness (see especially 15.7, 16.4). It is normally a desirable virtue, but—like trustworthiness—can easily turn into the vice of intolerance, rudeness, or excessive rigidity when not possessed by a true gentleman (5.24, 13.18, 17.8).

Virtue (*de* 德). "Virtue" works as a rendering for this term because it refers to moral worthiness ("virtue" in the more common sense) as well as the particular "power" residing in a person or thing—the original sense of the Latin *virtus*, still preserved in modern English in such expressions as, "by virtue of his great intelligence, he was able to solve the problem." Virtue in the early Shang context referred to a kind of attractive, charismatic power residing in a ruler who had won the endorsement of the ancestral spirits. This power could be perceived by others, serving as a visible mark of the spirits' favor, and its attractive qualities allowed the ruler to both acquire and retain supporters. This sense of Virtue was inherited by the Zhou, who saw it as a gift from Heaven for proper ritual conduct, and by Confucius, although for Confucius it was no longer the sole prerogative of the ruling class: *anyone* who genuinely embraced the Way could obtain Virtue from Heaven. In both Western Zhou texts and the *Analects*, however, it is the power of Virtue to attract people in a noncoercive, almost magical way that allows a moral ruler to govern by means of wu-wei or "effortless action." See especially 2.1, 4.25, 7.23, 12.19, 14.42, and 15.5.

(The) Way (*dao* 道).   Referring literally to a physical path or road, *dao* also refers to a "way" of doing things, and in the *Analects* refers to *the* Way: that is, the unique moral path that should be walked by any true human being (6.17), endorsed by Heaven and revealed to the early sage-kings. More concretely, this "Way" is manifested in the ritual practices, music, and literature passed down from the Golden Age of the Western Zhou.

wisdom, wise (*zhi* 智, 知).   An important virtue that seems to involve a cognitive understanding of the Way, as well as an ability to accurately perceive situations and judge the character of others. See especially 2.17, 5.7, 6.22–6.23, 14.14, 14.28, 15.8, and 15.33.

wu-wei 無為.   Meaning literally "no-doing" or "nondoing," wu-wei serves as both individual spiritual ideal and political ideal for Confucius. It might be best translated as "effortless action," because it refers not to what is or is not being done, but to the *manner* in which something is done. An action is wu-wei if it is spontaneous, unself-conscious, and perfectly efficacious. The state of wu-wei represents a perfect harmony between one's inner dispositions and external movements—and thus is perceived by the subject to be "effortless" and free of strain—as well as a state of harmony between the individual and Heaven, which means that a person in the state of wu-wei also possesses Virtue. In the political realm, wu-wei refers to ruling by means of Virtue. Wu-wei is therefore an effortless form of rulership whereby the ruler merely makes himself correct and thereby wins the spontaneous fealty of everyone in the world. For wu-wei as personal ideal, see especially 2.4, most of Book Ten, and 14.13; as political ideal, see especially 2.1, 2.21, 8.18–8.19, 12.19, 13.6, 15.5, and 17.19.

BIBLIOGRAPHY

For a more extensive annotated bibliography, including a survey of secondary scholarship on the *Analects*, please visit www.hackettpublishing.com.

Other Important English Translations of the Analects

Ames, Roger and Rosemont, Henry. 1998. *The Analects of Confucius: A Philosophical Translation*. New York: Ballantine Books. (Includes the Chinese text, extensive introduction and bibliography, and notes on the Dingzhou fragments of the *Analects*; follows a rather untraditional interpretation of the text.)

Brooks, E. Bruce and Brooks, A. Taeko. 1998. *The Original Analects: Sayings of Confucius and His Successors*. New York: Columbia University Press. (Follows the Brookses' radical reorganization of the text and includes the Brookses' own commentary on individual passages; the translation is at times awkward, but is perhaps the most precise and scholarly one available in English.)

Dawson, Raymond. 1993. *Confucius: The Analects*. Oxford: Oxford University Press. (Very solid, traditionally oriented translation, but with little annotation.)

Huang, Chichung. 1997. *The Analects of Confucius*. New York: Oxford University Press. (One of the few translations to provide some traditional commentary and alternate readings of passages [in the form of footnotes]. Also seems to be based on Cheng Shude's edition of the text; often follows the Han commentators, but sometimes adopts Zhu Xi's readings, all without attribution.)

Lau, D.C. 1992. *Confucius: The Analects*. New York: Penguin Books. (The classic and most commonly read translation, originally published in 1979; generally follows Zhu Xi's interpretation without attribution. Second edition [published by Chinese University of Hong Kong in 2001] includes Chinese text.)

Legge, James. 1991a. *Confucian Analects*. Taipei: SMC Publishing. (Reprint of Legge's classic translation, originally published in 1893; includes Legge's own helpful commentary and some citations from traditional commentators, especially Zhu Xi.)

Leys, Simon (a.k.a. Pierre Ryckmans). 1997. *The Analects of Confucius*. New York: W.W. Norton. (An elaborated version of Ryckmans' 1987 French translation of the *Analects* [published by Gallimard], with additional notes aimed at the English-language reader. Very fresh and original in style, although occasionally at the expense of literalness; helpful, though sometimes somewhat idiosyncratic, annotation.)

Soothill, William. 1910. *The Analects of Confucius*. Yokohama: Fukuin Printing Company. (Contains extensive comments from the translator, as well as Zhu Xi's commentary more or less in its entirety [in both Chinese and English].)

Waley, Arthur. 1989. *The Analects of Confucius*. New York: Vintage Books. (Originally published in 1938, this is perhaps the smoothest and most literary of *Analects* translations, with excellent notes; generally eschews Zhu Xi and follows the pre-Tang commentators.)

Translations of Other Early Chinese Texts Cited in Commentary and Appendices

Graham, A.C. 1990. *The Book of Lieh-tzu: A Classic of Tao*. New York: Columbia University Press. (Translation of the *Liezi*.)

Hightower, James. 1952. *Han Shih Wai Chuan: Han Ying's Illustrations of the Didactic Applications of the* Classic of Songs. Cambridge, MA: Harvard University Press. (Translation of the *Exoteric Commentary*.)

Ivanhoe, P.J. 2002. *The Daodejing of Laozi*. New York: Seven Bridges Press.

Karlgren, Bernhard. 1950a. *The Book of Documents*. Göteborg: Elanders.

———. 1950b. *The Book of Odes*. Stockholm: Museum of Far Eastern Antiquities.

Knoblock, John. 1988–1994. *Xunzi: A Translation and Study of the Complete Works*. 3 vols. Stanford, CA: Stanford University Press. (1988: vol. 1; 1990: vol. 2; 1994: vol. 3.)

Knoblock, John and Riegel, Jeffrey. 2000. *The Annals of Lü Buwei*. Stanford, CA: Stanford University Press.

Lau, D.C. 1963. *Lao-tzu: Tao Te Ching*. New York: Penguin. (Translation of the *Laozi*.)

———. 1970. *Mencius*. New York: Penguin.

Legge, James. 1967. *Li Chi: Book of Rites*. 2 vols. New York: University Books. (Translation of the *Record of Ritual*, originally published in 1885.)

———. 1991b. *The Shoo King (The Chinese Classics, vol. III)*. Taipei: SMC Publishing. (Translation of the *Book of Documents*, originally published in 1865.)

———. 1991c. *The She King (The Chinese Classics, vol. IV)*. Taipei: SMC Publishing. (Translation of the *Book of Odes*, originally published in 1871.)

———. 1991d. *The Ch'un Ts'ew with the Tso Chuen (The Chinese Classics, vol. V)*. Taipei: SMC Publishing. (Translation of the *Annals* and *Zuo Commentary*, originally published in 1872.)

Liao, W.K. 1959. *The Complete Works of Han Fei tzu: A Classic of Chinese Political Science*. 2 vols. London: A. Probsthian.

Mei, Yi-Pao. 1980. *The Works of Motze*. Taipei: Wen chih ch'u pan shê. (Translation of the *Mozi*.)

O'Hara, Albert. 1981. *The Position of Women in Early China According to the Lie nu chuan*. Westport, CT: Hyperion Press. (Translation of *Biographies of Exemplary Women*.)

Rickett, Allyn. 1985. *Guanzi: Political, Economic, and Philosophical Essays from Early China*. 2 vols. Princeton, NJ: Princeton University Press.

Shaughnessy, Edward. 1996. *I Ching: The Classic of Changes*. New York: Ballantine. (Translation of a version of the *Book of Changes* unearthed in 1973.)

Steele, John. 1917. *The I-Li or Book of Etiquette and Ceremonial*. 2 vols. London: Probsthain & Company.

Waley, Arthur. 1960. *The Book of Songs*. New York: Grove Press. (Translation of the *Book of Odes*.)

Watson, Burton. 1968. *The Complete Works of Chuang Tzu*. New York: Columbia University Press. (Translation of the *Zhuangzi*.)

Wilhelm, Richard and Baynes, Cary. 1950. *The I Ching or Book of Changes*. Princeton, NJ: Bollingen.

Brief Selection of Secondary Scholarship

Dawson, Raymond. 1981. *Confucius*. New York: Hill and Wang. (Short introduction to Confucius, the *Analects*, and Confucianism in Chinese culture.)

Fung Yu-lan. 1952. *A History of Chinese Philosophy*. 2 vols. Princeton, NJ: Princeton University Press. (Standard account of history of Chinese thought, from earliest times up to the twentieth century.)

Graham, A.C. 1989. *Disputers of the Tao: Philosophical Argument in Ancient China*. LaSalle, IL: Open Court. (An excellent general introduction to early Chinese thought, with a chapter devoted to Confucius.)

Ivanhoe, P.J. 2000. *Confucian Moral Self Cultivation*, Second Edition. Indianapolis, IN: Hackett Publishing. (Excellent short, clear introduction to the thought of Confucius, Mencius, Xunzi, Zhu Xi, Wang Yangming, and Dai Zhen.)

Loewe, Michael, ed. 1993. *Early Chinese Texts: A Bibliographical Guide*. Berkeley, CA: Institute of East Asian Studies. (Standard reference work for early Chinese texts.)

Loewe, Michael and Shaughnessy, Edward, eds. 1999. *The Cambridge History of Ancient China: From the Origins of Civilization to 221 B.C.* Cambridge, UK: University of Cambridge Press. (Collection of essays on early Chinese history up until the Qin unification.)

Munro, Donald. 1969. *The Concept of Man in Early China*. Stanford, CA: Stanford University Press. (Discussion of early Chinese conceptions of the self.)

Nivison, David. 1996. *The Ways of Confucianism*, ed. Bryan van Norden. La Salle, IL: Open Court. (A collection of essays on early Confucianism.)

———. 1999. "The Classical Philosophical Writings." In *The Cambridge History of Ancient China*, ed. Michael Loewe and Edward Shaughnessy, 754–812. Cambridge, UK: Cambridge University Press.

Schaberg, David. 2001. "'Sell It! Sell It!' Recent Translations of *Lunyu*." *Chinese Literature: Essays, Articles, Reviews* 23: 115–139. (Comparative reviews of Ames and Rosemont, Lau, Dawson, Leys, Huang, Hinton, and Brooks and Brooks.)

Schwartz, Benjamin. 1985. *The World of Thought in Ancient China*. Cambridge, MA: Harvard University Press. (Classic introduction to early Chinese thought, with a chapter devoted to Confucius.)

Van Norden, Bryan, ed. 2002. *Confucius and the* Analects: *New Essays*. New York: Oxford University Press. (Wide-ranging anthology on various aspects of the *Analects*.)